D0885860

How to Read the Bible Without Losing Your Mind

How to Read the Bible
Without Losing Your Mind

A Truth-Seeker's Guide to Making Sense of Scripture

KENT BLEVINS

WIPF & STOCK · Eugene, Oregon

HOW TO READ THE BIBLE WITHOUT LOSING YOUR MIND
A Truth-Seeker's Guide to Making Sense of Scripture

Copyright © 2014 Kent Blevins. All rights reserved. Except for brief quotations in critical publications or reviews, no part of this book may be reproduced in any manner without prior written permission from the publisher. Write: Permissions, Wipf and Stock Publishers, 199 W. 8th Ave., Suite 3, Eugene, OR 97401.

Wipf & Stock
An Imprint of Wipf and Stock Publishers
199 W. 8th Ave., Suite 3
Eugene, OR 97401

www.wipfandstock.com

ISBN 13: 978-1-62564-065-9

Unless otherwise noted, all scripture quotations are from the New Revised Standard Version Bible, copyright 1989, Division of Christian Education of the National Council of the Churches of Christ in the United States of America. Used by permission. All rights reserved.

Scripture quotations marked (CEV) are from the Contemporary English Version Copyright © 1991, 1992, 1995 by American Bible Society, Used by Permission.

Manufactured in the U.S.A.

For Teresa Gail

I, the Lord, invite you
to come and talk it over.

—Isaiah 1:18 (CEV)

Contents

Foreword by Glen H. Stassen | ix
Preface | xiii
Acknowledgments | xv

1 To Be a Truth-Seeker | 1

2 Map for a Journey or Fortress to be Defended? | 22

3 Storybook or Textbook? | 39

4 Biblical Authority is *Bottom-Up* | 70

5 A Model for Reading, Reflecting On, and Living
in Tune with the Bible | 92

6 Applying the Model—Letting the Bible Shape
Our Moral Horizon | 121

7 Applying the Model—How Can the Bible Speak
to Contemporary Issues? | 155

8 Following Jesus with Heart and Mind | 180

Study Guide Prepared by Gail Peace | 193
Bibliography | 201

Foreword

KENT BLEVINS ASKS THE questions that will not be silenced. He longs for a faith community characterized by intellectual honesty and free and open discussion. He thus helps us face questions many of us have thought were impertinent: are there contradictions in the Bible? Are there contradictions between the Bible's pre-scientific worldview and our present scientific worldview? Are there contradictions between the ethical assumptions of the culture that influenced some early biblical teachings and what we now know as biblical teachings in line with the Lordship of Jesus Christ? He does this thoughtfully and respectfully.

Throughout, Kent is helping us develop "a truth-seeking spirit." The outcome is a more confident, growing selfhood in a community of dialogue with our friends and fellow church members, including honest conversation in areas where we see things differently.

Kent helps us develop an attitude of humility that serves the search for truth well. He moves us toward openness, curiosity, and diligence. He helps us avoid pride, closed-mindedness, and laziness. In fact, he models these attitudes of growth in himself. He says "The measure of the Bible's authority for us is the extent to which we use it as a guide for discovering the whisperings of God in the stories of faith communities that have preceded us and allow that knowledge to shape the direction of our own faith communities going forward."

The Bible is narrative, like the narrative of creation and the narrative of Noah and the Ark and the Gospel narratives of Jesus; and it is prophetic proclamations of justice like the prophet Isaiah, on whom Jesus meditated extensively; and it is teachings like the Ten Commandments and the Sermon on the Mount. Each of these brings together different strands of tradition, with somewhat different emphases. They are not simply one homogeneous set of doctrines. They are therefore much more interesting, if we dig in, as Kent shows us how to do. And they put us in touch with God's inspiration in our lives.

But because Kent is so thoughtful, so honest, so continually asking probing questions, the positive payoff for faith and for sensing God's inspiration in our lives comes later rather than earlier in the book. First Kent leads us to face the questions honestly. Only then can he bring us to the positive payoff for faith. So let me give you a glimpse of where we are headed before the book finishes, in Kent's own words:

> A picture of a relational God who enters into covenant, makes promises, hears the cries of those who suffer, acts to protect the weak and vulnerable, is merciful, forgiving, and compassionate, and expresses "steadfast love," is an exceptional image worth exploring. If those communities that produced the Bible had anything unique or extraordinary to offer the rest of humanity in relation to our understanding of God, this latter portrait is where it is to be found.
>
> When we look at the prophetic material, we find strong reinforcement of the idea that God has a special concern for the poor and vulnerable. A strong case can be made, therefore, that the unique contribution of the Hebrew scriptures to any conversation about the nature of God and the intentions of God for this world lies in their portrayal of God as loving creator who desires shalom as the pattern for human relationships. God's love for God's creation grants worth and value to it, including those parts of God's creation that seem not to have any particular usefulness to human beings.

Furthermore, the Bible's message has a unity:

> Jesus did not stand outside of, but rather fully within, that tradition. Jesus begins his ministry in Luke with a quotation from Isaiah (see Luke 4:18–19), and when John the Baptist sends two disciples to inquire of Jesus whether he is "the one who is to come, or are we to wait for another?" (7:19), Jesus responds with references drawn from Isaiah: "Go and tell John what you have seen and heard: the blind receive their sight, the lame walk, the lepers are cleansed, the deaf hear, the dead are raised, the poor have good news brought to them" (Luke 7:22).
>
> Jesus's critique of the religious leaders and institutions of his day echoes the critique of the Old Testament prophets . . . . The prophetic concern for justice, including special attention to the cries of those who suffer, finds clear resonance in the New

Testament generally and is unquestionably present in the portraits of Jesus contained in the Gospels.

Correct theology does not seem to be the focal point around which Jesus organized his band of followers. Even a doctrine as central to Christianity as the trinity is not explicitly mentioned in the Bible. For those who are Christians, the central focus is Jesus. The criterion for measuring Christian faithfulness is not close adherence to a doctrinal standard or evidence of denominational loyalty, but rather the extent to which we are faithfully following Jesus.

I want to add a testimony of my own to what Kent has written about the narrative of creation in Genesis 1. (My own scholarly career began as a nuclear physicist.)

Kent writes insightfully that the Bible's narrative of the forming of creation in seven days was the basis for the command in Exodus 20:9–10: "Six days you shall labor and do all your work. But the seventh day is a sabbath to the LORD your God; you shall not do any work—you, your son or your daughter, your male or female slave, your livestock, or the alien resident [immigrant] in your towns." No other culture had such a command, focusing on justice for the powerless, and on their need for a day of rest. Other cultures focused on the privileged, and neglected the powerless. This concern for rest for weary workers totally fits the picture of a "God who enters into covenant, makes promises, hears the cries of those who suffer, acts to protect the weak and vulnerable, is merciful, forgiving, and compassionate, and expresses 'steadfast love.'"

Furthermore, the Genesis narrative is a rejection of the many gods, including sun, moon, and stars, in the rival Babylonian culture. It says "these are no gods at all; they were all created by the one God." That is its point, besides caring for the relatively powerless.

Once we see these points, and get over a literalistic fixation on the Bible's poetry of seven days, we become open to what I think is a remarkable, awesome realization:

I was sitting in the second floor of our seminary library, reading an article that mentioned science's Big Bang understanding of the origin of the universe. Astrophysicists almost all agree now that the universe began about thirteen billion years ago, when all matter in what became the universe was compacted in one enormously hot, energetic, unbelievably compact concentration. In that intense concentration, the nuclear and gravitational binding forces were so unimaginably powerful that nothing could exist but nuclei of hydrogen and helium, and some deuterium. Their electrons would be stripped off. Suddenly it exploded, and has been expanding ever since. A huge burst of light immediately took place, and the pieces began expanding into stars and galaxies, including our little earth, into the darkness, as the universe itself began expanding.

I looked up from my reading, around at the Fuller students, who come from many different nations around the world. They were each reading different articles or books, thinking complex, internationally and individually different thoughts about their reading. I looked out the windows, and saw buildings, and cars driving down Union Street. In awe, I thought of the amazing development from that intense nuclear concentration to the whole universe, and then to water and earth where vegetation could grow, and then to fish, birds, and animals, and then to the complexity of human beings whom I was seeing around me. Even if you were an atheist, you would be moved with awe at how all this complexity was produced from the Big Bang to now.

Genesis 1 begins: "In the beginning when God created the heavens and the earth, the earth was a formless void and darkness covered the face of the deep, while a wind from God swept over the face of the waters. Then God said, 'Let there be light'; and there was light." I thought of the Spirit of God, leading the development forward from simple hydrogen and helium nuclei to the amazing complexity of what we see around us. Almost unbelievable. But we see it did happen. We are here.

Having this in mind, we can read Genesis 1 as remarkably like what actually has happened. I am not suggesting that the purpose of Genesis 1 is to give us a scientific description of the details of what happened. Its purpose is to tell us, among other things, that God, God's Spirit, is the Creator, and these stars and sun and moon are no gods at all. But if we read it with the Big Bang in mind, and with a sense of the amazing complexity that has gradually developed from then to now, it draws from us awe at the complexity and gratitude for what we now have in our lives.

I ask you to read Kent Blevins's book with a commitment to the "truth-seeking spirit" that he is calling us to, and with openness to the inspiration from God's Holy Spirit that shines through the diverse narratives, prophecies, and teachings of the Bible. I invite you to become more open to inspiration from "the loving creator who desires shalom as the pattern for human relationships."

Glen H. Stassen
Lewis B. Smedes Professor of Christian Ethics
Fuller Theological Seminary
Pasadena, California

Preface

DISCUSSIONS OF THE BIBLE'S meaning and authority often seem to be situated in a context of struggle and contention. A dispassionate examination of the matter often seems impossible. Particularly disturbing, in my view, is the fact that more and more Christians seem to see a conflict between rational inquiry and the claim that the Bible can be a source of truth.

This book is based on the premise that following Jesus does not require suspension of one's intellectual capacities. Christian discipleship is not opposed to honest and open questioning. Passionate faith and passionate truth-seeking are complementary rather than contradictory. Fear, defensiveness, and failure to honestly engage points of view different from our own are antithetical to both faith and truth-seeking.

Although I believe I can successfully defend the arguments I develop in this book in any academic forum, my intended audience is not primarily fellow academics. Every semester I have students in my introductory classes who ask, "Why haven't we heard this stuff in church?" No seminary or divinity school graduate will find the information contained in this book shocking or even surprising. In my experience, however, church members are seldom exposed to it. There are lots of reasons why the questions explored in this book are seldom raised in church. Fear is behind many of them.

Fear is not a place where most people want to live. Jesus calls us out of our fear and into an exciting journey of discovery. Truth does not bind; it frees (John 8:32). The search for truth cannot be left to academics and church leaders with graduate degrees. We are all called to take responsibility for our own truth-seeking journey.

To be clear, this book does not provide the kind of specific guidance for interpreting particular texts that one might find in a book that discusses the use of commentaries and Bible dictionaries, the nature of biblical manuscripts and issues of translation, information from archeological discoveries, the various sorts of disciplines that aid the process of interpretation, including literary criticism, source criticism, redaction criticism, form criticism, etc. It asks a more fundamental question: What is the nature of the truth contained in the Bible, and how can it be effectively discerned?

Chapter 1 discusses the process of truth-seeking and the sorts of attitudes needed if our search is to be genuine. Chapter 2 briefly describes how we got our Bibles, the nature of the material contained within them, and discusses implications for our understanding of the Bible's inspiration and authority. Chapter 3 looks at three specific problems the Bible presents for modern readers. Chapter 4 discusses the nature of the Bible's authority and suggests how its authority can be effective in shaping one's life. A method for reading the Bible with integrity, honesty, and with openness for receiving new insights is presented in chapter 5. Chapters 6 and 7 provide examples of how the model outlined in chapter 5 can be applied to specific contemporary issues. The last chapter returns to the nature of truth-seeking and argues that unless Christians find a way to take seriously the authority of the Bible, other authority sources will control the direction of their lives. The Bible is a rich mine of insight for Christians who understand the nature of its authority and who are willing honestly and diligently to enter into conversation with its content.

Scattered throughout this book the reader will encounter text boxes containing questions for reflection. These are opportunities for pausing and thinking more deeply about the ideas being presented. Chapter study questions can be found at the end of the book. They can be used for personal reflection or to facilitate group discussion if you are reading the book together with others. The premise behind this book is that Bible reading/study can be intellectually stimulating, devotionally rewarding, ethically and theologically challenging, pastorally comforting, and spiritually enriching. If this book encourages you to take the Bible with greater seriousness and to read it with increased diligence and attention, it will have accomplished its purpose.

Acknowledgments

ALTHOUGH THIS BOOK IS in reality the product of a lifetime of engagement with the Bible and with questions concerning its applicability to our contemporary context, the writing began with a sabbatical leave granted by Gardner-Webb University during the fall semester, 2012. The structure of the book and many of its chapters took shape during those months of leave from teaching responsibilities, and I can honestly say it would not have been written without the time afforded me during that semester. The idea for the book grew out of many years of teaching undergraduate and graduate students, as well as observing and participating in the lives of local churches. I sensed a need for a book like this, but in spite of the multitude of books on the market dealing with the Bible and its authority, I have been frustrated that there did not seem to be anything in existence similar to what I have done here. Church folk are not unintelligent or incurious. They do not need to be shielded from difficult questions. Questions are opportunities for exploration. I am grateful to the innumerable students and church-going folk who have been part of my own journey of exploration and who helped shape, whether they agree with it or not, the perspective I bring to the topics covered in these pages.

Early morning conversations with my former colleague, Ron Williams, provided a seedbed for the development and articulation of many of the thoughts contained in these pages. To those who read parts of the manuscript and offered helpful feedback I am particularly grateful, including Helen Tichenor, Shea Stuart, Cody Sanders, Scott Shauf, Steve Harmon, Joe Collins, Warren Kay, and Joe Webb. Lisa and Dean Allen allowed me to test some of my ideas on Wednesday nights with their church members. Thanks to Jeanie Groh for early copyediting assistance and to Rachael Bradley, my student worker, for the excellence of her work related to the general sort of assistance that made my life so much more manageable. Brandon McKoy provided helpful early advice on the world of publishing, as did also Joe Webb. To Joe Webb I owe an immense intellectual debt, since he alerted me to the vocabulary of hub symbols for describing the sorts of loyalties, values, beliefs, and assumptions I discuss in chapter 5. Our discussions concerning my project were always invigorating, Joe was always encouraging and gracious, and the breadth of his knowledge and his joy in exploring ideas were an inspiration. Thanks to Eddie Stepp for making possible relinquishment of my Department Chair responsibilities one year ahead of schedule.

My experience with the good people at Wipf and Stock, and especially Assistant Managing Editor Christian Amondson, has been overwhelmingly positive. I find their publishing model highly attractive, and am grateful to them for taking what I have written and making it available to you, the reader.

Glen Stassen wrote the foreword, for which I cannot sufficiently express my gratitude. My debt to Glen extends back to my days of graduate study, first as I sat in his master's level classes on Christian ethics, and then later as he supervised my doctoral studies. I was his grader for master's level classes for a couple of semesters. Glen shaped my intellectual journey in powerful ways, but more significantly he was a model for me of someone who took with utmost seriousness our call as Christians to be followers of Jesus. His work in establishing peacemaker groups led me to establish such a group in my own church. That action gave me tangible hope that the church could be a place of transformation rather than reactionary resistance to any and every prospect of change. Our work together in the Louisville Council on Peacemaking and Religion gave me hope for the possibilities for effecting change within the larger society.

Glen's books exploring the themes of incarnational discipleship, just peacemaking, transforming initiatives, and the need for a "thicker Jesus" who can both motivate us to action as well as challenge our false loyalties are evidence of his aptitude for keen analysis, sharp insight, and eloquent expression. The fact that he was the recipient of the 2013 Baptist World Alliance Denton and Janice Lotz Human Rights Award is a testament to the fact that he is not only a hearer but also a doer of the word (Romans 2:13; James 1:22). Glen preached on the occasion of my ordination more than thirty years ago; I still remember that he chose as his text a passage from Mark 10. He has been my teacher and mentor; he powerfully influenced the direction of my life. He possibly will not agree with all that I have written, but I hope he finds what is on these pages to be within the spirit of his lifelong efforts toward encouraging us all to work harder at taking with seriousness the message and example of Jesus.

Gardner-Webb University has been a good place for stimulating my own theological reflection and development. Higher education institutions combining a clear Christian commitment with a robust and unabashed stance in favor of academic freedom and an open search for truth are becoming something of a rarity these days. No institution is perfect, and the story of my journey contains its share of pain suffered as a result of institutional dysfunction, but I am blessed to have colleagues at Gardner-Webb in virtually every academic discipline who challenge me and encourage me to be a better person. I am particularly blessed to have departmental colleagues who genuinely love and support one another. We are proof that collegiality, community, and fellowship do not depend on agreement in our opinions.

My parents and I disagree on many things, to their probable chagrin. They encouraged me in my questioning from an early age, however—a gift for which I will forever be grateful. They set an example for me of what love means in practice at a personal level. I never once witnessed an occasion when societal standards for proper relational boundaries prevented them from showing love toward another on an individual level. When they encounter another person in need, they do what they can to meet that need in a way that respects the autonomy of the other. I am grateful to be able to take this opportunity to thank them for being outstanding role models.

The relentless truth-seeking exhibited by my children is a source of gratitude and satisfaction. May they and those of their generation make great strides of progress toward the elimination of bigotry, narrow perspectives, and authoritarian assertions of power and toward the achievement of a society characterized by openness, respect, genuine dialogue, and justice.

My greatest debt of gratitude is owed to my wife, Gail. From her I have learned that the loftiest truth is relational truth and that honesty and vulnerability are prerequisites for its acquisition. She teaches me that acceptance of and love for another does not require agreement with the other's viewpoint. Her sensitivity to the pain of others helps keep me alert to issues of injustice and perspectives I likely would otherwise miss. Her joy and laughter reveal to me a celebration of life that does not deny or ignore injustice and heartbreak. She helps me keep a proper perspective so that small things remain small things and more important things are kept in view. Life is tenuous. Change is inexorable. Each day we have together is cause for rejoicing. This book is dedicated to her, with all my love.

1

To Be a Truth-Seeker

SOME OF MY EARLIEST memories are memories of church. I remember dressing up on Sundays. I remember being in Sunday School classes with other kids. I remember sitting through sermons I did not understand, drawing pictures, fidgeting, and sometimes going to sleep with my head on a parent's lap. I remember learning Bible stories.

Those stories spurred questions in my young, inquisitive mind. My parents and Sunday School teachers would explain things as best they could, but often their answers seemed to me to be inadequate. Rather than satisfying my curiosity, the answers often only served to spur additional questions. Even the answers provided by ministers sometimes seemed less than satisfactory, while at the same time there often seemed to be a hint in many of the responses that my questions were impertinent—that I ought to be satisfied with the authoritative word of a teacher or minister and not ask further questions. The questions would not be silenced, however, and my search for answers has continued throughout my life. I have settled on my own answers to many of the questions I have had along the way, but new questions always seem to arise and there always seem to be new directions to explore.

As an adult, I have encountered many Christians who share a similar experience of having had questions that did not seem to receive adequate answers from those in positions of authority in the church. Like me, they have often had the impression that certain questions are considered by others in the church to be disrespectful, or inconvenient, or perhaps beyond the boundaries of what one is permitted to ask. As in my own experience, the questions for them would not be stifled.

Often such Christians continue to attend church faithfully and to participate fully in the community life of their local congregations. There can sometimes be a disconnection, however, between what the church calls on them to affirm and what they actually believe. They live with an ongoing tension, often afraid to reveal their true thoughts, sometimes harboring feelings of guilt, but unable to accept some ideas that seem to have the status of *what all Christians believe*—at least as far as the Christians they know are concerned.

For others the tension leads them in a different direction. The rigidity of the Christianity they have experienced, or the intellectual hollowness of the church's responses to their questions, or perhaps the inability of those in church as they have known it even to allow candid questioning leads them away from church. Theirs is not a rejection of Christianity *per se*, but they long for a faith community characterized by intellectual honesty and free and open discussion.

This book is written for Christians with inquisitive minds. It calls for us to be honest with our questions. It rejects the notion that Christian faith requires us to lobotomize our intellects. It addresses, in particular, issues related to the Bible and how Christians can use the Bible as an effective guide for living while at the same time acknowledging that many of the assumptions and beliefs of those who produced the biblical writings are no longer valid in today's world.

Whether you have read the Bible from cover to cover or never opened its pages, it has had a vast influence on your life. The Bible's influence on Western culture has been so massive that one can fairly say that some knowledge of the Bible is necessary in order to be considered an educated person. There is value in studying the Bible even if your only concern is to learn something about its importance in shaping history, culture, art, music, literature, politics, and the English language. For Christians, however, the Bible is much more important than an interesting piece of literature.

Christians claim that the Bible is inspired and has a special authority for them. This book is an exploration of what that means—or perhaps more correctly, what it can plausibly mean for someone who desires to have an informed, coherent Christian faith. I write from a Christian perspective primarily for a Christian audience, but I will not be speaking secret Christian-code. Whatever your level of knowledge concerning the Bible, you will be able to understand the information presented here and the arguments developed and can draw your own conclusions on the basis of the evidence. In other words, Christian faith commitment is not necessary for understanding the arguments, but my primary purpose is to assist Christians searching for a rationally coherent view of the Bible's inspiration and authority.

How can modern Christians claim that the Bible is inspired? In what way can we claim that it is authoritative for us? How, practically speaking, can the Bible serve as a source of truth? The pages that follow will explore these and similar questions, examine evidence, and draw conclusions on the basis of the evidence. The Bible itself will serve as the primary data source. We will explore the Bible's content and draw some conclusions about how twenty-first century Christians can appropriately use it as a guide for their lives.

The topic of the Bible's authority is a central concern for Christian belief, yet it has generated so much controversy and confusion that many Christians are reluctant to discuss it openly. As a result, many Christians find themselves insecure and unsure about what they believe concerning the Bible and its inspiration and authority. Many books have been written on the subject, yet clarity among Christians in this area seems to be diminishing rather than increasing. I have yet to find a single book that provides a systematic exploration of the subject that is scholarly yet accessible, appreciative of the importance of the Bible as an authority source for Christians yet honest about the Bible's peculiarities and special challenges, and that takes seriously those challenges while attempting to develop a practical guide for reading the Bible with integrity in our modern world. This book seeks to fill that gap.

If you are confused about how to apply the Bible to your life in a practical way or if you are searching for a candid exploration of the Bible's inspiration and authority, I invite you to come along with me on this journey. I promise you will be challenged to think about what you believe. Whether you change your mind about anything or not, you will have a better understanding of the Bible that will help you feel more confident about why you believe what you believe. My fervent hope is that you will come away with renewed confidence in your ability to read the Bible with sensitivity to the nature of its origin and with clear guidance for how to apply its content to your life in an effective way.

As with any journey, we should make sure we have what we will need for the trip before we begin. The first thing needed is a certain perspective. This book examines a topic likely to arouse an emotional response within many. So before we begin our study of biblical authority and inspiration, we should think about how our emotions interact with our ability to think logically. We should consider what hindrances might interfere with the achievement of our goal. What are things we should keep in mind as we proceed?

As we explore the topic of this book, we will be looking for something we can claim to be true. Our assumption is that there are ways of understanding biblical authority and inspiration that are more coherent, more faithful to the text, and more rationally satisfying than other ways of understanding authority and inspiration. Put differently, some understandings are more truthful than others. So, if we want to discover things we can claim to be true, what should we keep in mind as we engage the questions and issues we will be examining?

First of all, we must be aware of our limitations. We are finite creatures, and our finitude affects us in several ways. We cannot pay attention to every stimulus received by our senses—we miss things. Our senses receive innumerable stimuli each and every day. Our brain selectively filters those stimuli and focuses our attention on a very small percentage of the whole. Our memories retain only a tiny portion of the enormous quantity of sensory data to which we are exposed every day.

We are self-centered; we focus on things that matter to *us*. Our rational capacities are never completely separated from our passions. Our emotions shape the things we choose to think about. For example, few of us will spend much time reading a book we consider boring, unless forced to do so by some external authority. On the other hand, most of us have had an experience of starting a book and then hardly being able to put it down until it was finished. We are selective in our choices. We pay closer attention and devote more time to things that interest us.

Not only do we selectively filter the experiences we have as we focus our attention on a tiny portion of the whole, the extent of our experience is limited by our finitude. Most people have experienced things I have not. In addition, our interpretation of our experiences is powerfully shaped by our culture in ways that are mostly hidden from our conscious awareness. We tend to view our own perspective as normative, but even a brief stay in another country reveals the relative character of much of our perception.

Even when my experience parallels that of someone else (say, for example, when my wife and I go to a concert together), we experience the event internally in different ways. If she likes it and I do not, is one view more truthful than the other?

We constantly attempt to systematize our experience. We process it, we analyze it, and we try to make sense of it—both consciously and unconsciously. This process of systematization allows us to speak intelligibly of our experiences in conversation with others. We do this so naturally that we rarely give any consideration to what is happening. Yet it is this process that largely makes us who we are and enables us to interact with others in meaningful ways.

Our different experiences, and the differences in the way we process those experiences, are part of what makes life so interesting. These differences among us do not always fall into the categories of *true* or *false*. One person's experience or interpretation of an experience is not necessarily more true than someone else's. They are simply different. However, when we try to generalize from our experience, these differences among us become problematic. When I attempt to make a truth claim that is valid beyond my own interior reality, I bump into the fact that my experience does not precisely match the experience of others.

So how can we make truth claims that are generally valid? Are we stuck with a relativism that says, "Your truth is truth for you, and my truth is truth for me?" As it happens, there are ways of checking our truth claims. Some things appear to be absolutely true (i.e., true for everyone in every place); other things appear to be absolutely false. And some things really *are* true or false in only a relative sense.

We err if we try to absolutize our own experience, just as we err if we believe everything is relative. Believing a falsehood does not make it true. The degree of passion with which I believe a falsehood does nothing to alter the fact that it is untrue. My belief that a very hot pot is actually cool will not prevent my hands from getting burned if I grab it without a potholder. My belief that the sun is shining in a cloudless sky will not prevent me from getting soaked if I step out into a downpour with no umbrella. Beliefs about things might (and often do) diverge from what is true of those things.

Beliefs, therefore, may be (and often are) mistaken. We have noted some of the reasons for this: (1) our experience is limited, (2) within our limited experience our perception is selective, and (3) we react emotionally to our experiences. In addition to these factors that complicate our ability to discern truth from falsehood, we tend to accept explanations provided by our culture and our primary communities. The way we view the world is shaped by the communities in which we are raised.

Of course, we understand why this happens if we stop to think about it. A two-year-old or six-year-old is not able to weigh evidence and draw conclusions in the same way that someone can who is twenty-five or forty-five. By necessity we largely accept the wisdom and knowledge of our elders as we are growing up. The result, however, is that we carry many unexamined assumptions with us from childhood into adulthood.

Anyone who has traveled internationally or spent time in a cross-cultural immersion experience knows that the way people think about things varies tremendously. One learns quickly, when in a different culture, that assumptions can be dangerous. When traveling or living in another culture, one never knows for sure *which* assumptions will be problematic even when one expects that one's cultural assumptions will cause difficulties. One learns that much of what we believe to be true about the world is in fact composed of beliefs we would not hold had we been born elsewhere.

The implications of this fact are so crucial to the investigation we wish to undertake that they can hardly be overstated. The people who learn to live successfully in a cross-cultural environment are those who come to understand that much of what we learn to assume about the world around us is not necessarily true in an absolute sense. Neither are those assumptions necessarily false. They are simply different from what people learn in other cultures.

For example, the physical distance separating two people conversing with one another may be interpreted differently in different cultures. From one perspective, the personal space may seem crowded. From another, the space may communicate a degree of coldness or distance. What is *correct* depends on the general understanding within one's culture. There is no objective standard for the correct distance one should maintain from someone with whom one is engaged in conversation. There are numerous cultural perspectives that have this quality about them—they are neither right nor wrong, neither true nor false, except as interpreted within a particular cultural framework.

When we speak of something that is *true*, however, we often mean that it has a feature that goes beyond culturally relative practices or beliefs. Something that is true is true for everyone. Whether or not it is believed by a majority of people in a particular culture does not affect whether it is true or false. As Vincent Ryan Ruggiero puts it in his book on critical thinking, "the truth about something is *what is so about it*—the facts in their exact arrangement and proportions . . . . Truth is apprehended by *discovery*, a process that favors the curious and the diligent. Truth does not depend on our acknowledgment of it, nor is it in any way altered by our ignorance or transformed by our wishful thinking."[1]

So far I have tried to make two main points: (1) there are truths and they can be discovered, and (2) we cannot trust that all of our beliefs are true. In order to discover the truth about things, we must be prepared to acknowledge that our beliefs may be false and we must stand ready to be corrected. We must hold our views tentatively. An insistence that our beliefs must be tentatively held does not place us in the camp of those who deny the existence of absolute truth nor are we saying that truth is unknowable. We are simply acknowledging that our search for truth is part of our life-journey. We can legitimately claim to have made some progress along the way, but there are many things that we do not know and many of the beliefs we presently hold may be (and probably are) incorrect.

When something or someone challenges one of our beliefs, therefore, no matter how passionately we hold the belief, no matter how certain we are of its truth, and no matter how widely shared our belief is within our own culture, we need to remember that we could be wrong. Reason tells us that we ought to be willing to have our beliefs tested. A reasonable response when one of our beliefs is challenged would be to say, "You could be right; make your case and let me see what I think about it." An attitude of humility serves the search for truth well. Of course, it is hard for any of us to admit that we are wrong. But that is precisely what we must be prepared to do if we are to make progress in our search for truth.

Closely related to humility is openness. Have you known people whose minds are so made up on a certain question or topic that seemingly no amount of evidence could ever change their beliefs? It is relatively easy for us to recognize closed-mindedness in others and to criticize them for it. Recognizing closed-mindedness within ourselves is much harder. Closed-mindedness is harmful not only because it prevents us from allowing our false beliefs to be challenged, but also because it effectively disengages us from the search for truth. Ruggiero, as we noted, says that truth-searching is a "process that favors the curious and the diligent." Closed-mindedness destroys curiosity. If we already know the truth, why should we bother

1. Ruggiero, *Beyond Feelings*, 36.

searching for it? Or why should we consider the veracity of a claim that challenges our perspective?

We need humility, openness, and curiosity. But, as Ruggiero points out, we also need diligence. Truth-searching is hard work. It involves brain-strain. Intellectual laziness is not an uncommon phenomenon, as evidenced by the high rate of student cheating on papers and tests. Many of us are not really interested in doing the work necessary to discover truth. We prefer short cuts. True knowledge of our world is not something that magically appears in our minds, however. We have to go out and search for it. We must expend some effort.

In our truth-quest for a satisfactory view of the authority and inspiration of scripture, we will need humility, openness, curiosity, and diligence. We will want to avoid pride, closed-mindedness, and laziness. We should recognize that the journey ahead may prove difficult. I might be able to admit that I should be receptive to consideration of new ideas, but when my beliefs are challenged I instinctively react in a defensive manner. We have already observed that admitting one is wrong can be difficult. That difficulty is exacerbated by the fact that there are differences in our emotional responses to different types of truth.

The answer to the question "what time does the ball game start?" will likely not be emotionally troubling to me, unless it creates a conflict between two highly desirable activities between which I must now choose. The search for answers to some other questions, however, may be gut-wrenching. Our emotional reactions can affect how open we are to ideas that conflict with dearly held convictions. Admitting we are wrong on one narrow point may be difficult enough, but if we sense, even vaguely or unconsciously, that admitting we are wrong on that point may call into question a number of other deeply held beliefs, the result can be terrifying. Fear can do more than simply inhibit our search for the truth. It can harden our opposition to viewpoints that seem to challenge our beliefs.

We cannot separate ourselves from our emotions, but a degree of emotional detachment is required if we wish to maintain the level of open-mindedness that the search for truth requires. I teach in a university, and many of the topics we examine in my classes are controversial. Class discussions can become emotional. A rising level of emotional engagement can be a good thing when it indicates that the topic being discussed is interesting to the students. Discussions of interesting topics can sometimes provoke intense anger, however. Why would students become angry in an academic setting where all class members are explicitly encouraged to develop their own viewpoints? What exactly is going on when that happens?

We more readily recognize what is happening when we observe it in someone else. The anger is a response to a perceived threat. When a belief that we hold intensely is no longer assumed to be true by those around us, we can no longer summarily dismiss challenges to its validity. We must defend it, and defending it can involve a lot of hard work. All the while, as we attempt to marshal evidence to support our belief, there is an unconscious—or perhaps conscious—voice in our head, asking us, "What if you are wrong?" That voice is frightening, because there is another question the voice also raises: "If you are wrong on this point, concerning which you were previously so certain that what you believed is true, what are *other* points where you may be mistaken?"

The search for truth can be frightening. It can be tough, it can be hard work, and it can turn our world upside down. So why engage in it? Why leave our comfort zone to head down roads that may cause us a lot of emotional turmoil?

In my judgment, part of the answer as to why the hard path of truth-searching is chosen by so many has to do with the fact that most people have an internal *something* that makes it hard for them to maintain beliefs they suspect are false. As scary as the search for truth is, most would rather choose honest wrestling with tough questions than continue to try to defend positions they sense are not defensible. Knowledge changes us. Once we pass through certain doors, there is no turning back. When beliefs we have previously held seem inadequate, pressing on until we find better answers to our questions is the only way out of the discomfort we feel. We remain unsettled until we begin to find a better way to understand things.

Another part of the answer has to do with human curiosity. Most people want to learn new things, expand their knowledge, seek answers to important questions, and integrate the knowledge they have into a worldview that helps them make sense of things in a more comprehensive way. Exploration, discovery, and the pursuit of knowledge are part of what makes us human. Human curiosity nudges us out of our comfort zone.

The discovery of new things, for most people, is intrinsically exciting. Imagine you are on a science class field trip to study the biodiversity of a local pond. Imagine walking around the edge of the pond, learning astonishing things under the tutelage of the trained eye of your teacher. As you observe cattails, frogs, tadpoles swimming in the water, flowers around the edge of the water, butterflies fluttering about, as you listen to the sounds of birds and insects and notice subtle yet significant differences between the kinds of plants and animals that inhabit the aquatic biosphere and those that inhabit the terrestrial biosphere and the gradations in between, you may find yourself amazed at the world that opens before your eyes as you see things you had never before imagined were there.

Now imagine looking through a microscope as you examine a slide containing living things invisible to the naked eye. Imagine your wonder as you consider the immensity of this invisible world and its importance for understanding the world in which we live. Think about what it must have been like to have been the first person to observe such tiny creatures. What would you have thought about them? What kinds of ideas would you start to formulate in your mind if previously there had been no conception among humans that such things existed?

The adventure of discovery and the drive to learn new things have been a part of the story of humans ever since humans have existed. The impulse to learn new things continues to this day. The Hubble telescope was placed in orbit around the earth so that we could expand our knowledge about the universe. Atom smashers have been constructed to facilitate learning about subatomic particles. Robotic rovers have been sent to Mars so that we can learn more about our neighbor planet. Aptly enough, the rover that landed on Mars in 2012 was named *Curiosity*. Why did we send it? Because we are curious. We want to learn new things. Increasing our knowledge of the world around us gives us satisfaction.

Try to imagine what it must have been like to have been the first person able to look through a telescope powerful enough to see a few of Jupiter's moons. Of course, you would not have known initially that you were looking at moons. The idea of moons orbiting other planets would not have existed. Your first presumption as you gazed at those faint lights would probably have been to think you were looking at stars. But watching them over several nights, you would have noticed that their movements were not at all star-like.

Suppose that subsequent observations led you to theorize that these objects were actually not stars at all but rather bodies orbiting Jupiter, and that your theory allowed you to predict the movement of these faint lights with remarkable accuracy. Imagine also that as you were pointing your telescope around the sky, you noticed some other surprising things, including the existence of mountains and craters on the moon and that Venus can be observed to move through phases much like the moon (crescent, gibbous, and full).

Imagine your excitement at such discoveries! You would be expanding human knowledge of the universe. You would be observing things never before seen. Suppose, however, that people objected to your findings, and that they objected not on the basis of observations which seemed to contradict yours, or on the basis of a theory which explained the data more effectively and elegantly than yours, but simply because your observations and your ideas about those observations contradicted long-established ways of thinking about the universe. Imagine being told that you *had* to be wrong and that you *could not possibly* be right.

This scenario actually happened. Through his observations in the early seventeenth century, Galileo was able to confirm predictions that had been made by Copernicus about one hundred years earlier. Galileo was condemned by the Catholic Church and placed under house arrest for the remainder of his life.

The kind of resistance to new ideas faced by Galileo is not uncommon. The resistance is more fierce when the new ideas seem to challenge the veracity of religious beliefs. We now know that abandonment of an Aristotelian cosmology did not necessitate a rejection of belief in God or belief in the Bible. Yet, at the time Galileo lived, fear led many people to oppose his ideas despite strong evidence in their favor. Inquisitions are fear-based responses. Attempting to silence one's opponents is not a strategy for discovering truth.

Looking back at Galileo with the advantage of hindsight, we can clearly see the errors of those who could not allow themselves to consider seriously whether he might have been correct. We would like to think that we have made progress—that today we are more open-minded in our search for truth than were people living in previous centuries, but the same dynamics present in the debates concerning Galileo are often present in modern discussions. These dynamics are especially prone to occur when the topics involve matters of religious concern, since such matters often involve intensely held beliefs.

A key difference between Galileo and his opponents was something we have already mentioned—the presence of an open-minded attitude versus a closed-minded attitude. There was something else going on, however, that we need to understand if we are to avoid a similar error in our own search for truth. When we refer to someone as closed-minded, we tend to assume that she or he is intentionally closed-minded, that the problem is not an issue related to the person's reasoning, but to the person's will—she or he is stubborn. We attribute a certain attitude to the person and we assume that he or she does not want to learn. We have already seen how fear can interfere with the learning process. Sometimes, though, neither stubbornness nor fear is the main problem—sometimes the approach we take to the discovery of truth causes difficulty.

Since ancient times, people have taken two different approaches to the discovery of truth. One approach starts with an assumption about what is true and attempts to deduce conclusions from that starting point. The other approach is to observe things and then try to come up with explanations for what one sees. There is nothing necessarily wrong with the first approach, unless one resists letting go of false premises when they are contradicted by the data.

In Galileo's day, many people had believed for hundreds of years that the earth was stationary and that all heavenly bodies orbited around it. That idea of a perfect universe occupied by perfect spheres orbiting in perfect circles with the earth at the center was challenged by Galileo's observations. In order to understand the resistance to Galileo's ideas, we have to understand the emotional attachment to the conception of a perfect universe that his ideas threatened. The threat had a religious component, since the perfection of the universe was thought to reflect the perfection of God, its creator. If the universe did not, in fact, fit this model of perfection, what were the implications for belief in a perfect God?

For many in the time of Galileo, it was *impossible* for his ideas to be correct. No observations were necessary. Abstract reasoning was sufficient. God is perfect. The universe is perfect. End of story. And not only was Galileo wrong on the basis of deductive reasoning, his ideas were clearly contrary to scripture and therefore heretical. The papal condemnation issued in 1633 states that Galileo rendered himself

> in the judgment of this Holy Office vehemently suspected of heresy, namely, of having believed and held the doctrine—which is false and contrary to the sacred and divine Scriptures—that the Sun is the center of the world and does not move from east to west and that the Earth moves and is not the center of the world; and that an opinion may be held and defended as probable after it has been declared and defined to be contrary to the Holy Scripture.[2]

2. De Santillana, *The Crime of Galileo*, 310.

Galileo's crime was not that he introduced new ideas or even that he over-turned long-held beliefs. As long as such challenges did not represent a threat to deeply held religious views of his day, there was no real problem. For example, the idea that the earth's gravitation exerts an equal accelera-tion force on objects, regardless of their mass, did not generate the same controversy in Galileo's day as his views concerning the motion of heavenly bodies, even though this idea also challenged the Aristotelian thinking that was the basis for people's understanding in Galileo's day. Galileo's transgres-sion was that some of his ideas threatened what were, for many, founda-tional *religious* beliefs.

Eventually, a different approach to increasing our knowledge began to gain preeminence as new technologies made more discoveries possible—discoveries that further challenged ancient ways of thinking. What we now call the scientific method became an important way to expand our under-standing of the universe. We began to recognize that our assumptions about the world could be radically challenged by the data of our observations.

The findings of science continue to challenge deeply held religious beliefs to this day. Science and the scientific method are not anti-religion, however. While it is true that religious beliefs tied to a view of the earth as flat or to a geocentric (earth-at-the-center) universe have been abandoned by most people, religion is still a strong force in the lives of many people in the modern world, including many scientists who fully accept the latest theories and assumptions of modern science.

There is much debate about the proper relationship between science and religion. Are they completely separate areas of inquiry? Are they neces-sarily in conflict? Is religion an arena of superstition, or at least unverifiable speculation, while science the arena of facts, data, and evidence? There are certainly differences between religious sorts of questions and scientific sorts of questions. Science cannot, and does not attempt, to answer the question of God's existence. Scientists sometimes weigh in with their views on the existence of God, but when they do so, they are not practicing science. On the other hand, as the case of Galileo illustrates, there is no question that scientific discoveries have an impact on religious beliefs. There can be no neat division into completely separate spheres (though some have argued for such a way of viewing the relationship between science and religion).

As John Haught has pointed out, both scientific and religious ques-tions originate from a "humble desire to know."[3] They both, in their own

---

3. Haught, *Science and Religion*, 21.

ways, engage us in the quest for truth. They both assume the world is intelligible. They both assume that there is "a real world, one that transcends mere wishing."[4] Both science and religion have standards of inquiry and methods for testing the veracity of claims, and since they both recognize the limitations of human finitude, they recognize that there ought to be a tentativeness in all of our truth claims. Long-held beliefs may need revision. Longevity of an idea is no guarantee of its veracity.

John Polkinghorne argues (as does Haught) that the view of knowledge adopted, "consciously or unconsciously, by scientists can properly be called 'critical realism.' The noun expresses the conviction that the scientists are indeed exploring a physical world whose nature 'out there' is independent of human social construction . . ., while the adjective acknowledges that physical reality is often partly veiled and obliquely encountered."[5] Both Polkinghorne and Haught argue that while there are significant differences between scientific investigation and theological inquiry, both kinds of truth-searching recognize the need for openness to alternative viewpoints and both require a readiness to hear (and possibly accept) arguments that challenge one's own perspective. As Polkinghorne states:

> We are able to attain best explanations of our experience, which we should treat with the utmost seriousness, but to claim to have achieved absolute proof and indubitable certainty is to go beyond finite human capacity. Absolutely coercive argument is not at our disposal . . . . Reason is not to be identified with the possession of indisputable proof, but with the careful search for well-motivated belief, whether we are concerned with science or with theology.[6]

There are those who disagree with this position. Usually they do so because they believe either science or religion ought to take precedence over the other. Some ask "Why should theology bow to science?" while others insist that science is the only source of true knowledge. If we see the two as being in irrevocable conflict, however, we cut ourselves off from entire worlds of knowledge.

Christians have no reason to fear science. The scientific progress of the last few centuries has certainly not destroyed Christianity. The remarkable increase in human knowledge that has come through scientific investigation has benefitted humanity in numerous ways. Certainly Christians have

4. Ibid., 20.

5. Polkinghorne, *Theology in the Context of Science*, 25.

6. Ibid., 36.

every right as well as the responsibility to add their voices to discussions about how knowledge gained from science ought best be put to use. The scientific quest, however, is a quest for truth, and as such ought to be celebrated and encouraged by Christians. It is a quest for knowledge about our physical universe and how things in this universe function. Scientific investigation is rooted in the human desire to learn and explore. From a Christian perspective, that desire was placed in us by God, the source of all truth.

When Christians, for theological reasons, resist accepting what is a scientific consensus, they resist this God-given desire to know. Rather than engage arguments openly with the kind of joyous curiosity that leads to the excitement of learning new things, they respond out of the insecurity that comes from the (often repressed) fear that they may be wrong. We have seen that the Catholic Church's response to Galileo was to demand submission to what it considered to be true doctrine. The question at his trial was not, "Is your idea better than our idea?" Rather the question was, essentially, "Do you accept our idea, or not? If yes, then all is fine and you may go on your way; if not, we will use the power available to us to suppress your views."

This same way of approaching issues is prevalent today, though usually—and fortunately—access to the kind of political power that would allow coercive methods for suppressing opposing viewpoints is absent. We should ask ourselves: what would attempting to suppress ideas with which we disagree accomplish? Why should we fear viewpoints that differ from our own? Can we legitimately claim that we honestly desire to know the truth when we are more oriented toward discrediting or quashing opposing viewpoints than investigating them open-mindedly to see whether they have merit? Carl Sagan has rightly observed that "the cure for a fallacious argument is a better argument, not the suppression of ideas."[7]

The desire to suppress viewpoints with which we disagree does not arise from a desire to discover truth, but arises rather from fear. Practiced truth-seekers listen respectfully to views that challenge their own ways of thinking about things. They pay attention to internal emotional reactions that indicate a stronger attachment to a viewpoint than may be healthy—especially strong negative emotions toward an idea that arise before there has been an opportunity to fully examine and comprehend the arguments on both sides. Truth-seekers welcome challenges as positive opportunities

7. Sagan, *The Demon Haunted World*, 429.

to learn. They do not immediately assume a defensive posture when they encounter disagreement. They do not see their task as defeating opponents or winning arguments, but rather welcome opportunities for discussion and dialogue.

Practiced truth-seekers tend to be more intellectually secure than those who would rather not expose themselves to new ideas. After all, a practiced truth-seeker knows what difficult intellectual struggle is like and has put in enough work to feel a relative sense of personal satisfaction in terms of the coherence of her or his beliefs. Because a practiced truth-seeker is constantly testing her or his beliefs and open-mindedly considering alternative viewpoints, there is a greater certainty that one's views can withstand challenge. The more one examines challenges to one's beliefs, the greater confidence one gains that one is on the right track. Even when one's beliefs change, there is a greater sense of confidence in one's ability to rightly discern truth.

Sometimes this attitude of self-assurance is perceived by others as arrogance. This is especially true when a practiced truth-seeker seems not to take certain arguments seriously. After all, have I not been emphasizing that truth-seekers should always be open to contrary viewpoints and respectful of other positions? There is a difference, however, between arrogance and a relative confidence in one's position. Once an idea has been thoroughly tested and been shown to be inadequate, there is little point in continuing to view it as an intellectually viable option. Scholars who spend lifetimes studying a subject disagree about many things within their disciplines of study, but they also have large areas of agreement and consensus. To dismiss certain ideas after thorough investigation is not the same thing as being dismissive.

No one today would seriously entertain an argument in favor of a geocentric universe, nor do we believe that ships sailing on the sea might fall off the edge of the earth. We have abandoned many medical practices that were common only a few hundred years ago. Our knowledge stands open for correction, but we have made progress in what we know. A truth-seeker does not need to spend time giving serious consideration to every belief that differs from her or his own. Nor does a truth-seeker need to personally test and confirm every truth she or he accepts as valid. We learn from those who have gone before us. The discoveries of previous generations do not need to be rediscovered in every future generation. Only when an accepted explanation begins to fail to explain new data does the search begin for a better explanation.

When there is consensus among those who have studied the evidence most diligently and when one has examined the evidence oneself such that one finds the scholarly consensus personally convincing, there is a satisfaction that comes from knowing that one's views are defensible in the arena of the highest levels of academic inquiry—even if one is not an expert in the subject. The burden of proof rests on those who hold opinions contrary to the scholarly consensus to show, on the basis of the evidence, why the consensus viewpoint is mistaken. Ill-informed opinions do not advance the search for truth.

Truth-seekers do not need to be experts in every field of inquiry. Nor do they blindly accept what someone else tells them. The data that is the basis for areas of consensus is there for anyone who wishes to examine it. Truth-seekers have a healthy respect for the work done by scholars, and they are willing to put in the time and effort to examine the evidence if they find themselves unprepared to accept the scholarly consensus. However, the degree of tentativeness must be greater, not less, when one's view diverges from the mainstream of informed opinion.

As I have already tried to make clear, truth-seeking has its unsettling aspects. A practiced truth-seeker will feel a certain dissonance with surrounding cultural assumptions, since truth-seekers recognize that not all of our cultural assumptions are truthful. In addition, there is no way to know where the truth journey will lead. How can one know ahead of time which beliefs one will eventually find to be inadequate and therefore necessary to abandon? Of course, as disconcerting as that thought might be, the alternative is to remain locked in an ignorance based on fear. Ignorance is not bliss. And it can be dangerous.[8]

The quest for truth is a prominent theme in human history. Most people like to think of themselves as truth-seekers. We like to think our beliefs are rational, coherent and correlated with the reality of the world around us. Most of us understand that if our goal is to be truth-seekers, we must be ready to change our position when data conflicts with it. From a strictly logical point of view, truth should not be perceived as threatening, nor should it be resisted. If we are mistaken, is not the sensible thing to admit we are wrong and change our belief so that it more closely aligns with the truth? Often, however, we are neither sensible nor logical. In practice,

8. See Kimball, *When Religion Becomes Evil.*

changing deep-seated beliefs can be a hard thing to do. The fact that we encounter ideas that seem threatening to us is not, in itself, a problem. A problem often arises, however, in the way we react to such perceived threats.

In Christian theological language, our tendency toward a distorted perspective (and actions based on such a perspective) and our need for ongoing correction are identified by the words *sin* and *repentance*. These words point to an important insight into the nature of our resistance to truth discovery. To paraphrase Col. Nathan Jessup in the movie *A Few Good Men*, sometimes "we can't handle the truth!" We resist it not on the basis of rational arguments, but because it challenges fundamental commitments that may need correction. Reinhold Niebuhr pointed out a key component of this sinful tendency when he noted that it must be understood as more than something that affects us as individuals—sin has a corporate dimension.

In *Moral Man and Immoral Society*, Niebuhr stated that "in every human group there is less reason to guide and to check impulse, less capacity for self-transcendence, less ability to comprehend the needs of others and therefore more unrestrained egoism than the individuals, who compose the group, reveal in their personal relationships."[9] Niebuhr clearly affirmed the importance of education: "a growing rationality in society destroys the uncritical acceptance of injustice."[10] Education alone is ultimately insufficient, however, since we need repentance from impure motives:

> [People] will not cease to be dishonest, merely because their dishonesties have been revealed or because they have discovered their own deceptions. Wherever [people] hold unequal power in society, they will strive to maintain it. They will use whatever means are most convenient to that end and will seek to justify them by the most plausible arguments they are able to devise. Nevertheless there are possibilities of increasing social justice through the development of mind and reason.[11]

We need to repent of sinful motives that block our search for truth, including selfishness connected with our desire to preserve our status or the status of groups to which we belong.[12] As we practice truth-seeking, we need to

9. Niebuhr, *Moral Man and Immoral Society*, xi–xii.

10. Niebuhr, 31.

11. Ibid., 34.

12. "Groups" here does not refer only to organizations we may be part of, though certainly they are included. The idea in this context is broader, encompassing group loyalties

pay attention when we notice an internal, emotional reaction to an idea or argument—especially when that reaction is strongly negative. The reaction itself can provide useful information. It may indicate a point where we feel a personal threat or a threat to a larger group to which we belong. If that is the case, we may need to consider whether our first response, before we even consider the merits of an argument, should be one of repentance.

In the chapters that follow, we will be looking for a view of the authority and inspiration of scripture that is rationally coherent. If you do not care whether your beliefs are rationally coherent, then this book is not for you. If you wish to engage others in conversation on this (or any other) topic, however, then rational coherence is a necessary prerequisite. Some Christians argue that faith does not need to be reasonable. In fact, some Christians seem to take pride in the idea of an unintelligible or irrational faith.

I agree that faith itself is not something that falls into the category of a logically derived conclusion. Søren Kierkegaard, a nineteenth century Danish philosopher, spoke of faith in terms of a *leap*—something involving the will rather than the intellect. I think Kierkegaard is correct in asserting that faith is not primarily an intellectual decision. Faith has the character of a choice.

A faith defined as contrary to reason, however, is problematic since there is no way to test its truth claims. How can such a faith be missionary? How can one attract others to adopt one's position if it is admittedly illogical and incoherent? There is a theological problem with such a position, as well. How can a Christian argue that the God who created us and gave us brains expects us to disengage those brains in the realm of religion? Could refusing to do the hard work necessary for discovering truth be seen, in fact, as disobedience to a God who gave us rational capacities? Are those who take pride in their lack of knowledge really doing anything more than boasting of their laziness?

We return to the question of how we know things. How can we make truth claims and how can we have relative certitude regarding those truth claims? Ultimately, knowledge is related to experience. I learn things based on my own experience as well as the experiences of others, both past and present. There is a correlation in this respect between religious knowledge and scientific knowledge. Although significant differences exist between

that have nothing to do with choices we have made (including aspects related to gender, ethnicity, nationality, age, etc.). These things are part of the particularity of our existence, and they have a powerful effect on how we view the world around us.

science and religion in terms of the kinds of experiences examined and the nature of the tests applied to them, the only way to advance knowledge in either area is to check one's interpretations of one's experience of the world against the experiences and interpretations of others. How else can one know truth, except through comparing one's experiences with those of others? Some argue that the best way to truth is to submit to one or another authority as the final arbiter of truth, but submission to an absolute and unquestionable authority provides little comfort, ultimately, that one's beliefs are correctly correlated with reality.

To find truth, we have to search for it. Truth-seeking, by definition, challenges previously held assumptions. Truth-seeking has no predetermined outcome. Truth-seeking requires respectful dialogue with those who have differing opinions. Truth-seekers ask, "What do you think about this?" and "What makes you say that?" Scientists are not immune to closed-mindedness, but at least scientists have rigorous rules for validating interpretations of the evidence. The tendency toward closed-mindedness is greater in the arena of religion, so we need to keep in mind some guidelines:

1. Questions are friends, not enemies.

2. We must practice open-minded and attentive listening to beliefs which differ from our own.

3. We should especially be attentive to the presence of negative emotional reactions (anger, fear), and be prepared to repent of motives and loyalties that distort truth.

4. Principles of logic and critical thinking can be helpful.

5. Changing our mind about something is not a sign of weakness, but rather a sign of progress.

6. Knowledge of the views of experts is helpful, especially in areas where consensus exists.

7. We need to practice giving clear explanations to support our views.

The last point is often not sufficiently appreciated. People frequently confuse the expression of an opinion with a justifying reason. "I don't like that restaurant" is an opinion, but it is not very informative. Is the problem a personal dislike of the type of food served (fast food versus vegetarian versus particular ethnic style of cooking, etc.)? Does the food tend to be overcooked? Undercooked? Is the wait staff rude? The prices too high? The atmosphere too noisy? When clear explanations are provided we can understand another's perspective more clearly. These kinds of explanations help us make sense of our experiences and help us relate our own experience to that of others.

We live in an increasingly polarized society. Many seem less interested in learning than in winning arguments, but shouting down an opponent or coercively eliminating opposition to one's position is not really winning. Truth requires no army for its defense. Truth wins non-coercively, through the power of its own persuasiveness. If seeking truth is important to you, and if learning more about the possibilities for viewing the Bible as a truth-revealing collection of writings sounds interesting, I invite you to keep reading.

2

Map for a Journey or Fortress to be Defended?

HAVE YOU EVER THOUGHT about how the Bible came into existence? Have you ever wondered where it came from? Did it just fall out of the sky? Was it written by one person? Many different people? Did God dictate the words to people who just wrote them down? Or did people write things that later came to be viewed by others as inspired? If the latter, who made decisions about which writings are inspired and which are not? We cannot have a proper understanding of the Bible's authority without understanding how we got our Bibles.

Although it might seem odd, we must begin by clarifying what we mean when we use the word *Bible*. There is no *one* Bible used by all Christians. In fact, there never has been agreement among all Christians about the content of the Bible. Differing branches of Christianity include different books in their Bibles. We need to examine a bit of history in order to understand how that happened.

Although there are some small differences, Roman Catholics and Eastern Orthodox branches of Christianity are in fairly close agreement about the content of the Bible. Eastern Orthodox Christians include only a few writings not in the Roman Catholic Bible (e.g., 1 Esdras, 3 Maccabees, and Psalm 151). Both Roman Catholic and Eastern Orthodox Bibles include books referred to as *deuterocanonical*. These were books contained in the Septuagint—a Greek translation of Jewish scriptures dating back as far as the third century BCE.[1]

Several hundred years before the appearance of the Septuagint, events took place that had a tremendous impact on the religious and cultural development of the Hebrew people. In the early sixth century BCE the Babylonians were the major superpower dominating Palestine. They asserted control over Judah by conquering Jerusalem, but not destroying it, in 597 BCE. Sometime around 590 BCE, Zedekiah, king of Judah, rebelled against Babylon by withholding tribute, provoking the Babylonians to send their army back into Palestine. They laid siege to Jerusalem in 587 BCE and conquered the city in 586 BCE. Jerusalem, along with many other cities in Judah, was left in ruins and many Jews were deported to Babylon.

Conditions in the region following the year 586 were harsh. Many of those not deported by the Babylonians decided to leave Palestine. A large number of Jews settled in Egypt. Many others emigrated from Palestine to Asia Minor. Before long, more Jews lived outside of Palestine than lived in it, and many of those living in the Diaspora outside of Palestine stopped speaking Hebrew.[2]

Following the conquests of Alexander the Great in the late fourth century BCE, Greek became the common language of the eastern Mediterranean region. Jews living in Alexandria, Egypt spoke Greek rather than Hebrew, and wanted a translation of the Hebrew scriptures in the Greek language. As a result, a Greek translation, which we today call the Septuagint, emerged roughly a couple of hundred years before the time of Jesus.

The Septuagint contained the books we find in the modern Hebrew Bible, including the five books of the Torah, the prophets, Psalms and other writings. However, the formation of the Jewish canon was still in a fluid state at this point. The Jews did not establish a definitive set of authoritative writings until somewhere around one or two hundred years after the time of Jesus.[3] When the Hebrew Bible was finalized, it did not include the deuterocanonical books contained in the Septuagint—books that were

---

1. BCE stands for "Before Common Era" and is used by scholars in place of the culture-specific term "BC" (Before Christ). CE (Common Era) is used by scholars rather than AD (*anno domini*).

2. *Diaspora* is derived from a Greek word meaning "to scatter" or "to disperse." It can now refer to any scattering or migration of a people away from their homeland, but in relation to the Jews refers specifically to the dispersal of the people that followed the destruction of Jerusalem in 586 BCE.

3. See Sanders, "Canon," 837–52.

considered to have some degree of authority by Alexandrian Jews at the time of the Septuagint's composition.

Why is this information important for Christians? The earliest Christians, of course, did not have a New Testament. But they *did* have writings they considered to be authoritative. Since Christianity grew out of Judaism, the writings they considered authoritative were the same writings Jews considered to be authoritative. As Christianity rapidly spread to Greek-speaking areas, it was natural for them to use the Greek Septuagint rather than Hebrew manuscripts of Jewish writings. When the New Testament Gospels quote from Jewish writings, the quotes are from the Septuagint.[4] For many early Christians the Greek Septuagint translation of the Jewish scriptures was their Bible. The Jewish scriptures were authoritative for them, and the specific writings considered authoritative were those contained in the Septuagint.

If the Hebrew Bible, when it was put into final form one-to-two-hundred years after the time of Jesus, had contained the same writings as the Septuagint, the Bibles of Christians and Jews would have had the same content (except, of course, for the Christian writings that appeared in the first and second centuries CE that eventually became part of the Christian New Testament). As it happened, however, the Hebrew Bible left out some of the writings contained in the Septuagint. From that point forward, the Hebrew Bible and the Christian Old Testament were different.

This difference generated discussion among Christians about how to regard those writings not included in the Hebrew Bible but which continued to be part of the Christian Old Testament. In the late fourth century, when Jerome produced the Vulgate (a translation of Christian scriptures into Latin), he referred to these writings as *apocrypha*. In his prologue to the writings, he made clear that he viewed them as having lesser authority.

Differences of opinion concerning the deuterocanonical works (another name for these writings) continued among Christians until the time of the Protestant Reformation. Luther considered them to be of lesser importance than the writings contained in the Hebrew Bible. He placed them between the Old Testament and New Testament in his *Luther Bible* German translation. Partly in response to the Protestant position, the Roman

---

4. In one famous instance, Matthew 1:23 follows the Septuagint's "virgin" translation of Isaiah 7:14. But the Hebrew word in Isaiah means "young woman" (not necessarily a virgin). Some Christian translations of the Bible follow Matthew when translating Isaiah, using the word "virgin" in Isaiah 7:14. Many modern Christian translations, however, let Isaiah speak for himself, translating the word in 7:14 as "young woman."

Catholic Church affirmed the deuterocanonical works as fully authoritative with the rest of scripture at the Council of Trent in 1546.

These differences between Catholics and Protestants are reflected in modern translations. The Catholic Jerusalem Bible, for example, includes the deuterocanonical writings as a part of the Old Testament, interspersed with other Old Testament writings. Some Protestant translations include the deuterocanonical writings in a separate section, while others exclude them altogether. The exclusion of these writings by Protestants from the Bible, however, was something new in the history of Christianity—it had not been done prior to the time of the Protestant Reformation.

Christians, therefore, disagree about the precise content of the Bible. This disagreement is not a peculiarly modern phenomenon. Christians have *always* disagreed about the precise content of the Bible. We cannot go back to a time when all Christians everywhere were in agreement on the content of scripture. This fact has implications for our study of the authority and inspiration of the Bible. Some of the ways Christians understand the authority of the Bible become immediately problematic in the face of this data. Did the Bible not come directly from God? Didn't God know what should be included in the table of contents? If the Bible is holy scripture, how can there be uncertainty about its content? If indeed there are multiple Christian Bibles, how can we decide *which* Bible is *the* Bible? How can we even talk about the authority and inspiration of the Bible if we are unsure about what is (or ought to be) included within its pages? We will come back to these questions later. For now, we turn our attention to the formation of the Bible.

There are many good books available that discuss the process of how the Old and New Testaments came into existence. For the purpose of our investigation, the point is that the Bible is composed of writings that appeared over hundreds of years involving many different authors and audiences. Although it was a complicated process, modern scholars have made great strides in figuring out the main pieces of the puzzle.

Both Judaism and Christianity consisted of communities of considerable diversity, which contributed to the production of writings composed within those communities that were likewise diverse. Much of the material of the Old Testament was transmitted orally over a long period of time before it was ever written down. Many of these oral traditions were first put in written form during the aforementioned Babylonian exile. The oral traditions from which the written material was derived reflected the pre-exilic diversity of various Hebrew communities. Some traditions originated in the northern kingdom, while others came from the southern kingdom.[5] Some were more ancient, while others were of more recent origin.

These traditions reveal different perspectives. For example, during the rise of the monarchy, some viewed the idea of having a king as a positive thing ordained by God.[6] Others viewed it as a sign of disobedience and a lack of trust in God, because God alone was supposed to lead them as a people. When the oral traditions were written down, the scribes did not always seem concerned about the discrepancies created when contrasting perspectives were juxtaposed. They simply wrote them down and let the diversity within the traditions stand. We will look at some specific examples in the next chapter.

The traditions of the Old Testament developed over hundreds of years within Jewish communities located in various places. That those traditions contain a variety of perspectives is only to be expected and is perfectly natural. Adding to the diverse perspectives of the Old Testament is the fact that the editors who helped shape the final product had their own viewpoints that affected the way they organized and presented the previously existing material. In short, the Old Testament is composed of many voices. Those voices are as diverse as the Jewish communities, existing over centuries, from which they arose. As we shall see, they are not always harmonious voices.

A similar thing could be said about the New Testament. The formation of what we now call the New Testament began as Christian writings were composed and began to circulate within early church communities (gospels, letters, apocalypses, etc.). That process took several hundred years. There was never a general council of bishops in the first thousand years of church history that specified an official content of the New Testament. The earliest list we have of New Testament books that matches our modern New Testament is from 367 CE, in a pastoral letter Bishop Athanasius wrote to churches in the area of Alexandria, Egypt. At that time, there was still

5. The twelve Hebrew tribes were led by a series of intermittent judges until first Saul—then David and Solomon—united the tribes around the tenth century BCE. Following Solomon's death ten northern tribes broke away from the two southern tribes. From that point, *Israel* refers to the northern kingdom, while *Judah* refers to the southern kingdom. The kingdom of Israel disappeared after it was conquered by the Assyrians in 722 BCE, but many of its traditions were preserved and incorporated into those of the southern kingdom of Judah.

6. Saul was the first king. See the previous note.

no general agreement about the content of the New Testament. Different Christian communities used different collections of what they considered to be authoritative writings. One scholar has pointed out that around the year 300 CE there were more than one hundred writings "considered as divinely inspired, potentially scripture, circulating in all parts of the Christian movement."[7]

Eventually, a particular viewpoint prevailed among Christians. A key difference between Christians and Jews in the process of canon formation was that among Christians the debate was influenced by imperial politics.[8] The victory of those representing what came to be viewed as an orthodox perspective over those who are regarded by the church today as heretics was won not only in the arena of arguments and debates, but through force and the power of the state.[9] Following Constantine's conversion to Christianity in the early fourth century, imperial power was used to coerce and stamp out dissenting points of view. Writings considered heretical were destroyed.

In the early centuries of the church, many different types of communities claiming the name *Christian* existed. These communities all professed to be followers of Jesus, but in many cases they had little else in common. Some of those communities emphasized the humanity of Jesus, denying his divinity, while others emphasized his divinity, denying his humanity. Some believed that Jesus was a man, but claimed Christ entered his body at his baptism and then left his body at the time of the crucifixion (thus the cry of Jesus on the cross: "My God, my God, why have you forsaken me?"). Others maintained that the Old Testament God was an evil being. Some insisted that Christians must follow Jewish customs and practices. Others believed that salvation could only be obtained through secret knowledge. These diverse forms of Christianity produced equally diverse writings that circulated among their communities. There were numerous gospels, acts, epistles and apocalypses.[10]

Christians who gained imperial support in the fourth century used the power available to them against those they viewed as their opponents. Today, most of the writings that originated among communities that came

---

7. Dungan, *Constantine's Bible*, 9. See also 69.

8. The process among Jews was influenced by political *events* (e.g., the destruction of Jerusalem in 70 CE), but did not involve direct meddling by the emperor, as was the case with Christianity.

9. The root meaning of the word *orthodox* is "correct belief." Often the specific content of what gets defined as correct belief is shaped by power relationships.

10. See two books by Bart Ehrman: *Lost Scriptures* and *Lost Christianities*.

to be regarded as heretical are available to us only in small fragments or in the quotations of orthodox writers who were arguing against them.

We cannot know how things might have turned out without Constantine's intervention. Would those voices representing the viewpoint that eventually prevailed have triumphed regardless? Very possibly. Almost certainly, however, the vitality of other expressions of Christianity would have made any attempt to define Christian orthodoxy more problematic. The power and prestige of the emperor contributed significantly to orthodox Christianity's numerical growth and stimulated the development of a centralized and hierarchical institutional structure that was new in its scope and influence. The shape of Christianity by the end of the fourth century was considerably different from what it had been two centuries or even one century earlier.

There has been much debate concerning whether Constantine's influence on the development of Christianity was ultimately positive or negative. As far as our inquiry is concerned, the point is that the New Testament, like the Old Testament, was formed through a process of selection from among numerous writings. Before a consensus was established concerning the proper boundaries of the New Testament (Which writings should be included? Which should be excluded?), attitudes were fluid toward works such as Hebrews, James, 2 Peter, 2 and 3 John, Jude, and Revelation (which were held in lesser esteem by some, but were eventually included), as well as the Shepherd of Hermas, 1 Clement, the Didache, the Epistle of Barnabas, the Acts of Paul, and the Revelation of Peter (which, among others, were considered authoritative by some, but were eventually excluded).

The Bible, thus, did not come to us as a gift from the heavens. Whatever view of its inspiration and authority we adopt should take into account the evidence that the Bible is the end product of a long history of development which, at the end of the day, never did produce a precise list agreed upon by all Christians. This point is fundamental for our subsequent arguments and conclusions and is uncontroversial among biblical scholars, yet we must admit that it is a difficult idea for many Christians to accept. For one thing, our use of the word *Christian* is broader than some would allow. Some argue that those from a tradition other than their own are not authentic Christians. Some evangelical Christians, for example, do not believe that Catholics are genuine Christians, while the Roman Catholic Church, until relatively recently, held that there is no salvation outside the boundaries of Roman Catholicism. Such positions allow one to declare victory in the debate over scripture by denying one's opponents the right to enter the arena of discussion, equivalent to merely asserting "I'm right and the rest of you are wrong" concerning which books ought to be considered canonical.

Others look at the evidence concerning the origin of the Bible and refuse to accept it because it challenges theological views upon which their faith depends. Their understanding of reality is theologically constructed in a way that prevents them from acknowledging the facts in front of them. Such persons, obviously, are not open-minded truth seekers. There are facts that stand before us and must be taken into account if we are honest with ourselves and respectful of the data. Those who fear the dissolution of a framework that has enabled them—up until now, at least—to make theological sense of the world are sometimes impervious to information that calls into question their assumptions.

To be clear, the fact that the Bible is a human product, with human authors who wrote within specific historical contexts does *not* mean that the Bible cannot also be considered to have a divine origin. But any claim for divine origin cannot be based upon a belief in direct delivery from God. Christians cannot make the same claim for the divine origin of the Bible that Muslims claim for the Koran or that Mormons claim for the Book of Mormon. The Bible was not directly dictated to anyone. Nor was it discovered on golden plates. Nor do we possess any of the original manuscripts. What we have are copies of copies of copies of material passed along for hundreds of years, none precisely matching the rest in every detail.

The fact that Christians cannot claim that the Bible was given miraculously directly from God does not signify any necessary diminishment of its (potential) significance and authority. As we shall see, its authority and inspiration are not dependent on any particular process through which it came into existence. Were that the case, religions that claim a miraculous origin for their scriptures as a sign of those scriptures' authority would seem to have an advantage over Christianity. Such a claim appears not to be a decisive factor in whether a person chooses one religion over another, however. Conversion rates for Mormons, Christians and Muslims do not seem to be much affected by the claims they make, respectively, regarding the divine origin of their scriptures.

There is another implication to be drawn from the data we have examined in this chapter. In relation to the Hebrew Bible, at the time the list of books deemed canonical was being decided by the rabbis, the real debate concerned a relatively small number of works. There was consensus about the Torah and the prophets, but much discussion about some of the writings. Likewise, a consensus developed relatively quickly in the early church concerning the authoritative status of the four Gospels found in the New Testament as well as most of Paul's letters. Some works, however, fell into a category of disputed writings as Christians disagreed about their status.

In other words, different works were regarded differently. This is an important point, since it fits with what we have said about the origin of the Bible and has implications for our understanding of the relative authority of different parts of the Bible. Some argue that every word of the Bible is equally authoritative with every other word. If the Bible had been miraculously delivered directly from God, such a claim would have plausibility. After all, if God is the direct source and author of each and every single word, is it not logical to say that each and every single word has equal divine authority? How could one say that one word spoken by God has more authority than another word spoken by God? How could one verse be placed above another in value or importance? Or one biblical book valued more highly than another? Any attempt to draw distinctions that in effect elevate some parts of the Bible over others would seem to be judging *God's Word* by a human standard.

As we have seen, however, the Bible was not miraculously given directly from God, and some of its content was scrutinized over a long period of time before finally being accepted as authoritative. Rather than a homogenous or flat Bible where every single word has equal authority with every other, we instead have a Bible with a varied landscape, containing hills and dales, peaks and valleys.

This is not a new idea. Five hundred years ago Martin Luther placed Hebrews, James, Jude and Revelation at the end of the New Testament due to his low opinion of those works. He said that James "wanted to guard against those who relied on faith without works, but was unequal to the task. He tries to accomplish by harping on the law what the apostles accomplish by stimulating people to love. Therefore I cannot include him among the chief books."[11] Elsewhere Luther said that in comparison to John's gospel, the Pauline epistles, and 1 Peter, James "is really an epistle of straw . . . for it has nothing of the nature of the gospel about it."[12]

We may disagree with Luther's assessment of James, but anyone who reads the Bible makes judgments about its content. I sometimes ask people

11. Luther, *Luther's Works*, Vol. 35, 397.
12. Ibid., 362.

in a church setting to write down a favorite Bible verse. In a group with as few as twenty or twenty-five people I will invariably get some repetition in the responses. How is it possible, with as many verses as are contained in the Bible, that a small group of people will produce identical favorite verses? On the other hand, I have yet to have someone list a favorite verse from the books of Leviticus or 3 John.

In practice, our Bibles are not flat, and we do not regard every verse as equally important to us or as having equal authority. If there were such a thing as a Bible-verse-reading-meter that could keep a worldwide record of the number of times each verse of the Bible was read over the course of a year, the results would show that every Christian gravitates toward some verses and not others. Many verses of the Bible, and indeed some entire books of the Bible, are virtually ignored by most Christians.

I do not intend to suggest that Christians may rightfully disregard some texts or that all opinions regarding favorite or less-than-favorite passages are equally valid. To handle the Bible with integrity, we must read it as it has come to us, including passages we may find to be less than inspiring, as well as others that may seem highly problematic theologically or morally offensive. The Bible we have has come to us through a centuries-long process involving worshipping communities with differing cultures, values, and assumptions. We will have more to say about how we ought to approach the reading of scripture, but for now we simply note the obvious: every Christian regards some parts of the Bible more highly than other parts.

Since we are speaking of the authority and inspiration of the Bible, we should say something about the meaning of these words. *Inspiration* is a broad term. We think of an inspiring sunset, or artists and musicians being inspired. The word communicates a sense of something that comes from beyond ourselves. In my own experience as a songwriter, I have sometimes asked myself after writing a song, "Where did that come from?" Even though songwriting, as any art form, involves discipline and work, there is also a sense that it comes to one as a gift, as it were, from somewhere (or someOne) outside of oneself. It involves an element of surprise—of the unexpected. And it leaves one with a sense of awe and wonder. From a theological perspective, inspiration has to do with a sense of the presence of God's spirit in our lives. The content of inspiration should be understood broadly, since it is a term that attempts to encompass the movement of

God's spirit among us. It cannot be contained within human boundaries, structures, or limitations.

John Cobb has said that

> there is no life at all except as God's Spirit participates in constituting us. It is that participation of the Spirit that leads to our being, in each moment, something more than the deterministic outcome of the forces from the past that also play so large a role in shaping us. The times when we think of ourselves as inspired are those when this creative novelty contributed by God's Spirit plays a particularly strong and effective role and is less inhibited than usual by the other causal factors in our lives.[13]

To speak of the Bible as inspired, therefore, means that it reflects the activity of God and thus tells us something about the nature of this God who is active in human history, as well as something about the claim of God upon our lives in the present and the call of God toward a particular sort of future. As Paul Achtemeier puts it,

> To say that Scripture is "inspired" means that God continues to address [God's] people through its pages in the present. For the Christian, the "inspired" Bible means that God spoke not only to our forebears in the history of Israel, and to the apostles in the founding generation of the Christian church, but that [God] also continues to address [God's] people through its pages, as they are read in public worship and private devotions.[14]

When we say that the Bible is inspired, we mean that it is part of the revelatory activity of God—not only in the production of the writings themselves, but within the history of those communities that produced the writings. We mean that the Bible is a result of God's initiative, and that it therefore contains truths about the nature of God and the intentions of God for humanity.

To say that the Bible is inspired is not to make any unique claim for the Bible. If inspiration, from a theological perspective, refers to the activity of God's spirit in the world, that activity is not limited to the pages of the Bible. Nor was inspiration a criterion in the consideration of which books to include in the Bible, as David Dungan has pointed out: "Inspiration was thought to be widely active in all branches of the Christian religion, not just among the orthodox . . . [so] *every* writing was thought by *someone* to be

---

13. Cobb, *The Process Perspective*, 71.

14. Achtemeier, *Inspiration and Authority*, 8.

inspired . . . . Since inspiration was a common, wide-spread phenomenon among Christians of all types, it could hardly help the orthodox in the critical task of separating genuine from forged apostolic writings."[15] Although Christians rightly speak of the Bible as inspired, inspiration refers to God's activity on a much broader scale than that involved in the formation of the Bible. Christians affirm the presence of God's spirit throughout the universe. The Bible is one result of that mysterious and marvelous activity.

The word *authority*, like the word inspiration, has a broad meaning. An authority on gardening is an expert who possesses a great deal of knowledge about gardening. Thus authority is associated with knowledge. A police officer has the authority to enforce compliance with the laws within a particular jurisdiction. Thus authority is associated with power or influence. The Bible, for Christians, possesses authority in both of these senses. It is a source of knowledge about God, and it has, potentially at least, the ability to influence one's life (to the extent that one takes it seriously).

The Bible's authority is a derived authority or a secondary authority. The truth toward which it points is a truth rooted in the history contained within its pages. We have already said that the Bible was not miraculously delivered straight from God. The Bible itself, therefore, is not a direct revelation of God. God did not speak it into existence. Nor did God deliver it fresh off of heavenly presses to Moses or Isaiah or Jesus. Ancient communities produced traditions that eventually were combined and collected in written form. Those communities claimed to discern the presence and activity of God within the stories, poetry, law codes, and other literary genres of their traditions. The Bible bears witness to the revelation of God in history. The nature of the Bible is not that of a systematic theological treatise, full of precision, clear argumentation, a set of clearly delineated doctrines, and neatly explained answers to our religious questions. The revelation of God in history is messy, mysterious, ambiguous, and wrapped within the assumptions and values of the communities within which it arose.

Interpretation, therefore, is both required and unavoidable. There are disharmonies among the stories preserved in the Bible and among the messages those stories communicate. Differing and even contrasting viewpoints existing within the communities that produced scripture are reflected in the pages of the Bible. We should try to keep our hearts and minds open to the ongoing revelatory activity of God as we seek interpretations that are truthful. Martin Luther correctly saw the necessity of interpretation (and

15. Dungan, 89.

possessed rather immodest confidence in the accuracy of his own interpretations). The following quote is from the preface to his translation of the New Testament into German:

> It would be right and proper for this book to go forth without any prefaces or extraneous names attached and simply have its own say under its own name. However many unfounded interpretations and prefaces have scattered the thought of Christians to a point where no one any longer knows what is gospel or law, New Testament or Old. Necessity demands, therefore, that there should be a notice or preface, by which the ordinary man can be rescued from his former delusions, set on the right track, and taught what he is to look for in this book, so that he may not seek laws and commandments where he ought to be seeking the gospel and promises of God.[16]

God's revelation is ongoing and not confined to a book or a set of books. Luther saw the need, in his own day, for a correction in the common thinking of church leaders and ordinary Christians. He received a particularly powerful insight helpful in his own journey and sought to communicate that insight to others.

The history of Christian theology is the history of a long succession of similar experiences of insight into the nature of God and of God's activity in the world. For example, the Nicene Creed is not found in the Bible. Augustine's discussion of original sin represents a novel reformulation of the meaning of the biblical material. Most modern understandings of Christ's atonement are based on post-biblical arguments and analogies. Many widely-held contemporary Christian beliefs are not derived directly from the pages of the Bible, but are rather the result of a long and ongoing history of applying the biblical witness to the experiences of Christian communities across past centuries. The revelation of God continues into the present. The insights of each succeeding generation are passed along to the next. The lens through which we read the Bible today is not the same lens possessed by Origin (third century) or Augustine (fifth century) or Aquinas (thirteenth century) or Calvin (sixteenth century) or even Karl Barth (twentieth century). What Christians see revealed in the Bible has changed over the course of the centuries.

This means that the Bible is a living entity. The message Christians have perceived as contained in its pages has changed over time. The process

16. Luther, *Luther's Works*, Vol. 35, 357.

of interpretation itself has a history.[17] God's revelatory activity becomes effective as the Bible is read by and influences the lives of Christians and the communities of faith to which they belong. The Bible has persevered as an authority source among Christians precisely because of its adaptability to the amazingly varied contexts within which Christians have lived over the past two thousand years. It serves Christian communities best when viewed as flexible, adaptable, and malleable.[18] It is not a helpful resource when it is rigidly and defensively used as part of an attempt to preserve old wineskins.[19] It is no help at all if it sits on a shelf and collects dust, its pages hardly ever opened. Too often Christians most vocal about defending the Bible's authority are not well acquainted with its content.

Many Christians today seem to have a protective posture in relation to the Bible, as though it needs safeguarding. We sometimes feel like we need to defend our territory and oppose those who challenge our ways of thinking. But when our attention is focused on guarding our turf, we cannot listen. And when other people are seen as opponents, we are not likely to believe we can learn something from sitting down and having a conversation with them. A defensive mentality, as though we are guarding a fortress against outside invaders, does not serve well the search for truth.

The Bible is not a treasure that needs defending, as though its truth is so fragile it cannot stand on its own. The Bible is a resource best wielded in the hands of truth-seekers.[20] It calls us to a journey of discovery. Perhaps a better image for understanding the function of the Bible as an authority source is to compare our faith journey to a voyage. The ship of discovery awaits, ready to sail, beckoning us to come aboard. The journey is not a solitary voyage; Christians are part of a community, and the Bible serves as a community authority. The Bible is like a map for our journey that opens up vistas and possibilities. Where do we wish to go today? What do we wish to explore? What new things await us? The image of a voyage helps us better see and understand both the diversity among Christians as well as the fact that Christians are not the only ones on this journey of truth-seeking. Those of other religious traditions have different maps, and part of

---

17. See, e.g., Grant and Tracy, *A Short History*; Pelikan, *Whose Bible is It?*; Kugel, *The Bible as it Was*; Kugel, *How to Read the Bible*; Lampe, *The Cambridge History of the Bible*, Vol. 1; and Ackroyd and Evans, *The Cambridge History of the Bible*, Vol. 2.

18. See Sanders' article on "Canon" cited previously.

19. See Mark 2:22.

20. See my comments about the characteristics of a truth-seeker in chapter 1.

our journey involves comparing maps, exploring points of similarity and difference.

Have you ever gone on a trip as part of a tour group for a week or so with people you had never met before? Did you enjoy meeting people from all walks of life and with different backgrounds? There is joy in sharing the excitement of going to new places with others who are also excited about seeing and experiencing new things. A sense of community can quickly form in such groups among people who have never been together before and who are often quite diverse.

Analogies inevitably break down when pushed too far, but they can be helpful when they clarify truthful aspects of abstract ideas. Thinking of the Bible as providing a map for our faith journey helps us preserve the sense of joy that is a part of exploration and discovery. Remembering that we are on this faith journey with others helps us remember that the Bible is a community resource. The Bible serves as a unique (though not the only) authority source for Christians in the sense that it testifies to a story within its pages that is regarded by Christians as *the* story of who God is and what God desires.

Stories are dynamic, open, and not limited to a single meaning or interpretation. The stories presented in the Bible are paradigmatic. They illustrate what God is doing everywhere at all times. They help us understand our present in relation to our past and our future. They help us sort out who we are and where we are, as well as whom we are called to be and where we are called to go. The stories of the Bible, for Christians, become part of our personal story. The past they relate is part of our own past. The Bible's authority is not an abstract, intrinsic quality that it somehow possesses independent of its hearers/readers. The Bible is authoritative to the extent that contemporary Christian communities allow it to change them and guide them. Its authority is authority-in-action as it shapes the beliefs, character and behavior of Christian individuals and communities.

Obviously, then, there is no point in speaking of the authority of the Bible for non-Christians. A non-Christian may well be edified by reading the Bible, or may find the stories it contains to be interesting. But it will be edifying or interesting in the same way that other non-biblical texts might be. Non-Christians have different maps for their truth-journeys. Similarly, the Bible cannot be authoritative for Christians who do not read it and who are unfamiliar with its content. Verbal affirmation of allegiance is not equivalent to the kind of engagement with the text that results in one's life being shaped and molded by its substance.

The Bible helps us check and validate our perceptions about God and God's activity when we take it seriously as a guide for our journey. It provides a common vocabulary for Christians and its stories become part of the common experience of Christians. Despite the incredible diversity that exists among Christians, the Bible provides a point of cohesion and unity. Just as there is incredible diversity among Spanish-speaking communities around the world, and yet, at the same time, a sense of shared heritage and culture, Christians also share a common heritage—one that finds concrete expression in our shared appeal to the authority of the Bible.

The commonality that exists among Christians does not reside in having the same beliefs derived from the Bible. Beliefs and doctrines have been focal points of acrimony and division among Christians as much as they have been threads of unity. Rather, Christians are bound together in the fact that they share the same stories told through the pages of the Bible. Of course, the stories of the Bible contain within them implicit beliefs, but those beliefs must be worked out in a process of interpretation, and as it happens, the number of beliefs that plausibly can be claimed to be universally shared by all Christians is actually quite limited.

Truth-seeking Christians seek to clarify their beliefs and sharpen their understanding. The Bible certainly aids them in that task. But as we have said, the stories of the Bible require interpretation. The authority of the Bible is not located in the specific content of the beliefs we may come to hold and profess individually and corporately as members of Christians communities, but rather in the fact that the Bible serves as a resource in the development and honing of those beliefs. And equally if not more importantly, the Bible serves as a resource for shaping the kinds of persons we are called to be, the kinds of communities we are called to create, and the sorts of actions that are consistent with such persons and communities.

The power of the Bible's authority is unleashed in the lives of Christian individuals and communities as we live out our desire to serve the God revealed in its pages. The authority of the Bible is an authority activated through a Christian faith commitment. By *faith*, I do not mean assent to a particular set of beliefs or doctrines (though many Christians, erroneously in my view, use the word in that way). Faith does not primarily describe an intellectual activity, though certainly faith involves the intellect. Faith, rather, describes a volitional commitment. Jesus did not quiz his disciples on their doctrine as a screening test for discipleship eligibility. He said, "Follow me." The commitment to follow Jesus is what makes one a Christian. The Bible is a fundamentally important resource and a primary authority source in helping us figure out what that commitment means in the concrete, ambiguous, messy, confusing, ever-changing context of our modern world.

Truth-seekers check their beliefs against an open-minded examination of the data. In the next chapter, we will take a look at some specific biblical texts. If the Bible is to have real authority for us, it must be the authority of the Bible we possess, not an abstract authority of an imagined Bible that does not exist. As strange as it sounds, many writers addressing the issue of the Bible's authority make assertions that are incompatible with the actual content of scripture. Our procedure will be first to examine the text, and then to think about implications for understanding the matter of the Bible's inspiration and authority.

3

Storybook or Textbook?

WE ARE READY TO turn our attention to the data of scripture. We have already noted that for Christians, the Bible is not just any writing. Christians view the Bible as an important authority source and read it with the expectation that God can and does speak through its pages. Anyone who reads the Bible with seriousness and diligence, however, will begin to notice discrepancies. These discrepancies were not invented by liberal scholars in order to discredit the authority of the Bible. Rather, they have existed as long as the Bible itself has existed. Modern scholars were not the first to notice them.

The discrepancies in the Bible were not a major problem for Christians before the modern scientific era. Modern academic disciplines such as archeology, literary criticism, and historical studies have increased our knowledge of ancient societies. This new knowledge has generated questions our predecessors could not have formulated. In addition, our modern worldview has changed the nature of our questioning as well as the kinds of responses we consider to be adequate. Explanations that may have satisfied someone living in the fifth or fifteenth centuries are no longer viable in our time.

Modern science tells us that the world was created 13.8 billion years ago. How does that information fit with the creation story in Genesis 1? Is one right and the other wrong? If we accept the conclusions of modern science, must we reject the Bible as no longer relevant? Or if we continue to affirm the Bible as pointing us toward truth, are we automatically put in opposition with science?

In this chapter, we will examine three types of problems that the Bible presents for modern readers: (1) the prescientific worldview of the Bible and its apparent conflict with modern science; (2) ethical perspectives that may have been perfectly ordinary hundreds of years ago, but seem highly problematic today; and (3) scripture contradicting scripture.

We begin with the third issue for a practical reason. We might not get very far in a discussion about whether an iron ax head really floated (2 Kings 6:1–7). Some will insist that it did, while others will insist that it could not—that such a thing is impossible. That kind of discussion seems to place the authority of the Bible in conflict with modern science, forcing Christians to choose between the two. Those who firmly believe the Bible cannot contain errors are highly resistant to arguments based on science or ethics. When a seeming conflict arises between modern science or modern ethical sensibilities, on the one hand, and what one understands to be biblical truth, on the other, many Christians will place their allegiance to biblical truth above modern truth claims.[1]

Evidence that the Bible directly contradicts itself, however, is harder to ignore. When there is a direct contradiction between one part of the Bible and another, the issue is not modern science versus the Bible, or the Bible versus modern ethical arguments, but rather the Bible versus itself. We either have to admit that the Bible contains contradictions, or find a way to resolve the apparent dilemmas. If we can honestly face the fact that the Bible contains internal contradictions and develop a perspective that nonetheless affirms the Bible's authority and inspiration, the issues of prescientific worldview and ethical difficulties can be simultaneously resolved.

The conundrums we are about to explore were not particularly troublesome for Christians in the pre-modern era. Today, we read the pages of scripture with a different worldview than persons living hundreds of years ago. We cannot avoid the particularities of our modern context. We need to keep in mind, however, that many of our questions would not have occurred to the biblical writers or to readers living in pre-modern times. In other words, these are modern dilemmas, but they are nonetheless real

---

1. The position taken in this book is that every truth claim must be respected and investigated. A truth-seeker cannot, therefore, reject a truth claim without exploring its merits simply because it challenges what one currently believes.

dilemmas for us. Christian faith lived in the modern world requires a response to these sorts of questions if we want to retain our credibility.

Although the particular questions we face today are different from ancient questions, the task of giving an intellectually coherent and satisfying account of our faith is nothing new. Christian thinkers have sought to present intelligible and convincing expositions of Christian faith since the time of Jesus. In the first centuries of Christian history, Christian apologists used the categories of Greek philosophy to make Christianity sensible to those living in the ancient near-eastern world. Christians attempt to systematize and offer an articulate exposition of their beliefs for at least two reasons: our intellectual curiosity spurs us onward in a journey of truth-discovery, and the Christian missionary impulse leads us to want to share with others the truth we have apprehended.

We always risk, however, an entanglement between Christian truth and intellectual or cultural untruths. Christian truth is not essentially connected to an affirmation of a geocentric universe, as was once thought. Nor is Christian truth essentially connected to the practice of circumcision, as some early Christians believed. The process of sorting out the essence of Christian truth is never-ending.

Critical analysis of the Bible is not the same as criticism of the Bible. I do not intend to criticize the Bible or present it in a negative light, but a careful reading of scripture reveals dilemmas of various sorts. When we notice these dilemmas and try to seek answers to the questions they raise, we are not exhibiting a lack of faith or an anti-Christian attitude. In fact, faith and a desire for understanding are interrelated. Anselm encapsulated this idea in his famous phrase, *fides quaerens intellectum* (faith seeking understanding). Love of God and a desire for more complete knowledge and understanding are not competing goals. Fear of asking questions or following the implications of one's discoveries is not a sign of a strong faith, but exactly the opposite. Faith and truth-seeking walk hand-in-hand.

If the examples below taken from the pages of the Bible seem disturbing to you or raise troubling questions for you, I encourage you to keep reading. We will have to clear away some untenable ways of viewing the inspiration and authority of the Bible before we will be able to build a better model for understanding how it can function effectively and authoritatively for Christians living in today's world.

> We cannot explore these questions without examining the text of the Bible. Before proceeding, I invite you to read Matthew 27:1–10. If you do not have a Bible handy, you can search for the text on the internet. Write down a summary of the passage and the order of events. Now read another account of the same events found in the book of Acts: Acts 1:15–19. Again, write down a summary of the events and the order in which they occurred. Now compare the two passages. What do you notice? Write down your observations.

The reports describing events surrounding the death of Judas contained in Matthew 27:1–10 and Acts 1:15–19 contain irreconcilable differences. In Matthew's account, the priests buy the field, but in the version of the story told in Acts, Judas buys it. In Matthew, Judas hangs himself, whereas in Acts there is no indication that Judas' death is the result of suicide. Both accounts agree that the field became known as the "Field of Blood," but for different reasons. In Acts, Judas buys the field before his death, while Matthew suggests that Judas hanged himself before the field was purchased.

These texts are contradictory. Both cannot be correct—either Judas bought the field, or the priests bought it. Either Judas hanged himself, or he fell headlong and his body burst open. Either the field was called "Field of Blood" because Judas died there, or it was called "Field of Blood" because it was purchased with blood money.

Do you consider these differences significant? Are you bothered by them? For an inerrantist, this kind of biblical contradiction presents an immediate problem. Inerrantists differ about what inerrancy means specifically, but no matter how they qualify their definition, inerrantists want to affirm that the Bible is without errors. The claim is more than an assertion that the Bible contains no errors; inerrantists claim that the Bible *cannot* contain errors. Observe the argument in the following quote from Millard Erickson:

> If God is omniscient, he must know all things. He cannot be ignorant of or in error on any matter. Further, if he is omnipotent, he is able to so affect the biblical author's writing that nothing erroneous enters into the final product. And being a truthful or veracious being, he will certainly desire to utilize these abilities in such a way

that humans will not be misled by the Scriptures. Thus, our view of inspiration logically entails the inerrancy of the Bible. Inerrancy is a corollary of the doctrine of full inspiration. If, then, it should be shown that the Bible is not fully truthful, our view of inspiration would also be in jeopardy.[2]

Rather than let the Bible shape his view of God, Erickson's view of God shapes his view of the Bible. He begins with assumptions about God and the way God works in the world, then draws conclusions about the Bible from those assumptions. Erickson is aware of the difficulties presented by the passage we just examined. He attempts to resolve the contradictions by proposing a scenario in which Judas both hangs himself and then falls headlong in the field. Erickson is silent on the other points of difference between the two texts. He simply affirms: "rather than giving fanciful explanations, it is better to leave such difficulties unresolved in the confidence, based on the doctrine of Scripture, that they will be removed to the extent that additional data become available."[3]

What additional data could possibly resolve the conflict concerning the purchaser of the field? What additional data would resolve the conflict regarding the origin of the name of the field? Either Matthew and Acts say what they say, or they do not. Erickson's presuppositions will not allow him to accept the evidence in front of his eyes that Matthew and Acts contradict one another, so his alternative option is wishful thinking: maybe someday, somehow, someone will figure out how to make the difficulty disappear. His answer is not an answer. Like the church in the days of Galileo, his question is not "Where is the truth?" but rather "Does this agree with my doctrine?" Doctrine takes precedence over evidence, so if the evidence contradicts one's doctrine, the evidence, rather than the doctrine, must be thrown out.[4]

Some inerrantists, in their treatment of discrepancies such as we find in this example from Matthew and Acts, seem to imply that the biblical authors really *did not* say what we think they say. They speak of the "inerrancy of the original writings." In other words, the original writings were without error, and if we had access to them, the discrepancies we observe in the Bible would disappear. The problem, of course, is that we do not

2. Erickson, *Christian Theology*, 251.

3. Ibid., 263.

4. Erickson dismisses the position of Dewey Beegle on page 259 of his book, for example, not on the basis of any rational arguments, but simply because Erickson considers his view to be unorthodox.

have access to any original writings. This view is intended to strengthen the foundations of an inerrancy position, since it honestly recognizes the contradictions that exist in the Bible. In actuality, however, it makes the problem worse, since the basis for one's claim about the truthfulness of the Bible now rests on non-existent documents. This position offers no foundation for affirming the truthfulness of the Bibles we *have*.

The inerrancy position is attractive to many because it holds out the prospect of some sort of guarantee that one's beliefs are founded on a secure basis. What could be more secure than a Bible without any errors? But if the foundation for one's belief is inaccessible (like the golden plates of Mormonism), then the text that one possesses (containing obvious contradictions) becomes *less* reliable, not more reliable. If we affirm the doctrine of inerrancy because we believe that without it the Bible cannot be viewed as inspired and truthful, yet we admit at the outset that all Bibles in existence today contain errors, how can our view of the inspiration of the Bible be sustained? If confidence in the basis of one's viewpoint is the goal, an "inerrancy of the original writings" position is the worst possible position to adopt since there can be no transfer of the presumed dependability and trustworthiness of the original documents to the actual writings we possess. This intellectual difficulty, however, has not prevented large numbers of Christian churches, denominations, colleges, and seminaries from insisting that members, students, and teachers affirm their agreement with doctrinal statements containing the phrase "inerrant in the original writings" or something close to it.[5]

A better view of the inspiration of the Bible starts with the Bible in our hands rather than a fantasy Bible that has never existed. We will return to this matter, but first we need to continue our exploration of the actual text of the Bible.

> Read Matthew 1:6–17 and Luke 3:23–31. In Matthew, start with David in verse 6 and make a list of the names in the genealogy down to Joseph (husband of Mary). For Luke, you will have to work backwards from David at the end of verse 31 to Joseph in verse 23. Now compare the two lists. What do you notice?

If you are reading ahead without doing the exercise in the preceding box, that is fine, of course, but doing the exercise is the best way to

5. For multiple examples, try an internet search containing that phrase.

experience the difference between the two texts. You will see that Luke has many more names than Matthew and that very few of the names in the two accounts match. Can both Matthew and Luke be correct? What do you think? The Bible contains a multitude of these sorts of inconsistencies. I encourage you to take the time to find a Bible and explore the sampling contained in the following boxes.

Old Testament examples:

1. Read Genesis chapter 10, verses 5, 20, and 31, and then read Genesis 11:1. Were there multiple languages, or was there only one language?

2. The Ten Commandments (literally, "ten words"; see verse 28) of Exodus 34 do not look at all like the Ten Commandments ("ten words"; see Deuteronomy 4:13) of Exodus 20 (or Deuteronomy 5), even though God tells Moses in Exodus 34:1 that "I will write on the tablets the words that were on the former tablets, which you broke." What do you think?

3. 2 Samuel 24 and 1 Chronicles 21 both report a census taken by David. In 2 Samuel, God commands David to conduct the census (see v. 1), whereas in 1 Chronicles, Satan "incited" David to take the census (v. 1). In addition, the numbers reported in the two accounts differ substantially (cf. 2 Sam 24:9 and 1 Chr 21:5).

4. Exodus 6:3 says that God did not reveal his personal name Yahweh (Hebrew: YHWH) to Abraham, Isaac or Jacob. Yet in Genesis 15:7 God says to Abraham, "I am the LORD [Hebrew: YHWH] who brought you from Ur of the Chaldeans, to give you this land to possess."

5. Joshua 11:16–23 says that Joshua conquered "the whole land" and that the enemies of the Israelites were "utterly destroyed" and "exterminated." Chapter 11 ends with this declaration: "So Joshua took the whole land, according to all that the LORD had spoken to Moses; and Joshua gave it for an inheritance to Israel according to their tribal allotments. And the land had rest from war." Yet Joshua chapter 13 begins by listing all of the lands that have not been conquered, and the book of Judges begins with the Israelites asking, "Who shall go up first for us against the Canaanites, to fight against them?"

New Testament examples:

1. Read Mark 6:8–11 and Matthew 10:9–15. Were the disciples to wear sandals, or not to wear sandals?

2. Compare Matthew 20:20–21 with Mark 10:35–37. Who addresses Jesus to ask him a favor?

3. Read John 2:13–17 and Matthew 21:12–13. Do you think the same thing happened twice in Jesus's life, once at the beginning of his ministry and again at the end?

4. There are a lot of variations in the stories concerning Jesus's crucifixion and resurrection. Compare Mark 16:5, Matthew 28:2 and Luke 24:4. Was the stone already rolled away with a young man in a white robe sitting on the right side, or did an angel descend from heaven and roll back the stone, or did the women find the stone rolled away, go in to find the tomb empty and then suddenly encounter two men in dazzling clothes standing beside them? Are we to believe John 20:2's report that Mary Magdalene ran from the empty tomb and reported to Peter the fact that Jesus's body was missing or Mark 16:8's version that she (and the other women) "said nothing to anyone, for they were afraid"?

There are dozens of examples throughout the Bible of inconsistencies similar to those contained in the boxes above. Their existence does not necessarily mean that belief in the inspiration of the Bible is untenable. However, they present immediate difficulties for any claim that the Bible contains no errors and for views of the Bible's inspiration that rest on such a claim.

These discrepancies exist. Anyone engaged in a careful study of the Bible will find them. They were not invented by atheists trying to destroy the Bible's authority. This is the Bible we have. This is the Bible, containing dozens of inconsistencies and discrepancies, which we are talking about when we discuss the issue of inspiration and authority. Whatever view of inspiration and authority we adopt, if it is to have integrity and be logically coherent and defensible, must start with knowledge of the content of the Bible that has been passed down to us. Abstract theories that presume some sort of nonexistent harmony and perfect alignment within scripture are intellectually dishonest and result in distortions of the Bible as it is contorted to fit into a prefabricated theological mold.

So let us be honest and recognize that the Bible contains real contradictions. These contradictions are not merely apparent (i.e., resolvable if we had further knowledge). They have existed for as long as the Bible has existed, and they are not going away. As truth-seekers, let us base our thinking about the Bible's inspiration and authority on an acceptance of the data in front of us. Our beliefs should rest on an honest acknowledgement of the facts.

Modern scholarship has tremendously increased our understanding of the Bible and its message. Biblical scholars have devoted lifetimes to the study of the biblical text and we can learn much from their efforts. One of the great insights of modern biblical scholarship is the dependence of the Bible on pre-existing written sources. For example, as scholars have studied the synoptic Gospels (Matthew, Mark, and Luke), they have concluded that Matthew and Luke seem to have used Mark as a source in the composition of their Gospels. Matthew and Luke also have a lot of material in common that is not from the gospel of Mark, which has led scholars to conclude that Matthew and Luke both incorporated material from another source that we no longer have. Scholars have given this hypothetical source the name Q (from the German word *Quelle*, meaning *source*).

Old Testament scholars have reached a similar conclusion regarding the first five books of the Old Testament. The Documentary Hypothesis claims that the content of Genesis through Deuteronomy is the result of a complex blending of a number of different written sources (each preceded by long oral traditions), with different geographic and historical origins. Scholars who develop such theories are not using hocus-pocus tricks. They reach their conclusions on the basis of the evidence in front of them. This evidence can be examined by others, and if an explanation proves convincing to a broad range of scholars, it becomes the consensus view until and unless another, better explanation comes along. In other words, scholars do not accept a particular explanation because it is doctrinally correct. They accept it because it seems to account for the data in a reasonable way. There is a tentativeness to their views. In some areas, there are explanations that have been around for a while, have withstood a great deal of scrutiny, and are widely accepted. In other areas, a consensus may be lacking or the consensus that exists may be tenuous.

These scholarly explanations do not involve smoke and mirrors, nor are they locked in a secret vault. Anyone who wishes to expend the necessary time and effort may examine the same evidence and draw her or his own conclusions. Obviously, we do not have the space here for a detailed analysis of the scholarly evidence for the Documentary Hypothesis. There are plenty of places one can turn for those kinds of explorations.[6] If the Documentary Hypothesis is true, however, there are implications for our understanding of the Bible and our view of its inspiration. It is worth exploring at least one Old Testament text in some detail, therefore, so you can see for yourself some of the reasons why the Documentary Hypothesis is so powerful in explaining what we find in the first several books of the Old Testament.

Read the story below about Noah, the ark, and the flood that covered the earth. I suggest you take some notes as you are reading, even if you think you are already familiar with the story. Outline the story, including the main points and any information you deem pertinent. You will be able to understand my argument much more clearly if you do this exercise before proceeding.

> The Lord saw that the wickedness of humankind was great in the earth, and that every inclination of the thoughts of their hearts was only evil continually. And the Lord was sorry that he had made humankind on the earth, and it grieved him to his heart. So the Lord said, "I will blot out from the earth the human beings I have created—people together with animals and creeping things and birds of the air, for I am sorry that I have made them." But Noah found favor in the sight of the Lord.

> Then the Lord said to Noah, "Go into the ark, you and all your household, for I have seen that you alone are righteous before me in this generation. Take with you seven pairs of all clean animals, the male and its mate; and a pair of the animals that are not clean, the male and its mate; and seven pairs of the birds of the air also, male and female, to keep their kind alive on the face of all the earth. For in seven days I will send rain on the earth for forty days and forty nights; and every living thing that I have made I will blot out from the face of the ground." And Noah did all that the Lord had commanded him.

6. For an excellent brief introduction to the main lines of argument, see the chapter "Collection of Evidence" in Friedman, *The Bible with Sources Revealed*.

And after seven days the waters of the flood came on the earth. The rain fell on the earth for forty days and forty nights. And the LORD shut him in. The flood continued for forty days on the earth; and the waters increased, and bore up the ark, and it rose high above the earth. The waters swelled and increased greatly on the earth; and the ark floated on the face of the waters. The waters swelled so mightily on the earth that all the high mountains under the whole heaven were covered; the waters swelled above the mountains, covering them fifteen cubits deep.

Everything on dry land in whose nostrils was the breath of life died. He blotted out every living thing that was on the face of the ground, human beings and animals and creeping things and birds of the air; they were blotted out from the earth. Only Noah was left, and those that were with him in the ark.

And the waters gradually receded from the earth. At the end of forty days Noah opened the window of the ark that he had made. Then he sent out the dove from him, to see if the waters had subsided from the face of the ground; but the dove found no place to set its foot, and it returned to him to the ark, for the waters were still on the face of the whole earth. So he put out his hand and took it and brought it into the ark with him. He waited another seven days, and again he sent out the dove from the ark; and the dove came back to him in the evening, and there in its beak was a freshly plucked olive leaf; so Noah knew that the waters had subsided from the earth. Then he waited another seven days, and sent out the dove; and it did not return to him any more.

And Noah removed the covering of the ark, and looked, and saw that the face of the ground was drying. Then Noah built an altar to the LORD, and took of every clean animal and of every clean bird, and offered burnt-offerings on the altar. And when the LORD smelled the pleasing odor, the LORD said in his heart, "I will never again curse the ground because of humankind, for the inclination of the human heart is evil from youth; nor will I ever again destroy every living creature as I have done. As long as the earth endures, seedtime and harvest, cold and heat, summer and winter, day and night, shall not cease."

Now read another story about Noah and the flood. Once again, I suggest you take some notes as you are reading. Some aspects of this story will be similar, but you may notice some striking differences. I suggest you again make an outline of the story. You will be better prepared to compare the two stories if you do.

> These are the descendants of Noah. Noah was a righteous man, blameless in his generation; Noah walked with God. And Noah had three sons, Shem, Ham, and Japheth. Now the earth was corrupt in God's sight, and the earth was filled with violence. And God saw that the earth was corrupt; for all flesh had corrupted its ways upon the earth. And God said to Noah, "I have determined to make an end of all flesh, for the earth is filled with violence because of them; now I am going to destroy them along with the earth. Make yourself an ark of cypress wood; make rooms in the ark, and cover it inside and out with pitch. This is how you are to make it: the length of the ark three hundred cubits, its width fifty cubits, and its height thirty cubits. Make a roof for the ark, and finish it to a cubit above; and put the door of the ark in its side; make it with lower, second, and third decks. For my part, I am going to bring a flood of waters on the earth, to destroy from under heaven all flesh in which is the breath of life; everything that is on the earth shall die. But I will establish my covenant with you; and you shall come into the ark, you, your sons, your wife, and your sons' wives with you. And of every living thing, of all flesh, you shall bring two of every kind into the ark, to keep them alive with you; they shall be male and female. Of the birds according to their kinds, and of the animals according to their kinds, of every creeping thing of the ground according to its kind, two of every kind shall come in to you, to keep them alive. Also take with you every kind of food that is eaten, and store it up; and it shall serve as food for you and for them." Noah did this; he did all that God commanded him.
>
> Noah was six hundred years old when the flood of waters came on the earth. And Noah with his sons and his wife and his sons' wives went into the ark to escape the waters of the flood. Of clean animals, and of animals that are not clean, and of birds, and of everything that creeps on the ground, two and two, male and female, went into the ark with Noah, as God had commanded Noah.
>
> In the six-hundredth year of Noah's life, in the second month, on the seventeenth day of the month, on that day all the fountains of the great deep burst forth, and the windows of the heavens were opened.

On the very same day Noah with his sons, Shem and Ham and Japheth, and Noah's wife and the three wives of his sons, entered the ark, they and every wild animal of every kind, and all domestic animals of every kind, and every creeping thing that creeps on the earth, and every bird of every kind—every bird, every winged creature. They went into the ark with Noah, two and two of all flesh in which there was the breath of life. And those that entered, male and female of all flesh, went in as God had commanded him. And all flesh died that moved on the earth, birds, domestic animals, wild animals, all swarming creatures that swarm on the earth, and all human beings.

And the waters swelled on the earth for one hundred and fifty days. But God remembered Noah and all the wild animals and all the domestic animals that were with him in the ark. And God made a wind blow over the earth, and the waters subsided; the fountains of the deep and the windows of the heavens were closed, the rain from the heavens was restrained.

At the end of one hundred and fifty days the waters had abated; and in the seventh month, on the seventeenth day of the month, the ark came to rest on the mountains of Ararat. The waters continued to abate until the tenth month; in the tenth month, on the first day of the month, the tops of the mountains appeared. And [he] sent out the raven; and it went to and fro until the waters were dried up from the earth.

In the six hundred and first year, in the first month, on the first day of the month, the waters were dried up from the earth. In the second month, on the twenty-seventh day of the month, the earth was dry. Then God said to Noah, "Go out of the ark, you and your wife, and your sons and your sons' wives with you. Bring out with you every living thing that is with you of all flesh—birds and animals and every creeping thing that creeps on the earth—so that they may abound on the earth, and be fruitful and multiply on the earth." So Noah went out with his sons and his wife and his sons' wives. And every animal, every creeping thing, and every bird, everything that moves on the earth, went out of the ark by families.

Now that you have finished, compare your outlines and your notes. What do you notice? Although these stories, if read independently, are entirely coherent and contain no internal contradictions, when compared, we see some differences. For one thing, the first story consistently uses "the LORD" when speaking of God, whereas the second story simply says "GOD." In the first story, the announcement from Yahweh to enter the ark comes to Noah seven days before the flood begins and Noah, his family, and all of the animals (including seven pairs of clean animals and seven pairs of birds) go into the ark the same day (i.e., seven days before the flood begins). In the second story, instructions are given for building the ark, only two pairs of animals and birds are mentioned, and the flood begins on the same day Noah, his family, and the animals enter the ark.

In the first story, the inhabitants of the ark are in the ark for seven days before the flood begins, then for forty days and forty nights, then for another seven days, then for another seven days, for a total of sixty-one days. In the second story, the inhabitants of the ark are in the ark for more than a year. In the first story, Noah sends out a dove. In the second, he sends out a raven. In the first story, Noah builds an altar and performs sacrifices (this is the story that includes seven pairs of clean animals), whereas in the second story there are no sacrifices (sacrifices would presumably have caused immediate extinctions).

What is the origin of these two stories? Actually they are both found verbatim in Genesis 6:5–8:22, except not as you have read them here. In the Bible these stories are blended and interwoven, as if someone did a cut-and-paste combination. The first story that speaks of God as "the LORD" uses "YHWH" (Yahweh) for the name of God, while the second story uses "Elohim" when speaking of God. Scholars refer to the source from which the first story is derived as the "Yahwist" source and the source that produced the second story as the "Priestly" source due to its concern elsewhere in the Torah with priestly themes. These two sources are among four main sources scholars have identified in the Torah (there is much discussion about other possible less-prominent sources). Apparently the editor(s) of Genesis had available two stories from different sources. Rather than exclude either one, both were blended together.

If the Bible contained only the story from one of these sources, there would be no contradictions in the biblical story of the flood. But two stories have been intermingled. The Old Testament contains many examples of this kind of blending of ancient traditions. Some interpreters have attempted to contort the biblical text in all sorts of ways to force it into a mold of complete and perfect harmony. But the text resists that kind of rough treatment. In the case of the story of Noah, the simplest explanation—that we have two sources that have been blended and that retain points of differ-ence—removes the difficulty presented by contradictions within the overall story as we find it in Genesis. When separated into two stories as we have done above, *internal* contradictions disappear. What remain are the contra-dictions *between* the two stories—stories that arose as part of sources that developed within differing historical, geographical, and cultural contexts.

Our purpose here is not to review the wealth of evidence support-ing the Documentary Hypothesis, including the fact that the sources consistently employ styles of Hebrew language that come from different time periods, consistently use different terminology, are consistent in their content, etc.[7] The evidence is available, should you wish to expend the effort to examine it. As Friedman says, "the combined weight of the evidence . . . should make it clear why this explanation of the biblical origins has been so compelling for more than a century. And, whether one agrees with this explanation, questions it, or challenges it, one will have in front of him or her the evidence to address."[8]

Recognizing that the Bible contains a blending of sources that are not always harmonious means that we admit that the Bible contains internal contradictions. We reach this conclusion on the basis of the biblical text itself. Our view of the Bible's inspiration must begin with the data of scrip-ture, not some abstract assumptions about what we think inspiration must mean. A careful reading of the Bible leads us to conclude that inerrancy is not a logically defensible position. The idea of inerrancy contradicts the plain content of scripture. As we shall see, affirming the inspiration and authority of the Bible requires no acceptance of its inerrancy.

Erickson is flatly mistaken when he asserts that "if the Bible is not in-errant, then our knowledge of God may be inaccurate and unreliable."[9] This is an argument based in fear—an attempt to scare Christians into agree-ment with one's position. Rather than encouraging an open-minded, posi-tive, and exciting exploration of the evidence, it pushes one into a defensive stance. Truth-seekers are not controlled by fear. They follow the evidence in front of their eyes and the urgings of their heart. For the truth-seeking Christian, the Bible is an important source of knowledge about the charac-ter and purposes of God and its value is neither erased nor diminished by the fact that it contains contradictions.

7. See Friedman, *The Bible with Sources Revealed*.

8. Ibid., 31.

9. Erickson, *Christian Theology*, 246.

As an aside, it may be worth noting the historical context within which the emphasis on the Bible's inerrancy arose. I have already pointed out that the rise of modern science caused questions to be posed in relation to the Bible that were never previously asked. The Catholic Church tried to suppress the views of Galileo and others, but with the rise of nation-states and the tremendous changes occurring in the western world in the eighteenth and nineteenth centuries, the Church had an increasingly difficult time asserting its authority. When one's *actual* authority is threatened, one may be tempted to *declare* one's authority more aggressively in an effort to maintain one's power.

Such was the case in relation to the Roman Catholic Church when, in 1870, it defined the doctrine of papal infallibility. Protestants, having no pope, turned to avowals of the Bible's authority. Conservative Protestants felt threatened by ideas such as evolution and the challenges of historical and critical biblical scholarship in the late nineteenth and early twentieth centuries. A collection of essays in twelve volumes entitled *The Fundamentals* (source of the word "fundamentalism" to describe the movement) was published from 1910 to 1915. These essays defended traditional doctrines and attacked perceived threats, including many of the discoveries of modern scholarship. Eventually, defense of biblical inerrancy came to be seen by many conservative Protestants as equivalent to defense of the Bible.

Defenders of inerrancy have caused grave harm in the personal lives of many Christians. If the only problem with belief in inerrancy were that it has become as indefensible in our modern world as was the Catholic Church's resistance to the idea of a heliocentric (sun-centered) solar system, we could dismiss those who defend it as deluded or blinded by their theological prejudices. However, when the defenders of inerrancy claim that their position is the only possible position for a true Christian, they create a false dilemma.[10] Christians reared within a tradition that equates genuine Christianity with assent to the doctrine of inerrancy face a difficult struggle when they recognize the doctrine's weaknesses. They have been told that rejection of inerrancy is tantamount to a rejection of the Bible's authority and, in effect, Christianity itself. Yet, when they acknowledge the undeniable contradictions contained in the Bible, the doctrine of inerrancy becomes something that can no longer be affirmed in good conscience.

---

10. "False dilemma" is a type of logical fallacy, also called the "either/or fallacy," in which only two options are presented or considered when in fact there is at least a third and perhaps more alternative positions.

What is an honest, truth-seeking Christian to do when faced with such a dilemma?

Once one concedes that the Bible contains contradictions, there is no possible return to a prior state of ignorance. Too often when that threshold is crossed, the Christian community we have known and that has provided us spiritual nurture and sustenance says to us, in effect, "You are no longer one of us." What are Christians in such a situation supposed to do? Where can they turn? The community that has sustained them and supported them in their faith journey will only continue fully to affirm them as *belonging* (having the status of members-in-good-standing) if they deny within themselves a truth that will not be stifled. Some mistakenly believe that abandonment of Christianity is the only option open to them if they refuse to lobotomize the portion of their brains that makes possible higher-level thinking.

When those who grow up with a type of Christianity that defends inerrancy encounter real problems with the text, they are tempted to throw out the authority of the text completely. They do not see how it is possible to combine discrepancies in the text with any concept of the truthfulness of the text. The result, all too often, is that such truth-seeking Christians leave the faith. Rather than an inerrantist approach being a way of defending the authority of the text, as is so often claimed, its practical result is often to lead people toward an abandonment of Christianity.

Many inerrantist Christians, consciously or unconsciously, seem to sense this truth. That is apparently why a number of Christian institutions seem to be designed to create a kind of "Christian bubble" that minimizes contact with the exterior, secular world. Home schooling, Christian educational institutions, Christian bookstores, Christian radio and television stations and a plethora of other self-identified Christian organizations and institutions in many instances represent an attempt to create an insulating barrier, keeping challenges to true faith at bay. Calls for sanctioned public Christian prayers in public schools and government entities, for the posting of the Ten Commandments on public property, and for teaching alternatives to evolution in public schools are attempts to extend the bubble into the public square, making not just Christianity, but *a particular version of Christianity*, the established and government-supported religion.

In the United States, at least, some Christians have been highly successful with such tactics (though certainly not as successful as they would like). Their approach, however, is necessarily reactionary and defensive.

Any weaknesses in the ideological system could result in a collapse of the entire edifice, as we have just observed in our discussion of the doctrine of inerrancy. Thus, this brand of Christianity is constantly threatened by those who are genuine truth-seekers, since truth-seekers are open-minded, like to ask questions, and tend to challenge dogmatic assertions. Inerrantist Christians tend to focus on trying to squash threats as they arise. The truth, however, is difficult to suppress.

Although inerrantist Christians tend to disagree, it is certainly possible for a follower of Jesus to conclude that the Bible contains contradictions and errors and at the same time remain a follower of Jesus. So far, we have presented evidence to show that a careful reading of the Bible cannot avoid the conclusion that there are irreconcilable internal inconsistencies in the Bible. For inerrancy to be shown to be false, all that is required is one example of such a contradiction. In fact, however, an entire book could easily be filled with nothing beyond an examination of example after example of internal biblical discrepancies or self-contradictions.[11] We have shown that many of these places of tension within the text are easily explained when we recognize that the Bible is a product of multiple sources that do not always agree.[12] There are other issues that arise when open-minded truth-seekers carefully examine the content of the Bible, however, including issues related to modern science and ethical difficulties raised by the text.

The non-scientific worldview of the Bible seems to pit the truth of the Bible against the truth of modern science. Incidents are described in the Bible which, from a modern perspective, we would conclude are impossible. We already mentioned at the beginning of this chapter the example of the iron ax head that floats (2 Kings 6:1–7). Joshua 10:12–13 tells the story of a battle during which Joshua called upon God to stop the sun in the sky so that the battle could continue and the Israelites could take "vengeance on their enemies." According to the text, the "sun stopped in mid-heaven, and did not hurry to set for about a whole day." In 2 Kings 20:8–11 (see also Isaiah 38:8) Isaiah gives a sign to Hezekiah that Hezekiah will be healed. The sign is that the sun will move backward in the sky, which, according to the text, happens.

Genesis 1 and Genesis 2 contain conflicting accounts of the creation of the earth. In chapter 1, the order of creation is first light, then a dome or

11. For one example, see Sullivan, *Toward a Mature Faith*.

12. *Explained* does not mean *explained away*. In other words, the tensions have not disappeared. But now we understand why they are present.

firmament, then dry land and vegetation, then the sun, moon, and stars, then sea and air creatures, then land creatures, then human beings. In the second chapter, the order is a man (Adam), then a garden (vegetation), then animals and birds, then a woman (Eve). Besides the differences in the order of creation, how is it scientifically possible for there to be vegetation before the sun, moon, and stars are created? Does modern science believe it is plausible for vegetation and animal life to have appeared on earth in between the appearance of the first human male and the first human female?

Plenty of additional examples could be given. Think about the story of Noah's ark for a moment. Is it possible for a pair from each animal species on the earth to fit onto a single vessel? Whether they were in the ark for sixty-one days or for more than a year, could they have carried aboard sufficient food to have survived that long? What would prevent some of the animals from eating some of the other animals? Is it possible for water to cover all land on our planet? Is there evidence that such a thing ever occurred?

Christians who would never accept such a story as historically reliable were it to appear in the Upanishads (ancient Hindu writings), ancient Chinese mythology, or Native American traditions are ready to defend every detail as literally true because it is in the Bible. We have seen, however, that defending every detail is impossible, since the details differ. Once one concedes the truth that the Bible contains irreconcilable internal conflicts, attempts to defend the literal truth of the Bible against the claims of modern science become pointless.

Modern science has challenged the truth of many traditional Christian beliefs. But do these challenges represent a threat to Christianity itself? Many scientists who accept the evidence for evolution and for a universe that is billions of years old as overwhelmingly convincing are also Christians. Obviously, then, modern science and Christianity are not necessarily in conflict. As was the case in relation to the internal contradictions contained in scripture, the challenges of modern science are only threats to a particular variety of Christianity—one that insists that a literal reading of the Bible is an essential aspect of true Christian faith. But as we have already seen, any attempt to defend a literal reading of the Bible is a cause lost before one ever engages the challenges of modern science. The multiple traditions contained within the Bible are self-contradictory.

So what point is there in arguing that the earth can be no more than ten thousand years old (dating based on the number of human generations contained in the Bible going back to Adam) against the massive amount of scientific data suggesting our solar system is roughly 4.5 billion years old? The scientific evidence is there for anyone to explore. Genuine truth-seekers, if they have cause to dispute the conclusions that the vast majority of scientists have drawn from the evidence, will propose an alternative explanation for the data and allow it to be examined in scholarly forums. They will open-mindedly await the verdict of a scholarly consensus as others look at the evidence from the perspective of the alternative proposal.

No such alternative explanations of the evidence have been found to be convincing. In fact, as we gain more data, scientists are able to date the age of our universe with ever greater precision and are charting in greater detail the evolutionary history of human beings.[13] New tools such as molecular biology and genome analysis are shedding new light on questions related to human origins. Data from the Hubble Telescope has greatly enhanced our understanding of the universe. Additional data, as it has come in, has supported rather than refuted the overall scientific consensus, though sometimes reshaping it in significant ways. New data has narrowed the range of plausible explanations, but it has not overturned the scientific consensus that the universe we live in is almost unimaginably ancient.[14]

Why are more Christians not aware of this information? Because in the United States the number of Christians who wish to construct a bubble-world that excludes information deemed objectionable has grown fairly large. Even if one does not live entirely within the bubble, one is affected by it. School boards, for example, have tried to restrict the teaching of evolution. Even though they have generally been unsuccessful, they have created a climate in which the teaching of evolution is not robustly implemented. Few high school graduates in the United States have a rudimentary understanding of the theory of evolution and the evidence supporting it. The gap between the views of the scientific community and those of the general population in the United States on this topic is astounding. Gallup polling shows that over the past thirty years, persons who believe that "God created human beings pretty much in their present form at one time within the past 10,000 years or so" have consistently constituted between 40

13. For a succinct, readable introduction to the evidence for evolution, see Coyne, *Why Evolution is True.*

14. For example, not too long ago scientists debated whether the universe would cease expanding and begin to contract, eventually collapsing into a "big crunch." We now know that the expansion will continue.

percent and 50 percent of the US population.[15] The US National Academy of Sciences, on the other hand, supports the teaching of evolution and opposes the teaching of creationism.[16] Why this gap? The Gallup poll shows a correlation between belief in evolution and higher levels of education, as well as a correlation between belief in creationism and high levels of church attendance.[17] When an inadequate science education at the primary, secondary and even higher levels is combined with a cultural environment that reinforces a certain understanding of the Bible, its teachings, and the relation between those teachings and one's faith, non-scientific ideas and anti-scientific attitudes are more likely to flourish.

Science is a truth-seeking enterprise. Certainly scientists are not without their prejudices, but ultimately those prejudices must bow to the weight of evidence. A new theory will naturally encounter resistance, but if it has explanatory power it will eventually gain adherents. Of course, science has limitations on the parameters of its investigations. Science cannot prove or disprove the existence of God. A scientific answer cannot be provided for philosophical questions about morality or the highest human virtues. Science cannot explain why the universe is here. However, science can tell us a great deal about how the universe operates, how it developed and changed over time, and what the future of the universe looks like in general terms. As it examines the physical world in which we find ourselves, science, ideally at least, is open to challenges, stands ready to accept alternative explanations should they prove more powerful, and establishes procedures designed to reduce the influence of bias. Modern science has had an incalculable influence on our world and the way we view it because it has helped us learn so much about this world and how it functions.

Science does not have to be viewed as in conflict with religion. The Catholic Church's condemnation of Galileo was unnecessary as a defense of Christianity and ultimately proved to be an embarrassment requiring an apology. The same fate awaits any attempt by Christians to make a scientific argument on the basis of a theological belief. Perhaps within the isolation of a Christian bubble one can sustain a belief that evolution is a theory

15. "Evolution, Creationism, Intelligent Design," http://www.gallup.com/poll/21814/evolution-creationism-intelligent-design.aspx.

16. "Evolution and Creationism in Schools," http://www.nationalacademies.org/evolution/InSchools.html.

17. Newport, "In U.S., 46% Hold Creationist View of Human Origins," http://www.gallup.com/poll/155003/hold-creationist-view-human-origins.aspx.

without foundation and that the earth is actually only a few thousand years old, but outside the bubble such beliefs have not been persuasive.[18]

I find it telling that in all my many years of teaching, among the hundreds of adherents of young earth creationism who have sat in my classes, I have never encountered a single defender of creationism who did not also hold inerrantist Christian beliefs. I also find interesting the fact that those who oppose so vigorously the scientific consensus on the narrow points of evolution and the age of the universe generally seem to be quite accepting of the findings of science and its technological achievements in areas not perceived to be in conflict with their faith.

We have seen that the Bible contains internal contradictions and we have seen that many stories in the Bible contain descriptions of events that one would have to say, from a modern scientific perspective, could never have happened. Before we look at how the Bible can be viewed as inspired and authoritative while at the same time honestly recognizing these realities of the text, we need to examine another area where the clash between the ancient culture represented in the pages of the Bible and that of our modern world is acutely evident.

A careful reading of the Bible quickly reveals some disturbing ethical conundrums. Slavery was accepted in the Bible. Women were regarded as property. The ancient Israelites were commanded by God, according to the text of the Bible, to engage in what we would today call ethnic cleansing. Were it possible to regard the ethical sensibilities of the ancient cultures reflected in the pages of the Bible as simply different from our own, but not necessarily an ideal for us to follow in our own time, we could happily ignore verses such as Psalm 137:9: "Happy shall they be who take your little ones and dash them against the rock!" But a difficulty arises because the God reflected in the pages of the Bible seems either to command or to be involved in things that our modern world regards as horrifying.

We have already mentioned internal difficulties in the text of Joshua. Few modern scholars believe the kind of total conquest described in passages such as Joshua 11:16–23 actually occurred. As we have seen, other texts in Joshua and Judges contradict the picture presented there. Yet the theological difficulty of the passage is not removed by categorizing the story as imagined history rather than actual history. Verse 20 says that "it was

18. Supporters of teaching intelligent design as an alternative to evolutionary theory have been unable to make their case in court, for example. See the opinion handed down by Judge John E. Jones II in *Kitzmiller et al. v. Dover Area School District.*

the LORD's doing to harden their hearts so that they would come against Israel in battle, in order that they might be utterly destroyed, and might receive no mercy, but be exterminated, just as the LORD had commanded Moses." As the people prepare to enter the Promised Land, Moses gives them instructions from God: "But as for the towns of these peoples that the LORD your God is giving you as an inheritance, you must not let anything that breathes remain alive. You shall annihilate them—the Hittites and the Amorites, the Canaanites and the Perizzites, the Hivites and the Jebusites—just as the LORD your God has commanded" (Deut 20:16–17). When the Israelites fail to destroy everything as God instructs ("kill both man and woman, child and infant, ox and sheep, camel and donkey" 1 Sam 15:3) as happens in 1 Samuel 15, God rejects Saul as king over Israel: "Because you did not obey the voice of the LORD, and did not carry out his fierce wrath against Amalek, therefore the LORD has done this thing to you today" (1 Samuel 28:18).

In the Exodus stories, Moses often intervenes to plead with God. In effect, Moses has to talk God out of destroying the very people God has only shortly before rescued from slavery in Egypt. Here is a text from Exodus 32:9–14:

> The LORD said to Moses, "I have seen this people, how stiffnecked they are. Now let me alone, so that my wrath may burn hot against them and I may consume them; and of you I will make a great nation." But Moses implored the LORD his God, and said, "O LORD, why does your wrath burn hot against your people, whom you brought out of the land of Egypt with great power and with a mighty hand? Why should the Egyptians say, 'It was with evil intent that he brought them out to kill them in the mountains, and to consume them from the face of the earth'? Turn from your fierce wrath; change your mind and do not bring disaster on your people. Remember Abraham, Isaac, and Israel, your servants, how you swore to them by your own self, saying to them, 'I will multiply your descendants like the stars of heaven, and all this land that I have promised I will give to your descendants, and they shall inherit it for ever.'" And the LORD changed his mind about the disaster that he planned to bring on his people.

In Numbers 16:20–22, Moses and Aaron again have to talk God out of destroying the "whole congregation":

> Then the LORD spoke to Moses and to Aaron, saying: Separate yourselves from this congregation, so that I may consume them in

a moment. They fell on their faces, and said, "O God, the God of the spirits of all flesh, shall one person sin and you become angry with the whole congregation?"

In this instance, the anger of God is assuaged when the households of Korah, Dathan, and Abiram (including "their wives, their children, and their little ones") are taken "down alive into Sheol; the earth closed over them, and they perished from the midst of the assembly" (see verses 27–33). The text adds that "fire came out from the LORD and consumed the two hundred fifty men offering the incense" (verse 35). Just a few verses later, God is again ready to destroy the entire congregation of the Israelites. This time, Aaron quickly runs to make atonement for the people, but he is too late to save fourteen thousand seven hundred people who die from a plague sent from God, according to the text (see verses 41–50).

God's wrath can appear somewhat arbitrary to modern readers of the Bible. In 2 Samuel 6, as David is bringing the ark of the covenant to Jerusalem, the text says that "Uzzah reached out his hand to the ark of God and took hold of it, for the oxen shook it" (verse 6). One might think that steadying the ark so that it does not fall would be viewed in God's eyes as a helpful thing and that God would, if anything, express appreciation to Uzzah for his assistance. But verse 7 tells us that the "anger of the LORD was kindled against Uzzah; and God struck him there because he reached out his hand to the ark; and he died there beside the ark of God."

The famous story of Abraham and his near-slaughter of his son Isaac is found in Genesis 22:1–19. If you have not read this story, I encourage you to take a few moments to do so. What can we make of a story such as this? How would you describe Abraham's actions? What do you think of the picture of God presented here? The interpretation given to this story by many Christians is that we find here a demonstration of Abraham's tremendous faith. Christians who see the story in this way are following the lead of the New Testament book of Hebrews: "By faith Abraham, when put to the test, offered up Isaac. He who had received the promises was ready to offer up his only son, of whom he had been told, 'It is through Isaac that descendants shall be named for you.' He considered the fact that God is able even to raise someone from the dead—and figuratively speaking, he did receive him back" (Heb 11:17–18).

Apparently in the view of Hebrews, then, Abraham's faith consisted in his confidence that if he killed his son Isaac, God would raise him back from the dead. Others say that Abraham knew that God would not allow him to go through with the sacrifice. But the story as it stands implies that Abraham fully intended to kill his son. Any interpretation that claims otherwise removes the tension from the story. Was Abraham really only pretending that he was going to kill his son? The whole point of claiming that the story is an illustration of Abraham's faith rests on the assumption that Abraham *fully intended to kill his son* and that he indeed *would have killed his son*.

And what about the picture of God we see presented here? Is God a God who requires an absolute blind obedience? Does true faithfulness consist in a willingness to commit any act, including killing an innocent person—indeed, even killing one's own son? Is any action legitimate, as long as we believe it is commanded by God? Is God a God who toys with us, asking us to do things God does not truly want us to do, simply to see what our reaction will be? For those who believe God can foresee our reactions, why bother? Does God not know our hearts without having to test us like this?

Imagine a modern-day Abraham. What would your response be if someone told you he would be taking his son off on a camping trip next weekend and that he would be packing a butcher knife because God had told him to kill his son? Would you praise him for his wonderful faith? Or would you call the police? Why should our reaction to a story in the Bible be any different than our reaction to a similar circumstance today? If we are horrified by the notion that a father would kill his son, why should we override that revulsion so that both Abraham and God get a free pass, simply because the story is in the Bible and not in the local newspaper? Many Christians are either not honest with their feelings in relation to this passage, or else fail to take seriously the ethical conundrum that it presents.

The Bible contains attitudes toward women that have become increasingly problematic from a modern perspective. In the Old Testament, women were often considered property. A woman was owned by her father until (in a financial transaction) ownership rights were transferred to her husband. Though from a modern perspective we might judge being treated as property in a negative light, in ancient times for a woman to lose her status as property was even worse. The most vulnerable persons in ancient Israelite society were those outside of a household, i.e., widows and orphans, as well as aliens or strangers—what we today would call foreigners or those who did not grow up as a part of the local community. Since widows were not the property of a man, they existed outside of the ancient economy and lived a precarious existence.

The tenth commandment in Exodus 20:17 includes wives as part of the property list: "You shall not covet your neighbor's house; you shall not covet your neighbor's wife, or male or female slave, or ox, or donkey, or anything that belongs to your neighbor." The version of the Ten Commandments in Deuteronomy 5 represents a slight improvement, since the wife is separated from the other items of the property list.

Deuteronomy 22:28–29 provides instructions for what should happen if an unengaged virgin is raped: "the man who lay with her shall give fifty shekels of silver to the young woman's father, and she shall become his wife" (see also Exodus 22:16–17). In this case the father's property has been damaged (his daughter's value has decreased since she is no longer a virgin), so payment of a fine sets things straight. There was no consideration of the woman's feelings in the matter. Similarly, in Deuteronomy 22:13–21 instructions are given for a situation in which a "man marries a woman, but after going in to her, he dislikes her and makes up charges against her, slandering her by saying, 'I married this woman; but when I lay with her, I did not find evidence of her virginity'" (13–14). If, following an investigation by the town elders, the elders conclude that the man's charges are false, the man must pay the woman's father one hundred shekels of silver. The man's accusation, in other words, is not really against the woman. His charge is that the father delivered damaged goods. What happens to the woman? She "shall remain his wife; he shall not be permitted to divorce her as long as he lives" (Deut 22:19).

In the story of Tamar in Genesis 38, Tamar's husband Er dies. Tamar's father-in-law, Judah, then marries her to another of his sons, Onan, but Onan also dies (actually, the text says that God put both Er and Onan to death). Rather than marry Tamar to his son Shelah, Judah sends her to live "in her father's house" since he was afraid that Shelah "too would die, like his brothers" (38:11). After a while it becomes evident to Tamar that Judah has no intention of marrying her to Shelah (Judah had claimed that Shelah was too young and needed to grow up a bit). So Tamar hatches a plan—she disguises herself as a prostitute and positions herself along the road she knows Judah will travel. Judah sees her, does not recognize her because her face is covered, assumes she is a prostitute, and has sexual relations with her. Several months later Tamar is discovered to be pregnant. When Judah finds out about it, he is ready to have her burned since she has "played the whore" (38:24). Tamar, however, presents the items Judah had given her in pledge until he could send a baby goat as payment for sex—his signet and cord and staff. The story concludes: "Then Judah acknowledged them and said, 'She is more in the right than I, since I did not give her to my son Shelah.' And he did not lie with her again."

There are many interesting things we could point out about this story. The reason we include it here, however, is that it illustrates the double-standard in ancient Israel with regard to rules for men and rules for women. Tamar was charged with a crime for which the penalty was capital punishment. She had put at risk the property claims of her owner and was pregnant with seed of unknown origin. Killing Tamar would not only punish her for her crime; it would eliminate the contamination of her unborn child.

The story takes an ironic turn, however, when Judah recognizes that he is the father and that *he* is the guilty party, not Tamar. But of what was he guilty? He was guilty of not providing Shelah as a husband for Tamar. There is not a hint of condemnation in this story for the fact that Judah had sexual relations with a prostitute. Why not? In the Old Testament, sexuality morality was associated with protecting the property rights of males. Prostitutes were not property belonging to another male. Prostitution violated no Old Testament moral code. Our modern ideas about marriage and rights of women were completely unknown in ancient societies.

Christians tend to be selective in Bible verses they choose to put on bumper stickers or refrigerator magnets. Among verses from the book of Proverbs, 3:5–6 is a favorite text ("Trust in the LORD with all your heart, and do not rely on your own insight. In all your ways acknowledge him, and he will make straight your paths"). I have yet to see the following text displayed in a calendar or on a magnet or bumper sticker: "A prostitute's fee is only a loaf of bread, but the wife of another stalks a man's very life" (Proverbs 6:26). What is the message of this proverb? If you violate another man's property rights, you will die; if you want sex, prostitutes are relatively cheap. Proverbs was addressed to a male audience; there was no notion that the instructions contained in Proverbs applied to females (even though many modern translations render the oft-repeated word for *son* with the more inclusive word *child*).

The very meanings of words in the Old Testament are shaped by the cultural values of the ancient world. When I ask my students to define adultery, they usually respond with some version of "sexual relations between a married person and someone other than that person's spouse." They are often surprised to learn that the Old Testament view of adultery was quite different. Since women were viewed as property in the Old Testament, the definition of adultery was understood in terms of a property rights violation. Here is the definition of the biblical term for adultery from the *Anchor Bible Dictionary*: "Sexual intercourse between a married or betrothed woman and any man other than her husband. The marital status of the woman's partner is inconsequential since only the married or betrothed woman is bound to fidelity."[19] In a patrilineal society, paternity mattered. Sexual relations between a married man and a prostitute did not constitute adultery in the biblical understanding of the term.

The New Testament also contains passages that are, for many in our twenty-first-century world, problematic. 1 Timothy 2:11–15 states the following: "Let a woman learn in silence with full submission. I permit no woman to teach or to have authority over a man; she is to keep silent. For Adam was formed first, then Eve; and Adam was not deceived, but the woman was deceived and became a transgressor. Yet she will be saved through childbearing, provided they continue in faith and love and holiness, with modesty." According to Genesis 3, both Eve and Adam ate of the fruit and were subject to punishment (see especially Genesis 3:6), but setting aside that discrepancy, this is a verse that fewer and fewer Christians in our society today attempt to follow with any seriousness.

Here is a similar text from 1 Corinthians 14: "As in all the churches of the saints, women should be silent in the churches. For they are not permitted to speak, but should be subordinate, as the law also says. If there is anything they desire to know, let them ask their husbands at home. For it is shameful for a woman to speak in church. Or did the word of God originate with you? Or are you the only ones it has reached?" (verses 33b–36). Again, for the most part, this verse tends to be ignored by Christians today.

Many other ethically problematic texts from the Bible could be mentioned. In previous centuries slavery was defended in the United States on the basis of the Bible (see, for example, Leviticus 25:44–46). Those who opposed slavery could not do so on the basis of any explicit biblical condemnation of the practice.

The Bible does not always reflect our modern notion of individual responsibility and accountability. In Joshua 7, Achan transgresses, but his punishment entails the destruction of his entire household, including "his sons and his daughters, with his oxen, donkeys, and sheep, and his tent and

19. Goodfriend, "Adultery," 82.

all that he had" (Joshua 7:24–26). 2 Kings 2:23–25 tells a story about some "small boys" who taunted Elisha, calling him "baldhead." Elisha "cursed them in the name of the LORD. Then two she-bears came out of the woods and mauled forty-two of the boys." Is God the kind of god that sends bears to maul small children because God's prophet is overly sensitive about his lack of hair?

Are the guidelines provided for dealing with a stubborn son in Deuteronomy 21:18–21 relevant for us today (if he continues to disobey his parents, they are to bring him before the elders, who then "shall stone him to death")? What should we do with verses like Exodus 21:15 ("Whoever strikes father or mother shall be put to death") or Exodus 21:17 ("Whoever curses father or mother shall be put to death")? Why, in the story of the exodus from Egypt, does God kill all of the firstborn babies in Egypt (see Exodus 12:29–30)? Since the Pharaoh was the one preventing the people from leaving, why not kill Pharaoh?

How many Christians ignore Leviticus 19:19 ("nor shall you put on a garment made of two different materials")? How many ignore Leviticus 20:18 ("If a man lies with a woman having her sickness and uncovers her nakedness, he has laid bare her flow and she has laid bare her flow of blood; both of them shall be cut off from their people")? And of those who ignore Leviticus 19:19 and Leviticus 20:18, how many are quick to hold up Leviticus 20:13 (which falls between those other two verses) as fully relevant for our own time—though perhaps not to the extreme of demanding capital punishment ("If a man lies with a male as with a woman, both of them have committed an abomination; they shall be put to death")?

In practice, most Christians ignore much of the Bible. Many of those most adamant in defending its authority seem to be relatively unfamiliar with its content. Those who defend a literal reading of scripture are often unaware of the extent to which their use of the Bible is selective—both in terms of their knowledge of the Bible's content as well as in relation to their application of the Bible's content to practical concerns in their lives.

What can we conclude from these observations? What are the implications for our understanding of the Bible once we admit that it possesses internal contradictions, reflects a pre-scientific worldview, and contains within its stories some portraits of God that are ethically and theologically problematic?

One alternative, of course, if we find these ideas troubling to our faith, is to refuse to accept the evidence in front of us. We can let our theological commitment to an error-free Bible override the overwhelming data we have briefly considered in this chapter. We can continue to spend a great deal of energy in an unnecessary attempt to sustain what, in our own minds, is an essential component of our faith. Rather than engaging in an exploration of the questions raised by the text of the Bible, our response can be defensive, motivated by fear rather than the excitement of discovery. Rather than recognizing the truth toward which the accumulation of the evidence points, we can attempt to silence the questions in a piecemeal fashion, hoping to maintain the illusion of coherence in spite of nagging doubts.

If we find ourselves afraid to walk through the door toward which the evidence points, we have good reason for our fear. If our faith is integrally connected to a belief that the Bible must be inerrant, any admission that the Bible contains errors will result in the collapse of our faith. The real question, then, is whether our faith rests on an adequate foundation. Perhaps letting go of an inadequate faith will allow us to find something better—a place where fear and defensiveness are no longer necessary.

Our faith does not have to be defensively oriented. Think about the reactions of people in Jesus's day to his teaching and healing. Those who had most difficulty receiving his message positively were those who were most concerned to make sure that his message conformed to their presuppositions about God and God's plan. They were the *most* religious, not the least religious. Those who had no institutional religious structures or doctrines to defend were the most receptive to his message.

Leaving behind belief in an error-free Bible is in no way leaving behind Christianity. It is, in fact, to walk through the door of new possibilities for a vibrant and energizing faith. Jesus did not ask those he called to be his disciples whether or not they believed in an error-free Bible. In fact, he did not ask them anything about their beliefs. He simply invited them to follow him.

I do not intend to suggest that beliefs are unimportant. Quite the opposite! All I am suggesting is that our beliefs ought to be derived from sustained reflection upon our spiritual authority sources. We ought to allow the data of scripture to guide the formulation of our beliefs rather than allow beliefs we bring with us to the Bible to distort what we find there. How can the Bible function in an authoritative way if I have already determined what I believe before consulting it?

The evidence from the Bible itself suggests to us that it is a collection of documents accumulated over many centuries and that it is composed of multiple sources that are sometimes self-contradictory. There is nothing ex-traordinary in recognizing that these documents reflect the knowledge and values of the cultures that produced them—values that clash with many of the values of our contemporary world. The Bible does not necessarily cease to be an authority source for Christians when we honestly recognize that it is not a history textbook or a science textbook. The measure of the Bible's authority for us is the extent to which we use it as a guide for discovering the whisperings of God in the stories of faith communities that have pre-ceded us and allow that knowledge to shape the direction of our own faith communities going forward. The Bible provides a window into a story that has been told and re-told. For Christians, this story becomes *our* story, and it powerfully shapes the course we chart as we add our own chapters to the ongoing saga.

4

Biblical Authority Is *Bottom-Up*

IN THE PRECEDING CHAPTER we saw that the Bible is not a modern scientific textbook. It reflects the pre-scientific worldview of the ancient cultures that produced it. In addition, we cannot regard the Bible as we would a modern historical work. We cannot claim that the Bible provides an accurate historical account with regard to every detail, since when we read it we observe internal contradictions between parallel accounts. An inerrancy position that claims the Bible contains no errors is, therefore, unsustainable.

Does this mean, however, that the Bible is untruthful? Those who try to force the Bible to fit the inerrancy mold do so because they fear that an admission of a single error or falsehood in the Bible will invalidate any claim that the Bible contains truth. After all, if one freely admits that there are errors in the Bible, how can one distinguish between what is truthful and what is not? If part of it is wrong, how can any of it be helpful?

Such an either/or fallacy creates a false dilemma by narrowly restricting our choices. To say that a biblical text is not scientifically or historically accurate in every respect in no way precludes the possibility that it contains profound truth. For one thing, we need to recognize the diversity of the kinds of literature contained in the Bible. Besides narrative accounts, the Bible contains poetry, laws, wisdom literature, prophecy, letters, gospels, apocalyptic literature, etc. The truth of a poetic utterance or a song is not the same as the truth of a wisdom saying or of a letter.

This book does not attempt to examine in detail the different kinds of literature contained in the Bible. There are many good study Bibles, commentaries, Bible dictionaries, articles, books, and study guides available today that can assist one in obtaining a better understanding of a particular passage of scripture. Attention to historical context, literary context, type of literature, authorship, audience, canonical context, the cultural situation in which the text originated, and any difficulties peculiar to the passage are all important for gaining a richer understanding of a biblical text. Scholars spend lifetimes working in these areas, and the fruit of their labor is accessible to us. We are blessed to have a tremendous amount of knowledge available in our day to help us in our study of the Bible.

Bible study requires effort and care. Of course the Bible may be read devotionally without much concern for matters of authorship or dating of the text. But knowledge of such things adds to our understanding and increases the insight we are able to gain from reading the Bible. Just as importantly, knowledge gained from scholarly study helps us avoid misreading a text. Some interpretations are illegitimate. There are guidelines that can help us handle biblical texts with integrity. These guidelines are not mysterious; special expertise is not a requirement for engagement with a biblical text.

In my introductory Bible classes, students must write a paper on a specific passage. They begin by reading the text in a variety of translations. Then they read surrounding chapters to get a sense of the broader context. They consult the footnotes and study notes contained in the study Bible we use as one of our textbooks. They read the study Bible's introduction to the biblical book containing their text. Eventually they are required to consult other resources such as Bible dictionaries, single-volume commentaries, multi-volume commentaries, and scholarly articles related to their passage.

Anyone can do this. The only things required are time, careful reading, and reflection. The more of those one is willing to expend, the deeper and richer will be one's understanding of the text. Many churches have Bible study groups, and often such groups use excellent literature to assist them in their understanding of scripture. As a general rule, the more resources consulted, the greater will be the variety of perspectives one will encounter and thus greater also the possibilities for new insight and learning. Resources that can assist us in our reading of the Bible are accessible, and for a proper understanding, they can be indispensable. The best resources do not tell us "what the text means," but rather help us understand the background and context of a passage and offer suggestive possibilities for exploration and reflection.

My point is that reading the Bible with integrity does not require a divinity school degree. The tools we need are readily available. In the middle ages, a common belief was that if one randomly opened the Bible three consecutive times to texts that were similar, one could be assured of a clear message from God.[1] In the year 1208 Francis of Assisi (founder of the Franciscan movement) and two of his companions are said to have utilized this method on one occasion when seeking divine guidance. Although in the case of Francis one could say that this technique had a profound and positive influence on the direction of his life (as it had previously in the life of Augustine), this method of seeking guidance from scripture by opening the Bible and placing one's finger on a random verse has obvious problems.[2] Is the Bible a kind of magic book? Can randomly selected verses help me know which car to buy or whether I should accept a particular job offer?

Handling the Bible with integrity in our contemporary context means that we must have some respect for the knowledge we have gained concerning the authorship, background, genre, audience, context, etc. of the text we are reading. The author of Isaiah 7:14, for example ("Therefore, the Lord himself will give you a sign. Look, the young woman is with child and shall bear a son, and shall name him Immanuel") was not thinking of Jesus at the time the text was written, even though Matthew quotes this verse from Isaiah and applies it to Jesus (Matthew 1:23).[3] Isaiah 7:14 makes perfect sense in the context of the situation in Judah during the time of Ahaz and Isaiah. Isaiah tells Ahaz, "For before the child knows how to refuse the evil and choose the good, the land before whose two kings you are in dread will be deserted" (Isa 7:16). The use of this text in Matthew is an issue for the interpretation of Matthew, but Isaiah 7:14 must be understood on its own terms and within its own context.

We began this chapter by asking whether the fact that the Bible contains scientific and historical inaccuracies necessarily implies that it cannot convey significant truth. To illustrate our answer to that question, let us

1. See Spoto, *Reluctant Saint*, 71.

2. See Vauchez, *Francis of Assisi*, 39. The three texts which Francis randomly selected were Matthew 19:21 ("If you wish to be perfect, go, sell your possessions, and give the money to the poor, and you will have treasure in heaven"), Luke 9:3 ("Take nothing for your journey"), and Matthew 16:24 ("If any want to become my followers, let them deny themselves").

3. Jesus was born a few hundred years following the composition of this verse. To claim that the author had Jesus in mind when referring to a child named Immanuel would render the verse meaningless to people at the time of its composition.

take a look at the first chapter of Genesis. The first chapter of Genesis is controversial because it seems to contradict so directly the claims of modern science about how the world came into existence. If the world was not created literally as described in Genesis 1, should we dismiss chapter 1 of Genesis as untruthful? Are we foolish to think that Genesis 1 could be inspired or its words authoritative for us?

I do not intend to present a comprehensive analysis of this text. To do so would require, for example, some exploration of the picture of the world as it was seen in the ancient culture that produced this text, including the fact that in that ancient picture, the earth existed in a kind of bubble, with waters above and below (thus the sky was blue because of the waters above; rain fell when the "windows of heaven" were opened). A quick look at this chapter will be sufficient to illustrate my main point, however.

> Your understanding of the following section will be greatly enhanced if you stop and read the first chapter Genesis, which is the first book of the Bible. Go ahead and read the first three verses of chapter 3 as well, since scholars believe they go together with the verses in chapter 1 (chapter and verse numberings were added long after the texts were composed, and sometimes the dividing points between chapters or verses is a bit awkward). Perhaps as you are reading you can write down any interesting elements you notice.

There is a regular order to things and a pattern that is repeated in the first chapter of Genesis ("And God said"; "And there was evening, and there was morning"; "And God saw that it was good"). One of the intriguing things about this story is that there is only one god. That fact may escape our notice entirely, since monotheism is such a common perspective in our own day. But monotheism was a minority view in the ancient world. A related aspect is that the sun, moon, and stars created on the fourth day are not associated with divine beings. They are simply part of the created order, created at God's command. Some other ancient creation stories describe the world (and human beings) coming into existence almost as an accident—the result of battles among the gods. In Genesis, God speaks. God intends. Things happen as a result of God's intention.

Another aspect of the story that often seems unremarkable to my students is the repetitive "and God saw that it was good." Many religious perspectives, including many ancient religious perspectives, have a fundamentally negative view of the created order. In Genesis, God repeatedly affirms the goodness of creation. Verse 31 says, "God saw everything that he had made, and indeed, it was very good." The goodness of the physical creation is a significant theological principle that has not always been adequately appreciated in the thinking and actions of Western Christians.

Scholars have discussed at length the meaning of *image* in verses 26–27. We have an example here of a highly suggestive word with multiple possible interpretations. I think we err when we try to restrict its meaning too tightly. Can it mean that we are called to share in God's creative activity? Is it connected with the word *dominion*, and does it therefore mean that God shares God's power over and care of the world with humans? Is it related to our rational abilities? Does it mean we share the personal, relational character of God? Is it connected to the freedom we have as human beings to make choices and to control, within limits, our destinies? Does it have something to do with our capacity to love? Whatever the meaning of God's image in these verses, the text affirms that it is present in both male and female. Genesis 1 thus affirms a fundamental equality between men and women (and, indeed, among all persons).

In verse 28 God blesses the newly created humans and gives them a task. Work is a good thing when connected with the care and nurture of our world and when it allows us to use our gifts and abilities productively for the common good. Humans were not intended by God to sit around and be idle. Finally, God blesses and hallows the seventh day, and then God takes a break ("God rested from all the work that he had done in creation"). Modern readers tend not to find anything unusual about this statement in Genesis 2:3. We are used to a five-day work week. We cannot imagine not getting weekends off. But in the ancient world the lower classes (i.e., almost everybody) did not enjoy weekend breaks. Work days were uninterrupted.

This passage is cited in Exodus 20 as justification for the command to rest on the sabbath: "the seventh day is a sabbath to the LORD your God; you shall not do any work—you, your son or your daughter, your male or female slave, your livestock, or the alien resident in your towns. For in six days the LORD made heaven and earth, the sea, and all that is in them, but rested the seventh day" (Exod 20:10–11). The wealthiest and most powerful did not require a day off since they had choices about their time and the way they could use it that were unavailable to most people. This text was not good news to them. Rather, it was good news to slaves and children and livestock and common working people who otherwise had no rest. In other words, the sabbath command was not simply a religious command; it had political and social implications. It was directed against the interests of the powerful, who would have preferred that slaves and laborers not have a day off, and offered a respite to those who otherwise would not have had it.

Terence Fretheim has noted that "while seven-day patterns of various sorts are present in ancient Near Eastern texts, no sabbath day or seven-day week or seven-day creation account has been discovered."[4] We have here in the literature of the Hebrew people something exceptional. A foundation for the biblical theme of concern for the weakest and most vulnerable is laid here in the first chapter of the first book of the Bible, even though the theme is not made explicit until later.

Is there any truth in the first chapter of Genesis? If our criterion for judging the truth of the Bible is limited to whether it coheres with modern scientific truth or historical truth, Genesis fails. The world did not literally come into existence in the way that Genesis describes. Alternatively, if we take a position that says that error in one area invalidates all truth claims in any area whatsoever, Genesis likewise fails. This position says that once we admit that the perspective of Genesis assumes an ancient cosmology that is no longer intellectually viable in our modern world, nothing in Genesis can speak to us or be trusted.[5] According to this view, once one admits that the text is contaminated with error, there can be no basis for sorting out error

---

4. Fretheim, "The Book of Genesis," 346.

5. Of course there are plenty of creationist Christians who reject the modern scientific consensus about the formation of the universe. On the other hand, Christians who reject creationism sometimes take the position that the Bible is concerned with religious matters, not scientific questions. We should be careful, however, not to try to resolve the science and religion debate by claiming that the Bible does not speak to science. As Fretheim points out, "these chapters are prescientific in the sense that they predate modern science, but not in the sense of having no interest in those types of questions. . . . Despite claims to the contrary (often in the interest of combatting fundamentalism), such texts indicate that Israel's thinkers were very interested in questions of the 'how' of creation, and not just questions of 'who' and 'why'" (Fretheim, 337). The interesting point here is not the *content* of Genesis, but rather the *pattern* it provides for a way of thinking about the world around us. As Fretheim notes, "Israel's theologians . . . recognized that the truth about creation is not generated simply by theological reflection; we must finally draw from various fields of inquiry in order to speak the full truth about the world. The key task, finally, becomes that of integrating materials from various fields into one coherent statement about the created order. In effect, Genesis invites every generation to engage in this same process" (Ibid.).

from truth. If there is mold on one piece of bread, the whole loaf must be tossed.

But why should we assume that Genesis has nothing to say to us simply because its cosmological assumptions are those of its own time? Should we really be surprised that Darwin's theory of evolution is not found in the Bible? If we are willing to admit that Genesis is not a modern science book or history book, much can be gained from reflection on its message, as we have just seen. There are, of course, challenging hurdles that must be overcome. Especially challenging are passages that seem to make God responsible for, or at least condoning of, actions that are, to modern sensibilities, horrendous. We must be honest in recognizing that some texts are shocking and horrifying to our modern ears, and we must take seriously the challenges that biblical texts sometimes present to us.

My approach toward discovering the nature of the truth we get from the Bible and the way in which that truth is mediated to us is *bottom-up* rather than *top-down*.[6] In other words, I want to let the evidence of scripture and the data of our experience shape our perspective, rather than starting with theological presuppositions to which we must conform our conclusions. Many approaches to the topic of the authority and inspiration of scripture begin by assuming that the Bible is authoritative by virtue of the fact that God is its source. Though there may be human authors involved, God is the ultimate author. To speak of the Bible as *inspired* is simply another way of saying that God is the author/source of the material contained in the Bible. Since God is the ultimate author, the writings are inherently authoritative. From this perspective, the issue in relation to a problematic text is not, "does this really come from God?" but rather "how do I correctly interpret this message from God?"

I find it interesting that such top-down approaches claim to represent a higher view of the inspiration and authority of scripture and tend to criticize bottom-up approaches for "picking and choosing" which texts to privilege. They claim that bottom-up approaches allow subjective human judgments or extra-biblical (outside-the-Bible) criteria to be elevated over

---

6. Scholars often refer to this distinction with the words *inductive* (bottom-up) and *deductive* (top-down). Of course, the distinction between these two is more complicated than I imply here, but the general difference in approach is important. An inductive approach begins with experiences and observations and tries to see patterns and connections. It is open-ended, attempting to allow the evidence guide our exploration. Deductive approaches begin with truth claims and examine the implications of those claims. I do not intend to suggest that deductive approaches are never valid.

the authority of the text itself. All readers of the Bible make judgments concerning its content, however. Any claim to possess a special interpretation key that can magically unlock the correct or true interpretation of a text is either dishonest or naive. There is no abstract interpretation, no unbiased perch from which we can look down upon a text and read an unfiltered message from God.[7] The higher view of authority and inspiration claimed by top-down approaches is, in reality, nothing more than an attempt to assert God's approbation for one particular viewpoint.

What, then, is a better way to understand the matter of authority? In a bottom-up approach, we address this question by looking at how the matter of authority works in practice in a broad range of areas in our lives. How, exactly, do things become authoritative for us? When we say something is authoritative, what do we mean? Authority is not a word that we typically use in everyday conversation, but the concept is important and the authority sources in our lives shape us in powerful ways, whether we recognize it or not. I am using the word *authority* in the sense of things that influence us, consciously or unconsciously. The authority sources in our lives are the things that sway us to head in one direction and not another, to value this thing and not that thing, to take this action and not that action, to want to be one kind of person and not another. They may be narrowly focused or broad and general, and they change over time.

For most of us, when we were young our parents were the most powerful authority source in our lives. They controlled our universe, provided for our needs, and passed along to us, in thousands of small ways, their wisdom and their worldview. As we grew older, other authority sources began to compete with the authority of our parents. Middle school friends became the most important authority source in relation to our appearance. Teachers became an additional authority source that sometimes confirmed and sometimes was in tension with the values and wisdom we had received from our parents. If we grew up in church, the pastor, Sunday School teachers, or others in the church community probably became meaningful and respected authority sources.

---

7. See Swartley, *Slavery, Sabbath, War and Women*. Swartley's book surveys the range of Christian interpretations that have been proposed in relation to four issues. His research is a powerful reminder of the complexity of the interpretative task, as well as the influence of non-biblical factors in our interpretation: "We are subject to particular influences from our culture and history. We tend to use the Bible to reinforce what we believe" (203).

As we grew into adulthood, the number of competing authority sources multiplied, and the tension among those authority sources multiplied as well. For most of us, no single authority source is absolute in the sense that we agree perfectly with every utterance or every value expressed. As we mature into adulthood, we face increasing complexity in terms of the contrasts among those persons, principles, and things we value. As we sort out where we stand in the midst of that complexity, we develop our own unique personality, character, and beliefs.

We may have great appreciation for the wisdom of our parents and perhaps find ourselves in agreement with them on many things, but all of us experience points of tension and disagreement with our parents as we grow older. We will probably discover (eventually) that even in the case of those teachers we revere and respect most highly, our admiration and appreciation is combined with a recognition that we disagree on some points. Eventually we learn that *trusted authority* does not equal *fully in agreement with*. Good friends to whom we turn as trusted sources of advice are those with whom we can be honest; agreement is not a prerequisite.

Our level of maturity is linked to an ability to evaluate somewhat critically these competing authority sources. We have seen the danger of what can happen when an authority source is accepted too uncritically. Whether the authority source is a religious personality (Jim Jones, David Koresh, one's local pastor), a charismatic political leader (Adolf Hitler, Mussolini), or an ideology (an "ism" of one sort or another that becomes absolutized), our perception gets distorted when we lose our ability to judge authority sources with some degree of objectivity. Having a multiplicity of authority sources, therefore, is not only inevitable, but also helpful to the extent that the dissonance among them represents a challenge to assumptions that may need correction. A key question is not only the identification of our authority sources, but the relation among them in terms of which have greater priority.

In reality, genuine authority is always a bottom-up commodity rather than a top-down attribute. Our decision to trust one source and not another is freely made. I seek out and carefully consider a friend's advice because I value my friend's opinion and trust my friend to be honest yet caring—to speak truth in love. I turn to news sources I trust to be relatively unbiased. When my grown children ask me for advice, I know they seek my counsel not because I hold the title or attribute of *Dad*; they ask me because they value my opinion. Within an organizational hierarchy, subordinates will follow a leader's guidance if the leader is open, trusted, and respected. Leaders who attempt to accomplish their goals through coercion and power manipulation are seldom as effective.

Any position, office, or role has attached to it a potential degree of authority. The extent to which that potential will be realized depends not on some abstract quantity of power bestowed by the office or role, but on the character and personality of the person occupying it. Genuine authority is authority freely granted by those over whom one exercises some institutional or organizational power. Its direction is from the bottom up.

One can observe this phenomenon in churches. It often happens in a local church that someone with no official title or office possesses as much authority as those with official titles due to the respect people in the congregation have for that person. A leader in any organization knows that there can be a difference between official authority sources and unofficial authority sources. The power and authority of a leader is linked with the respect people have for that leader, whether in secular institutions or religious institutions. When persons in leadership positions in the church are involved in scandals, their authority and power are undermined.

Trust, openness, and respect are key ingredients for the exercise of authentic authority. Those with power can, and often do, become authoritarian in the exercise of their power, but when they do they become less effective. For example, when churches or other religious institutions (including religious educational institutions) impose a rigid creedal statement, those whose continued employment is thereby placed in jeopardy may decide to sign a piece of paper. To what extent, however, can the organization claim that the stack of signed documents it collects for its files represents free consent given with clear consciences rather than evidence of economic blackmail?

There is a clear distinction to be made between genuine authority and authoritarianism. Attempts to coerce consent indicate weak authority rather than strong authority. Ultimately, such attempts are self-defeating. Authoritarianism is top-down. Genuine authority is bottom-up. Forced acquiescence is not the same as freely given allegiance.

The elements required for the exercise of genuine authority are connected to the qualities required for truth-seeking, including especially an insistence on free response rather than coerced response. As Charles Kimball has rightly noted,

> Authentic religion engages the intellect as people wrestle with the mystery of existence and the challenges of living in an imperfect world. Conversely, blind obedience is a sure sign of corrupt religion. Beware of any religious movement that seeks to limit the intellectual freedom and individual integrity of its adherents. When individual believers abdicate personal responsibility and yield to the authority of a charismatic leader or become enslaved to particular ideas or teachings, religion can easily become the framework for violence and destruction.[8]

Genuine authority is inseparable from intellectual freedom and freedom of conscience. It is authority granted rather than imposed. It is authority earned rather than asserted. Genuine authority sources are trustworthy. We hold them in esteem because they have a track record of reliability.

Our authority sources are the result of choice combined with resonance. In one sense, we do not consciously choose our authority sources. Our authority sources are basically those things or persons we come to trust. The development of trust requires time. Once a respected authority source is discredited from our perspective, we cannot simply decide that we are going to continue to trust it or rely on it. We may continue to seek guidance or advice or information from it (depending on the extent of the disillusionment), but we will be more cautious about its dependability. Of course, there are no perfect authority sources, since no human being or human institution is perfect. A healthy degree of skepticism with regard to our authority sources is a good thing.

On the other hand, we exercise choice over our authority sources. Even though no authority source is perfect or absolutely reliable, there are institutions and people we come to trust more than others. We allow ourselves to become vulnerable as we make choices about where we place our trust. We entrust certain financial institutions with our money. We share personal information with friends. We open ourselves in myriad ways to the possibility of hurt and betrayal. Over time, we choose which persons and institutions we deem trustworthy.

My wife, Gail, is a key authority source for me. I value her opinion. We know each other well enough that I can fairly accurately predict her opinion in a lot of areas. She is not an automaton, however; we are both changing and developing and becoming. I can never assume that I know what she will say if I ask for her view about something. We sometimes surprise each

---

8. Kimball, *When Religion Becomes Evil*, 72.

other. We sometimes disagree. She is an authority source because I consult her opinion. She is also an authority source because she shapes the person I am becoming in all sorts of subtle, incalculable ways—both in relation to my thinking and my behavior. We do not give each other commands. Our relationship is not authoritarian. We both know that we would each give anything and everything for the sake of the other. Our authority over each other is not imposed—it is a special example of that choice combined with resonance that is true of all real authority sources.

I have been describing genuine authority as bottom-up. One could also describe it as inside-out. There is a gravitational pull toward those authority sources we recognize as truthful. Gail is much more intuitive than I am. Her truth-antenna captures a wavelength spectrum that mine only dimly apprehends. I trust her perceptions because I have experienced the accuracy of her perceptions. No authority source is perfect, since all authority sources available to us are finite. But the gravitational effect on us of some authorities is much stronger than others.

Think for a minute about the people or the things that are influential in your own life. What would you list as the sources for your values? What are the primary influences you would list as having shaped you into the person you are today? Who would you consult if faced with a crisis or major decision? How would you go about trying to make a major life decision (what process would you follow)?

> Your reflection will be enhanced if you actually, physically, write down your thoughts. Answer the questions in the preceding paragraph, then review your list and ask yourself whether you have left anything or anyone out. Think back to major turning points in your life and the way you approached those times. Once you are satisfied that your list covers the main sources of influence on your life, rank them in order of importance. Which would you place first, second, and so forth in terms of overall impact on your life?

Sometimes there is a discrepancy between our actual authority sources and our ideal authority sources. We sometimes claim certain things are important to us, but when we are honest with ourselves, we recognize that other sources have likely had as much or greater influence on us. I may say that I value fitness and health, for example, and I could write down authorities I might claim as the source of this value. But do I exercise regularly? Do

I eat healthy foods? Do I get enough sleep at night? If not, to what extent are the authority sources I would like to claim as important in my life truly effective in shaping my habits and the person I am becoming? And if the authority sources I would like to claim are not, in reality, my actual authority sources, what unacknowledged authority sources are exercising a more powerful influence on my life?

Authority sources are those things that are powerfully influential in shaping us and providing us with guidance. They are not authoritative because we declare them to be so. They are authoritative because there is evidence of their impact on our lives. What shapes the way you spend your money, for example? If you were to keep a record of how you spend every hour over the course of a week, what would be revealed concerning your use of your time? When you think about the things that are most powerful in influencing and shaping your life, do you feel like you need to change anything? Are you happy with the actual authority sources operative in your life?

Christians claim the Bible as an authority source. In reality, however, the Bible exercises little authority in the lives of many Christians, who are sometimes surprisingly unfamiliar with the stories and other content of the Bible. The Bible can serve as a kind of totem, symbolizing devotion and loyalty but having no real practical impact on our lives. Christians who are not practiced in reading and interpreting the Bible for themselves can become dependent on the interpretations of others. Personal responsibility for reading and interpreting scripture is abdicated, leaving one vulnerable to official interpretations of a minister or denominational statement. Other authority sources can become filters of the Bible's content, in effect superseding the authority of the Bible.

> Reflect a bit on how you use the Bible. In what way, exactly, can you say it exercises a powerful influence in your life? If the Bible functions as an actual authority source in your life, how did it achieve that status? What were the critical factors that resulted in the Bible being an important source of guidance for you? Is it powerful in a general kind of way—i.e., it provides you with some general principles that help you? Or does it provide more specific guidance, such as rules to follow? Do you use it in specific situations to help you make decisions? If so, how?

My approach is not to begin with declarations about what ought to be the Bible's place as an authority source for Christians. We should begin by asking ourselves how and to what extent the Bible serves as an effective, practical guide for our lives. Where is the evidence that the Bible shapes, molds, and guides our character and actions? If the Bible is not opened, if it is not read, if it is not studied, if its stories are not allowed to seep into the background of our consciousness, if there is no wrestling with its content, if it presents no challenges to the way we live our lives, then pronouncements of its authority fall flat. So-called high views of biblical authority are compatible with lives that evidence no real practical biblical influence.[9] If the Bible has any real authority in a person's life, it will be evident in the messiness of daily living.

Top-down approaches to biblical authority focus on abstract arguments and declarations of allegiance. Professions of belief are given greater weight than evidence of practical, effective influence. A bottom-up approach, on the other hand, looks for places where there is evidence that the Bible is taken seriously, then asks, "What is going on here?" What can we learn when we examine carefully the lives of those who display convincing evidence that the Bible has served as a primary authority source for them? What is different about their view of the Bible's authority, or of inspiration, or what is different in the way such persons use the Bible? If we can identify people we agree show evidence that the Bible is truly an effective authority source in their lives, perhaps we can identify common characteristics or principles that we can apply in our own lives.

Where do we look to find people we can agree show evidence in their lives that the Bible is an important authority source, however? External signs of piety are not sufficient. Many Christians attend church regularly, pray often, and even read the Bible regularly without manifesting evidence of resistance to cultural values. A bottom-up approach looks for individuals and communities that have effectively resisted conformity pressures from the larger culture and that credit the Bible as an important source of guidance.

---

9. John Lee Eighmy pointed out the extent to which cultural values rather than biblical values shaped the history of the denominational tradition within which I grew up (i.e., Southern Baptist) in his book *Churches in Cultural Captivity*. Of course, no denomination is immune from the influences of culture, but the case of the Southern Baptist Convention is particularly ironic, given the obsession of its leaders with enforcing conformity to what is seen, from their own perspective, as a high view of the authority of the Bible.

Glen Stassen, in his recent book, *A Thicker Jesus*, identifies several individuals who clearly acted against the grain of their culture and the pattern of most Christians of their time in taking courageous stands in the face of great personal risk, and who are today recognized as heroes of the faith.[10] Stassen's focus is slightly different from mine; he examines their witness and writings for evidence of commonalities in their ethics. But his approach is similar enough that his research can be useful to us. His method is a sort of reverse-engineering: he looks at examples of people who evidence biblical values and influence, and then asks how they got that way.

If the Bible is truly influential in our lives, it shapes our daily living. We do not come to a point of crisis in our lives and suddenly turn to the Bible for guidance if it has not been a significant force in forming our identity prior to that time. A crisis does not create character; it reveals the character already present. Stassen mentions André Trocmé and his wife Magda as examples of persons who, acting in a time of crisis in congruence with the character already formed in them, saved many lives at great personal risk. Shortly after becoming pastor of a congregation in the French village of Le Chambon during the time when France was occupied by the Nazis, André and Magda led the villagers over a period of several years to take action to protect as many Jews as they could. Their efforts saved roughly 3,500 lives from extermination, an amazing number considering the fact that Le Chambon had roughly 2,500 inhabitants at the time.[11]

Looking for clues about what made Trocmé the kind of person he was, Stassen analyzed notes for fifty-nine sermons Trocmé delivered in his two pastorates *before* moving to the French village of Le Chambon. Of those fifty-nine sermons, Stassen says Trocmé preached forty-one from the Gospels: "Reading his extensive writings . . ., one is struck that he was especially committed to obeying God's will, that he saw God's will particularly revealed in Jesus, that he endeavored to love all of humankind, and that he practiced this love in his ministry in all three of his pastorates."[12] Stassen comments: "Trocmé endeavored to develop among his congregations a richer and thicker understanding of Jesus' teachings as portrayed in the Gospels."[13] Though Stassen says that Trocmé preached on topics other than

---

10. Stassen, *A Thicker Jesus*. See especially chapter 2, "The Three Dimensions of Incarnational Discipleship."

11. Ibid., 24.

12. Ibid., 25.

13. Ibid.

the way of Jesus, he says Trocmé "strongly emphasizes that we are to go the whole way in following Jesus."[14]

Stassen finds a similar emphasis on Jesus in the writings of others he examines, including Karl Barth and the Barmen Declaration of 1934, Dietrich Bonhoeffer and his early and sustained opposition to Hitler, Martin Luther King Jr. and Clarence Jordan in relation to the civil rights movement in the United States, East German Christians involved in nonviolent resistance to Erich Honecker and the East German regime prior to the fall of the Berlin wall in 1989, Dorothy Day and the Catholic Worker Movement, and Muriel Lester and her work on behalf of the poor.

The evidence indicates that all of the people discussed in Stassen's book as examples of "heroes of the faith" took the Bible seriously and were shaped by it so powerfully that we are justified in saying that the Bible was authoritative for them. Stassen specifically delineates three characteristics he says distinguished their Christian faith—characteristics he says made a crucial difference in whether they passed the "tests of history." First of all, they all shared an "extensive attention to the actions and teachings of Jesus."[15] They understood Jesus as providing specific guidance, not general ideals or principles: "those who came through in these historical times of testing unequivocally interpreted Jesus' way as concrete and specific guidance to be followed."[16] Second, Stassen says they all "rejected a two-realms dualism in which Christ's Lordship is effective only for an inner spirituality, whether an inner dimension of selfhood, or only individual relations, or only internal to the church."[17] Finally, Stassen says that they all "called for repentance from letting some other lord, ideology, or nationalism take over their ethics and their loyalties."[18] To summarize, we could say that Christian faith seems to be more powerful and effective when loyalty to Jesus in all areas of life is able to take precedence over competing loyalties.

14. Ibid.

15. Ibid., 20.

16. Ibid., 21.

17. Ibid. Stassen uses the language of "Lordship of Christ" and "sovereignty of God" when discussing this second dimension of what he calls incarnational discipleship. If I understand him correctly, his point is to emphasize the universal character of God's creative, loving and redemptive activity. That point can be made without using the language Stassen uses, however, which in my view has had and continues to have harmful effects both in relation to the theological difficulties it creates, as well as in relation to the ethical positions sometimes associated with it.

18. Ibid.

We come here to a fundamental point: What do we mean when we say someone is a Christian? One possible definition is to say that a Christian is a person who has made a free choice to follow Jesus. Of course, this definition begs the question of what we mean by "follow Jesus," but clearly "follow Jesus" is a bottom-up definition. We are not Christian because we belong to a particular church or denomination, or because we have been baptized, or because we partake of the Eucharist, or because we can recite the Apostle's Creed. A Christian is one who is a disciple of Jesus, living a certain way, following the example Jesus set for us, attempting to put into practice Jesus's teachings.

Defining Christianity in terms of discipleship (following Jesus) has immense implications. When I ask my students to give me a definition of faith, their answers usually fall into one of two categories. One category is the notion that faith involves believing certain things. Faith has a particular content. There are two subcategories of this view. In one, faith is understood as rationally explicable and defensible. In the other, faith is viewed as being in tension with reason or even contrary to a strictly rational approach. On one occasion when I pointed out to someone the illogic of his religious beliefs, his response was, "Well, you've just got to have faith." Faith in this sense will express itself in a manner something like the following: "It may not be logical, or may even be illogical, but I believe it anyway." Faith understood as belief means that Christianity becomes defined in terms of accepting certain statements as true, whether one believes the statements have rational coherence or not. "Defending the faith" means defending the truth of what one sees as the content of faith. Evangelism means convincing others to affirm certain beliefs.

An alternative way of viewing faith is to understand it as a direction one takes in one's life. It is a road chosen, a commitment made, an orientation, a particular way of viewing the world. This second way of viewing faith is not unconcerned with beliefs, but beliefs are not the central focus. Faith understood in this second sense is closely related to the word *trust*. We choose to trust one thing rather than another as our north star to guide us and orient us on our journey. Used in this sense, we can say that everyone has a faith of some sort. Everyone has a primary value, an ultimate loyalty, a gravitational center that pulls one in a specific direction. This ultimate loyalty is not necessarily discovered in belief statements, but rather in the way we live. How do we spend our time? How do we spend our money? With whom do we associate? What is the orientation or direction of our lives?

Christian faith, according to this understanding, is a life oriented toward the God revealed most clearly in Jesus.

This second way of understanding faith seems more in line with the description of early Christianity as "the Way" (Acts 9:2). In addition, this understanding seems to take more realistic account of the enormous diversity among Christians. The theological affirmations that can claim universal acceptance among all Christians are surprisingly few. Furthermore, when Jesus called his disciples, he did not require them to affirm any doctrines. Correct theology does not seem to be the focal point around which Jesus organized his band of followers. Even a doctrine as central to Christianity as the trinity is not explicitly mentioned in the Bible. For those who are *Christ*ians, the central focus is Jesus. The criterion for measuring Christian faithfulness is not close adherence to a doctrinal standard or evidence of denominational loyalty, but rather the extent to which we are faithfully following Jesus.

Jesus confronts us with a choice. Whom will one serve? To what, or to whom, will one give one's loyalty? In which direction will one give one's life? This is the "leap of faith" that Kierkegaard described. It involves our whole being—intellect as well as emotions and desires. We choose. But we choose that which resonates. We make a decision, but the decision is in line with what seems *right* or *truthful* or *trustworthy*.

There is an important implication here regarding the importance of safeguarding the integrity of our choices. True choices are feely made, never coerced. As a Baptist, I am particularly concerned that Christians honor the voluntary character of faith by fighting to preserve the right of others to believe as they choose. We should never allow government to give preference to one religion over others and we should stand alongside those of other faiths who experience persecution for their beliefs. A top-down approach says, "Believe this, or else suffer the consequences." A bottom-up approach invites others to join in conversation where each can share perceptions of truth from differing perspectives. Unfortunately, Christians have too often been guilty of attempting to impose their beliefs on others.

Baptists were birthed with a concern for freedom of conscience. A key insight of Baptists (and Anabaptists before them) was that the true community of faith is composed of those who have made a free decision to follow Christ as Lord. Their rejection of infant baptism was based on the fact that infants are incapable of making such a free decision.[19] Thus they

19. In my opinion many if not most Baptist churches in the US today have abandoned

advocated believer's baptism. The issue which gave rise to Baptists was not the mode of baptism (immersion, sprinkling, affusion, etc.) but the subject of baptism—only believers should be baptized. True Christians, from a Baptist perspective, are those who freely follow Christ, and the true church is a community of such persons.

Since a decision to follow Christ is a matter of individual conscience, that decision cannot be coerced. From their earliest beginnings, therefore, Baptists defended religious liberty. Thomas Helwys, one of the first English Baptists, wrote what has been described by one historian as "the first statement of absolute religious liberty to be written in English."[20] Helwys stated in 1612: "Let them be heretikes, Turks [i.e., Muslims], Jewes, or whatsoever, it apperteynes not to the earthly power to punish them in the least measure."[21] Helwys wrote an inscription to King James I in the flyleaf of his book which included this statement: "The king is a mortal man, and not God therefore hath not power over ye immortal souls of his subjects, to make laws and ordinances for them, and to set spiritual lords over them."[22]

The prominent place given by Baptists to freedom of conscience is the source of the Baptist emphasis on the idea of separation of church and state. John Leland, Baptist minister in Virginia, wrote in 1791:

> Government has no more to do with the religious opinions of men, than it has with the principles of mathematics. Let every man speak freely without fear, maintain the principles that he believes, worship according to his own faith, either one God, three Gods, no God, or twenty Gods; and let government protect him in so doing, i.e., see that he meets no personal abuse, or loss of property,

---

this principle. Many Baptist churches baptize children at an age when they are clearly unable to make a mature decision about loyalty to Christ. Most of my Baptist students report that they were baptized when younger than ten years old. Almost all of those students report an experience later on when a more authentic choice was made about what direction their lives would take. The earlier "decision" was marked by coercive, if well-intentioned, pressure. Why the rush? Why not explain to children that the decision to follow Jesus is one they will be able to make when they are older? (In my experience among Baptists in other countries, almost never would someone younger than late-teens be baptized.) Perhaps part of the reason is fear—fear that their young souls will be damned to hell unless the church can get children dunked, and perhaps fear that unless the church can get them to agree to be baptized when they are young, it may fail to get them into the baptismal pool at all.

20. Leonard, *Baptist Ways*, 26.

21. Helwys, *The Mistery of Iniquity*, 72.

22. Helwys, in Freeman, McClendon, and da Silva, *Baptist Roots*, 84.

for his religious opinions. Instead of discouraging him with proscriptions, fines, confiscations or death, let him be encouraged, as a free man, to bring forth his arguments and maintain his points with all boldness; then, if his doctrine is false, it will be confuted, and if it is true, (though ever so novel,) let others credit it.[23]

Leland believed that truth is able to stand on its own in the realm of public discourse. Truth does not need to be propped up by the coercive power of government or ecclesiastical institutions. In fact, coercion is never a means through which truth can be conveyed, since truth must be apprehended freely. Leland was not afraid of novelty; new insights, if truthful, should be acknowledged as such. Leland would likely have agreed wholeheartedly with Carl Sagan's statement that "the cure for a fallacious argument is a better argument, not the suppression of ideas."[24] Leland left an important legacy; his "letters to and personal friendship with Thomas Jefferson and James Madison were highly influential in the passing of a bill that established religious freedom in Virginia (1786) and in the Bill of Rights that amended the Federal Constitution (1789)."[25]

Baptists rejected the idea of a parish church—i.e., the idea that all persons within a certain political territory are automatically members of an officially established denomination. Roman Catholics, Eastern Orthodox churches, Reformed (Presbyterian or Calvinistic) churches, Lutherans, and Anglicans (Episcopalians) all have been established churches in the past and all retain positions of political privilege even today in many countries where they have historically been predominant. These denominational traditions have accommodated to the constitutional separation of church and state in the United States, but they have had no clear theological basis for or historical track record of support for separation of church and state. Baptist theology, on the other hand, demanded advocacy for church-state separation. Such advocacy is in their DNA. It is directly connected to their foundational principles.

Obviously, denominations change over time, and today one can make a case that Baptists have become an establishment church in most areas of the southern United States. When the attainment of majority status provides access to political power, the preservation of principles forged in the fires of persecution as a minority group can prove difficult. Still, I consider

---

23. Leland, *The Rights of Conscience Inalienable*, 184.

24. Sagan, *The Demon Haunted World*, 429.

25. Freeman, McClendon Jr., and da Silva, *Baptist Roots*, 172.

their insight concerning the bottom-up character of genuine authority to be the most important contribution Baptists have made to the worldwide Christian community. The implications of this insight are so vast that they cannot, in my opinion, be overstated. Christians are those who freely choose to follow Jesus, having sensed in the person of Jesus—however dimly and incompletely—a resonance with the eternal truth of God's revelation and invitation to humanity. From the moment that choice is made, the Bible becomes an invaluable authority source as it points to Jesus and to the larger activity of God in the history of the Hebrews and the early church.

The Bible's authority, then, is inseparable from the authority exercised by Jesus Christ over the life of the Christian believer. If following Jesus is what makes one a Christian, the Bible is authoritative as a pointer toward the God revealed in Jesus. As Karl Barth put it, the Bible contains the Word in the words. The primary authority is Jesus. The Bible's authority is derivative from that primary authority.

This is an essential point. We have already observed that Christians do not appropriate the biblical material equally as far as its functional authority in their lives. As a practical matter, some parts function with greater authority in that they are better known, more closely studied, and held in higher esteem for providing practical guidance for Christian living. We have argued that the Bible is a distillation of material collected by communities of faith who believed that God was active in their history and who valued these writings as authoritative testimonies to that activity. For Christians, the supreme example of God's activity in history is seen in Jesus. Disciples of Jesus turn to the Bible because it points toward the God revealed in Jesus.

However, since the Bible is a collection of documents reflecting cultural assumptions that are in many instances vastly different from our own, since it includes various and sometimes conflicting perspectives, and since it represents an uneven apprehension of the light of God's revelation, we know there is work to be done as we seek to sort out the meaning of scripture for us today. The revelation of God is perceived through the eyes of faith in the messiness of history. That revelation is historically embedded, meaning there are intrinsic limitations to our ability to grasp it. If we keep those limitations in mind, however, we can make real progress in deciphering the truth contained in the pages of the Bible.

Whatever effective authority the Bible has for us is bottom-up or inside-out authority, not top-down or imposed authority. Top-down authority can display the family Bible on the coffee table as a symbol of allegiance without spending daily time reading and absorbing its message. Bottom-up authority engages the stories, teachings, poetry, laws, and prophetic utterances, etc., of the Bible in the hard work of seeking discernment and application. Top-down authority says, "The Bible contains no errors." Bottom-up authority is free to say, "These texts do not seem to agree; let's explore them further and see what we discover." Top-down authority says, "The Bible is God's perfect word." Bottom-up authority is free to say, "This text is disturbing; it doesn't seem to fit with the message of Jesus." Top-down authority says, "Here is what the text really means." Bottom-up authority says, "What are possible ways to understand this text? What would it mean to really practice what this text is saying?"

Christians affirm that the Bible contains truth about the nature and activity of God. Christians read the Bible with the expectation that the voice of God can be discerned within its pages. If the Bible is genuinely authoritative for us, it influences our faith journey. In fact, the Bible is a distillation of things deemed important in the faith journeys of communities that were seeking, in their own time, to discover truth about God's intention for them. Their faith journeys parallel our own faith journey, and the authority of the Bible becomes effective to the extent that the light of their journeys helps to illuminate our own way. Biblical authority, therefore, cannot be discussed apart from faith understood as whole-hearted commitment to follow the God revealed most fully in Jesus.

The English word *inspire* comes from a Latin word meaning "to breathe upon" or "to breathe into." When Christians affirm that the Bible is inspired, they affirm that the breath of God is found within its pages. That is not to say that the Bible is the only place where God's breath is felt, of course. But in the literature of scripture we find a testimony left by communities who claimed to have an encounter with a divine reality that transformed the nature of their story. As their record of that encounter resonates with our experiences of our own encounters with that same reality, the true nature of biblical authority is revealed.

5

A Model for Reading, Reflecting On, and Living in Tune with the Bible

WE HAVE SEEN THAT the Bible came into existence through a long process that included collecting, combining, and editing various traditions passed along over many generations. Our task now is to examine how something so diverse can be read with integrity and applied concretely to our lives such that it operates effectively as an authority source in both our thinking and living. As we proceed, we should remember that the true measure of the Bible's authority for us is not found in the claims we make about it, but rather in the extent to which it claims us as its truth is powerfully reflected in the way we live our lives.

> You might find it helpful to stop and reflect a bit on how, before now, you have handled problematic biblical texts such as those discussed in chapter 3. Do you tend to ignore them? Do you imagine that the Old Testament texts depicting God commanding total annihilation of cities, for example, are only relevant to ancient times and not to our own? If that is the case, how do you sort out which texts are relevant for us today and which are not?
>
> Some Christians respond to the difficulties presented in Old Testament passages by arguing that the picture of God presented in the New Testament is fundamentally different from the picture presented in the Old Testament. In the New Testament, according

to this view, we find a much clearer picture of God. This argument does not remove the difficulties, however.

Take a look at the following texts. What do you think is their meaning for us today? Are you consistent in the way you read these texts in comparison to the way you read other texts? What conclusions can you draw about your use of the Bible?

1 Corinthians 14:33b–36

Romans 13:1–2

Ephesians 6:5

Perhaps you have been aware of some of the difficulties presented by certain biblical texts but have not known what to do about them, other than to pick and choose the bits and pieces that seem useful to you. In this chapter we will develop a more systematic approach, based on the Bible we have rather than a fantasy Bible that does not exist. The Bible is a distillation of the experiences of communities of faith across hundreds of years of seeking, questioning, and exploring. It deals with ultimate questions with which human beings have struggled since before recorded history. Where did we come from? Is there a purpose to this world and to our lives? What lies beyond death? How should we live? How do we understand evil, and how can evil be overcome?

The Bible does not offer simple answers to these questions. It nonetheless provides a map that can guide our exploration. To call the Bible holy scripture is to make a claim that among the many voices contained within its pages one can hear echoes of the voice of God. Persons of faith claim that God's voice can still be heard today, even if mysteriously and enigmatically. Since the voice that spoke then is the voice that continues to speak, there is a resonance that reverberates across the centuries. When we expend the effort to place the questions arising in our own time and out of our own experiences in dialogue with the concerns and questions important to the biblical authors, those reverberations can be detected and can guide us and shape us in powerful ways.

We are more likely to detect God's voice if we prepare our ears to hear. Part of that preparation is honestly and realistically recognizing the magnitude of the challenges we face. We will never find the whisperings of the voice of God unless we learn to take seriously the multiplicity of voices present in the biblical material itself, in the history of its interpretation, and among contemporary Christians. Throughout the Bible we find contrasting traditions. There are pro-monarchy and anti-monarchy traditions from the days of Israel and Judah, for example. There is a Sinai covenant perspective (God's covenant with the Hebrew people is conditional; disobedience will result in punishment) and a royal ideology perspective (God's covenant is unconditional; the Hebrews will always be blessed and the Davidic dynasty is everlasting). The author of Chronicles reinterprets the Deuteronomistic History found in Joshua, Judges, Samuel, and Kings, omitting any negative information about David, in the process drastically altering the overall impression given to the reader.[1] Job and Ecclesiastes challenge the dominant Old Testament view that the righteous will be blessed and the wicked will suffer. Nahum and Obadiah celebrate God's judgment against enemy nations, while Jonah and Ruth speak of God's love for foreigners.

In the New Testament, James' view of faith requiring works contrasts with Paul's claim that "a person is justified by faith apart from works prescribed by the law" (Romans 3:28). Paul's view toward ruling authorities in Romans 13:1 ("let every person be subject to the governing authorities; for there is no authority except from God, and those authorities that exist have been instituted by God") contrasts with Revelation's portrayal of the Roman government as a "beast" in chapter 13. The view of women expressed in Galatians 3:28 ("there is no longer Jew or Greek, there is no longer slave or free, there is no longer male and female; for all of you are one in Christ Jesus") seems to be at odds with 1 Timothy's directive that women should "learn in silence with full submission" (2:11). The picture of Jesus presented in the gospel of John is vastly different from that of the other three canonical Gospels. Stephen Harris has said that John's gospel, when compared to the three synoptic gospels, "offers a different chronology of Jesus' ministry, a different order of events, a different teaching, and a distinctly different teacher."[2] Even when we compare Matthew, Mark and Luke, whose pictures of Jesus differ less radically from one another than they do with John's gospel, we find "distinctive literary portraits . . . that expressed their individual community's understanding of Jesus' theological importance."[3]

---

1. Michael Coogan calls the author of Chronicles a "revisionist historian, editing his sources and adding to them in support of his ideological program." See Coogan, *The Old Testament*, 454.

2. Harris, *The New Testament*, 215.

3. Ibid., 109.

A Model for Reading, Reflecting On, and Living in Tune with the Bible

If we compare listening for the voice of God to trying to tune an FM radio receiver to get clear reception rather than static, we must admit that an inherent difficulty in our task is that there seem to be multiple signals occupying the same wavelengths. In the same way that one sometimes picks up overlapping radio stations when driving in a rural area, the voices of scripture, the voices of Christian theologies expressed throughout the history of the church, and the voices of Christians today have always been and will continue to be polyphonic and often disharmonic. Christians sometimes lament the diversity that exists within Christianity today, believing that it represents some sort of fall from a prior state of unity and harmony. This view reflects a lack of knowledge of Christian history. The earliest writings we have in the New Testament (Paul's letters) provide evidence of vicious infighting and disagreements among those claiming the name of Christ.

The presence of so many conflicting viewpoints means that we must be cautious about elevating one strand or group of voices over others. We cannot pretend that the dissonant voices in the Bible do not exist and declare that the traditions we choose to emphasize represent *the biblical view* as though any alternative perspective is unbiblical. Unfortunately, this strategy is too often employed by Christians seeking to establish the supremacy of their position. Variations of the argument "I'm right because my view is biblical" are too often used to attempt to silence one's opponents. The reality is that there is no single biblical view.

There have always been groups of Christians who have claimed that the true voice of God is like a single melody—clear, comprehensible, and well-defined. The claims regarding where that true voice can best be found vary—prominent examples include church tradition, a particular denominational perspective, the Bible, the New Testament, or Jesus. All such claims are either delusions or deceptions, since a single voice cannot be found within church tradition, the Bible, the New Testament, or even the traditions concerning Jesus.

We must begin by honestly recognizing the difficulties involved in trying to say anything definitive about God. When we deny the possibility that certain voices could carry truth, even when they appear to us to be disharmonic, we cut ourselves off from possible new insights as well as the kind of correction we all sometimes need. On the other hand, we do not have to accept a relativism that says there is no divine voice discernible behind the many voices present in the Bible, nor does the existence of many voices make harmonies impossible.

Perhaps you are wondering how anyone, given the difficulties I have presented, can dare claim that it is possible to hear even an echo of the divine voice! However, if one believes that God is constantly interacting with every aspect of creation, and that God's interactions with humanity are especially significant due to our spiritual, moral, and cognitive capacities, then the claim that God's voice is embedded in every aspect of creation is not an outlandish idea. Readers of this book likely share my belief in God's presence everywhere at every moment. My belief in the reality of God's activity in this world cannot be asserted as indubitable, but neither is it without foundation. It is, to use Polkinghorne's phrase, a "well-motivated" belief.[4]

This chapter contains guidelines for helping us "tune our receivers" to hear more clearly the divine voice. I believe we can attain clarity on some points, but much of our knowledge will remain fragmented and incomplete. An inherent aspect of our existence as finite creatures is that God's voice is only available to us in whispers and sighs.

So why give so much attention to the difficulties involved? Because honesty demands it, because so few Christians are willing to admit or face these difficulties, and because the implications of this point will shape everything else we have to say. There has never been a time when all Christians were united, when they did not have major disagreements among themselves, or when Christian (or Hebrew) communities were free of internal conflict and power struggles. In the same way one observes an incredible amount of variety among Christians today, there has been an astonishing degree of variety among Christian communities throughout the history of the church back to the earliest traditions.

The claim that Christianity has always included a multiplicity of perspectives should not be surprising, but Christians often seem surprised by the idea that the Bible is subject to the same plurality of perspectives that characterizes modern Christianity. If we stop to think about it, however, the diversity characteristic of the ancient cultures that produced the Bible provides a point of contact with our modern world. The communities that produced the Bible were engaged in a process of questioning and searching. They dared to believe that God was active in their history and they interpreted their communal experiences in light of that belief. The particular issues they faced were often quite different from what we face today, but some of the important questions they raised are as relevant today as

4. Polkinghorne, *Science and Religion in Quest of Truth*, 13.

they were then. Their questioning produced no single answer, no definitive unambiguous response, but rather a multiplicity of perspectives. That fact suggests that the existence of multiple perspectives is not necessarily a negative thing.

On the other hand, my argument is that there are places where we must choose among the biblical voices. Our task is to search among the many voices for authentic echoes of *the* voice. Here again, the Bible itself provides an example for us, since later traditions elevated some, but not all, of the earlier traditions. Older material in the Bible was reshaped and applied in fresh ways to new situations by later writers.

The Documentary Hypothesis argues that the first five books of the Bible were composed primarily of four sources that were blended together to form the Torah. Although there has been much debate about the number of sources, their dating and origin, and which texts should be attributed to which sources, scholars agree that the Torah is composed of a blending of sources that interacted with one another. In addition, the editors who shaped them into their current form were not unbiased conduits who simply passed along the information they received. Instead, they actively stamped their own spin or slant on the material they transmitted, altering it for their own purposes.

The process of appropriating earlier traditions and reshaping it for a later audience and context continued throughout the Old Testament and into the New Testament. In the gospel accounts, Jesus quotes Old Testament passages, but the quotations are drawn disproportionately from the prophets, particularly Isaiah, thus emphasizing some Old Testament traditions over others. Jesus is depicted as offering new interpretative twists of Old Testament texts, often in conflict with religious authorities of his day.

In other words, the Bible itself provides warrant for elevating some texts over others and for interpreting texts in novel ways. We continue this practice every week in our churches, as certain primary texts appear more often in the liturgy and as the basis for sermons and homilies—which themselves attempt to draw new insight from what are often, for regular churchgoers, well-known passages. Biblical texts do not carry a single meaning; there is inexhaustible richness in the biblical material. The biblical canon is not a petrified archeological treasure, but rather a living, dynamic tradition. It continues to provide meaningful insight to contemporary Christian communities to the extent that we seriously and honestly utilize it as a resource for our own spiritual explorations.

Before we outline some steps that can guide our use of the Bible as a map for our spiritual journey, we need to mention some additional things to keep in mind as we spread our map before us and begin to plot our journey. First, we can observe not simply a multiplicity of perspectives in the Bible, but also a change of cultural beliefs and assumptions across the hundreds of years during which the biblical material was produced. Worship practices, including views regarding sacrifice, changed. The culture of the biblical communities shifted from agrarian to more urban. Contact with Persian culture during the Babylonian exile produced a number of important changes, including the rise of a concept of Satan as a non-human figure as well as development in ideas regarding angels and demons (the New Testament reveals much further development of these concepts).[5] Views regarding the afterlife changed. For most of the Old Testament writers, there was no heaven or hell and no concept of eternal punishment; everyone went to the same place—Sheol, a dark and damp place sometimes translated as pit or grave. Henotheism (belief in multiple gods, while worshipping one preeminent God) characterized early biblical perspectives; later writings reveal a change toward a stricter monotheism (there is only one God; there are no other gods).

Knowledge of these kinds of developments helps us understand better biblical texts within their historical contexts. It also reminds us that changes in theological perspective over time have always characterized human communities, including both the communities that produced the Bible as well as the communities that have utilized the Bible as scripture. The process of theological exploration and the introduction of creative novelty that we see in the biblical traditions and throughout the history of the church continue into the present. Different denominational traditions read the Bible in differing ways due to traditions of interpretation that are part of the history of those denominations. Even those who claim to be "nondenominational" reveal the influence of specific theological traditions in the way they read and interpret scripture. There is nothing wrong with this fact. Diversity is an aspect of our existence as human beings. We should remind ourselves of it, though, so that the particular slice of that history of theological development within which we find ourselves is not assumed too readily to represent in actuality *the* biblical view.

5. There are only four Old Testament references to Satan as a non-human personal being: Numbers 22:22, 32, Job 1–2, Zechariah 3:1–2, and 1 Chronicles 21:1.

Second, the order of the canonical books matters. The Bible does not give us an abstract set of theological truths. It provides a *narrative*, and changing the order in which books appear changes the nature of the narrative. It is false to say, therefore, that the Old Testament (excluding the Apocrypha) is the same as the Hebrew Bible simply because the books contained within each are the same, as Douglas Knight and Amy Jill-Levine point out:

> The order of the volumes tells us about the distinct stories told by the church and the synagogue. For the Christian order, ending with the prophets, the story is one of promise in the Old Testament leading to fulfillment in the New. This reading is confirmed when the New Testament then interprets the Old. It finds in the story of Adam and Eve an account of an irreparable rupture between humanity and divinity that only Jesus can reconcile; it finds in Isaiah's depiction of the suffering servant a prediction of the saving death of Jesus. For the [Hebrew Bible], the Prophets are not at the end, but in the middle. For the synagogue, although the events in Eden do create less than ideal conditions for human existence, there is no irreparable breach established that only the sacrifice of Jesus can repair. The human condition is not one of irredeemable sin apart from the Christ; the relationship between God and creation continues.[6]

Interpretation happens within the context of the overall narrative, and canonical order affects the narrative. Recognition of this fact raises our awareness of the importance of attentiveness to our view of the overall narrative and the impact that our view can have on our interpretation of particular texts.

Our third point is a consequence of what we have observed about the multiplicity of perspectives within the Bible and within the history of biblical interpretation. The variety of viewpoints within Christianity, both in the history of the development of Christian traditions as well as within the Bible itself, gives us permission to explore new possibilities for interpreting the biblical text today. Knowledge of traditional interpretations is certainly necessary and helpful if our study of the Bible is to be as thorough as it ought to be. A novel idea is not necessarily untrue, however. Nor are ideas that originate in traditions other than our own. Interpretations that are part of our own tradition may need correction. We have embarked on a journey of truth-seeking, not a defensive search for counter-arguments to use against those with differing positions. We are explorers, entering

---

6. Knight and Jill-Levine, *The Meaning of the Bible*, 46–47.

new territory with hopeful expectancy as we look for signs of the divine presence.

Many of the preeminent doctrines and theological ideas of Christianity are post-biblical developments, including the doctrine of the trinity, the idea of original sin, the various theories of atonement, various concepts regarding eschatology (last things, or end times), the debates regarding predestination and free will, discussions regarding the omnipotence and omniscience of God, and the doctrine of the full humanity and full divinity of Jesus. One can argue that the foundations for these notions can be found in scripture, but the ideas themselves were post-biblical developments. Many of these doctrines remain matters of debate among contemporary theologians. For example, we now recognize that most of the prominent thinkers in the history of the church were heavily influenced by Greek philosophical viewpoints. Classic orthodox formulations of the immutability of God (God does not change), the impassibility of God (God does not suffer), and the timelessness of God seem to owe more to Greek philosophy than to the Bible. The Bible itself continues to provide raw material for creative reformulations of many long-held orthodox beliefs.

Fourth, modern interpreters recognize to a greater extent than previous generations the importance of the perspective of the reader. The revolutionary implications of this insight have not yet been fully realized within the church, or even among scholars, for that matter. Liberationist and feminist theologians have helped us better understand the influence of one's social location in shaping one's reading of a text. On a more fundamental level, however, there is greater recognition today of the inherent difficulties involved in making objective truth claims. The pluralism of our modern world and the juxtaposition of differing cultures and religions have problematized our claims to possess absolute truth. The variety of perspectives within even a single religion, such as Christianity, gives one pause and leads us to wonder what is at the root of such diversity and whether an argument favoring some truth claims over others is sustainable.

This problem is intrinsic to our existence as human beings. Humans construct meaning out of their experiences, and though there is a communal dimension to such constructions, there is also a unique quality to the meaning constructions of every individual. No person sees things in exactly the same way as another.[7] Our varying perspectives shape what we

---

7. Joseph Webb, for example, has said that the basis for our modern understanding of the fundamental importance of pluralism lies in the recognition that "no two individuals,

see. Since no two people share exactly the same perspective, no two people see things in exactly the same way.

There are at least two important consequences of this fact. First, differences of viewpoint will *always* exist. The assumption that we can discover objective truth in the realm of religious beliefs has been shown to be without foundation. There is, simply stated, no objective ground upon which we can stand and judge the huge diversity of human perspectives. The limitations of our finitude rule out any possibility for claiming absolute certainty with regard to our apprehension of truth. Second, theological truth—the kind of truth we seek—cannot be directly apprehended. Any discovery of truth will only happen in conversation and dialogue with others who see things differently. As we engage in that conversation, we must bear in mind that frequently the basis for our disagreement with others is not erroneous or blurred perception. This is an essential point, since we need to understand the reason why people are so resistant to change in their theological or ethical beliefs. When someone disagrees with us, we tend to attribute the disagreement to ignorance or obstinacy. All that is required for the other person to "see the light" and accept the truth is a lucid explanation of the facts. If there is ongoing disagreement, the other person must be either a simpleton or willfully ignorant.

But what are facts for one are not at all facts for another. Another person may see with equal clarity a different set of pertinent facts and may have a very different framework for interpreting those facts. Simply enumerating counter-arguments likely will not result in another person recognizing the error of her ways and suddenly deciding that you are the source of great truth and wisdom. The way we view the world—the way we construct a complex set of symbolic understandings that help us make sense of the world—shapes the content of what we see.[8] What we see depends on where we stand.[9] When it comes to reading the Bible, this means that the perspective of the person reading the Bible is more determinative for the meaning derived from the text than any supposed objective content present in the text itself. If where one stands is critically important for what

---

even in the same familial or cultural setting, ever place exactly the same meanings or feelings into what we might take to be a 'common' community symbol." See Webb, *Preaching and the Challenge of Pluralism*, 21. Webb's discussion of symbolic interactionist theory in chapter 1 of his book is helpful in explaining "why we see things differently."

8. See Webb's discussion of "hub symbols" in chapter 3 of *Preaching and the Challenge of Pluralism*.

9. See Webb, *Old Texts, New Sermons*, especially chapter 1.

one sees, an important question will be whether some perspectives from which one might read the Bible are more truthful than others.

A truth-seeking approach to reading the Bible is cautious about any claim to possess *the correct* interpretation of scripture as though no other reading could possibly be valid. On the other hand, truth-seekers are able to identify some interpretive claims as false. We can make progress by narrowing the field of legitimate interpretations. The guidelines that follow are based on the presupposition that not all interpretative claims have equal validity. They also assume that the biblical material must be sifted—that from a modern perspective (the only perspective we have), there will be variations in the degree of insight different texts will provide.

The approach presented here rejects a *progressive revelation* view, as though God has been doling out bits and pieces of insight throughout history.[10] It also rejects a *recover the original meaning of the text* methodology, since any such quest will only reveal more about our own presuppositions than about any presumed inherent objective meaning present in the text. Though the revelation of God in Jesus is supremely important from a Christian perspective, the guidelines we will present reject a *just follow Jesus* view. Such a view devalues the greater portion of the biblical canon, tends to give insufficient attention to the impact of the agendas of the gospel writers on the shaping of their portraits of Jesus, and is susceptible to blindness regarding the biases present in our own depictions of Jesus.

The guidelines take into account the insight of many modern scholars who recognize that the diversity of the biblical material problematizes any claim to find within it an overarching theological theme or a unifying core that connects the various strands.[11] Rather than attempting to locate a singular correct interpretation, our goal is to discover interpretations that are legitimate, that handle the biblical text with integrity and respect, that are cognizant (as far as is possible) of the way our interpretation is shaped by factors outside the text, that are honest, that take seriously the views of

---

10. I believe we see some things more clearly in our time than they were seen in previous times (e.g., slavery is wrong), but that is different from saying that God has only recently revealed those things to us.

11. See, e.g., Knight and Jill-Levine, *The Meaning of the Bible*, xxi: "No one has satisfactorily for all or even most readers found the Bible's theological core, although themes such as 'covenant' and 'salvation' and 'God's holiness' remain popular . . . . Given the diversity of texts within the corpus, finding a theological core might be comparable to finding a singular meaning in all of Shakespeare's plays, or in human history, or even in a single life."

others and are thus aware of alternative views, that can be supported with good reasoning, and are coherent with our view of God (which is shaped and molded by our reading in a kind of feedback loop).

Christians read the Bible at different times for different reasons. Sometimes the purpose is devotional, other times liturgical, other times we want to learn more about a particular biblical book, or we look for guidance on an ethical or theological topic. The attitude and spirit with which we read will obviously be shaped by the motives we bring to the text. The guidelines below cannot be applied equally in all situations. They are relevant to all situations, however, even when not consciously applied in a particular instance. Whether our reading/hearing of the Bible is devotional, or communal participation in a liturgical reading, or listening to a sermon or homily, or studying a text in a more disciplined fashion, these guidelines can help us "tune our receivers" to more effectively detect the voice of God. Though I refer to the guidelines as steps, they are not steps in the sense of a sequential order to be followed. They are dynamic aspects of a complicated process, separated here only for reasons of description and analysis. Truth-seeking Bible reading includes all three aspects.

Step One: We begin with an ancient Greek aphorism: "know thyself." Since what we bring to a text shapes in powerful ways what we derive from it, critical self-awareness is essential. What are our most important values? What is their source? How do we see the world? What forces have shaped our perspective? Where do our loyalties lie? Unless we have some sense of our answers to these questions, we will tend to assume that our reading of the Bible is more objective than it really is.

Discovering the answers to such questions is not always easy. Joseph Webb, in his book *Preaching and the Challenge of Pluralism*, provides a method that can help us. Webb discusses "hub symbols"—our deepest values, those things that are most sacred to us, the self-evident *facts* that are assumed as part of the *way things are*, and the things that shape who we are and who we want to be.[12] These hub symbols are often hard to identify, for a variety of reasons. Webb says that approaching the task negatively is often the best way to uncover them. I need to honestly ask myself to consider

> what someone might say that would cause "me" to feel great intellectual or emotional pain. I really get upset or angry when someone tells me that—and there the blank may be filled in. When they talk about race or what women shouldn't do or about laziness or

12. See Webb, *Preaching and the Challenge of Pluralism*, chapter 3, especially 50–51.

> obesity or about patriotism or whatever, or when they tear down
> the church or deny the divinity of Christ or say this or that about
> the Bible—I get upset and defensive. Whatever "that thing" is or
> "those things" are that produce that reaction reveals the presence
> of one's own hub symbols.[13]

Hub symbols arouse our passions, both positively and negatively. The positive and negative emotional responses are the two sides of our attachment to these symbols. We can focus on the positive by asking ourselves questions such as: What do I affirm? What are my beliefs? What do I value most intensely? What are my deepest loyalties?

Our negative emotional responses, however, are often more obvious or more easily discerned than positive responses. They can be particularly helpful in detecting our hub symbols. When values or beliefs or assumptions that we affirm seem to us at some level (whether conscious or not) to be threatened, our negative reactions offer clues to their identity. Hub symbols involve deep attachments. Sometimes those attachments are to things or beliefs or values that we would not want to admit to others. Sometimes we cannot even admit them to ourselves. We can be surprised at what seems like a disproportionate response to a situation. When passions are stirred, hub symbols are present.

As important as it is to identify our hub symbols, we must go further, according to Webb. We need to "track them down":

> That is, one must take each one, as much as one can actually single
> them out, and search back in one's own life and experience to de-
> termine where one 'got it.' Where was its source, as far as one's own
> individual experience is concerned?[14]

Finally, we must "take control" of our hub symbols: "They do not lose their emotional power, nor their ability to produce intense pain when they are attacked. What one can do, however, is to experience that pain, be aware of what it is and what caused it, and then control one's reaction to the pain itself."[15] The increased self-awareness that results from this "tracking down" and "taking control" process can help us both reduce our emotional attachment to destructive or unhelpful hub symbols and, in the case of hub symbols we would like to see strengthened, can help us respond in more

---

13. Webb, *Preaching and the Challenge of Pluralism*, 59.

14. Ibid.

15. Ibid., 60.

constructive and creative ways than we might instinctively tend to do in situations when we sense they are threatened.

Let us look at an example that can illustrate how hub symbols work in practice. On the morning of December 14, 2012, 20-year old Adam Lanza shot his mother, drove a short distance, shot his way into Sandy Hook Elementary School in Newtown, Connecticut, then proceeded to kill 6 adults and 20 children before taking his own life. In the midst of the reactions of shock and grief, the event ignited a national debate on issues such as gun control, mental health, and violent video games. Passionate arguments erupted on various sides of these topics. When such events happen, we respond on the basis of our hub symbols. We are not neutral observers. We have pre-formed beliefs, commitments, loyalties, and understandings of reality that mold our interpretation of "what happened." We do not objectively debate these issues and dispassionately consider the various possible points of view. Even though we choose what we will say and what actions, if any, we will take as a result of an event such as the Sandy Hook killings, our emotional response to such events, and even to a large extent our perception of the event itself, is predetermined by our hub symbols.

Let us suppose, for example, that I am a member of the National Rifle Association. I own guns and hunt regularly, I am a strong defender of Second Amendment rights, and I am highly suspicious of laws that might restrict my individual freedom, such as gun control laws. In that case, I might respond to the national debate by suggesting that the solution to reducing violence in our schools is to place armed security guards in every school. This was precisely the position taken by NRA Executive Vice President Wayne LaPierre one week following the shootings. The threat is identified as a restriction of freedom. A passionate plea is made to defend against the threat.

Hub symbols predispose us to respond in certain ways, but they do not predetermine our actions or words. Not all gun owners or NRA members responded to the Sandy Hook shootings in the way that LaPierre did. In the aftermath of the Sandy Hook shootings, many gun owners argued that the Second Amendment is consistent with bans on the sale of assault weapons and large capacity ammunition clips, as well as requirements for licensing and mandatory training for gun owners. They were able to recognize that the defense of freedoms they value—freedoms to own guns and to hunt or target shoot using those guns—does not require opposition to every proposal to regulate gun ownership. They were able to take a more nuanced approach as they weighed their commitment to protect innocent human life against their desire to guard against infringement of their individual freedom. In some cases, Sandy Hook provided a catalyst that led them to change their position from general opposition to gun control laws to support for some types of gun control laws. A shift occurred, prompted by an experience that led to introspective examination and reconsideration of their hub symbols.

We can examine responses on the other side of the issue in the same way. Personal experience can powerfully shape our hub symbols. For example, Sarah Brady became involved in the gun control movement following the shooting of her husband, White House Press Secretary Jim Brady, in 1981 during an assassination attempt on Ronald Reagan. Her efforts, combined with those of others, resulted in passage of the Brady Act in 1993, which requires federal background checks for purchasers of firearms. Following the Sandy Hook shootings, Sarah Brady issued a statement which called for, among other things, "a real ban on semi-automatic assault weapons and on magazines of more than ten rounds."[16] Her response, given her personal experience and what we know about her efforts since her husband was shot, was predictable. Her hub symbols shaped the way she interpreted the killings in Connecticut.

Let us think about another example. Suppose that I do not own any guns, that I have work experience as a chaplain in a major trauma-center hospital where I witnessed every week the effects of gun violence, often the result of accidents at home involving children, and that for many years I lived in a European country with strict gun control laws where gun violence is extremely rare. Is my response to an incident such as the Sandy Hook violence likely to be more like that of Wayne LaPierre or Sarah Brady?

We can imaginatively extend this example. Suppose that I am outraged that so many six and seven-year old children were killed by an assailant who fired off several thirty-round clips with an assault rifle in the space of about fifteen minutes. And let us say that I see a post on a social media web site that says something like, "I think the answer is not regulating guns but regulating schools. We should put metal detectors in every school and every principal and assistant principal should be required to take firearm courses and carry a concealed weapon while at school." Suppose I immediately feel intense anger when I read this post, such that my initial reflexive desire is

16. Brady, "The Time for Debating is Over—We Need Action," http://www.huffingtonpost.com/sarah-brady/gun-control_b_2313088.html?utm_hp_ref=tw.

to respond with a post calling the other person an "ignorant, satanic, death worshipper." The anger that I feel, along with my impulsive desire to lash out at the other person, are generated by previously existing hub symbols. In the process of identifying, tracking down, and taking control of my hub symbols, I may decide that the high value I place on protecting human life is well-founded and something I want to continue to affirm. I may decide that support for more restrictive gun control laws is a reasonable, valid, and healthy way to support the value I wish to affirm. I may also conclude, however, that responding impulsively by lashing out at others who have a different point of view is not a healthy, constructive, or effective way to persuade others of the truthfulness of the value I hold so dearly.

We can extend this example further still. Suppose we want to have a discussion about this topic in a church Bible study group. The question for discussion can be posed as something like, "Does the Bible have anything to say to us about gun control?" Or we could ask more generally something like, "How should Christians respond to the issue of gun control?" Obviously, the Bible does not provide a specific answer. But many Christians claim the Bible can be used to help guide us in formulating a general response, at least, to this and other contemporary issues. If the Bible is an authority source for us, it has to be able to help us with questions like this.

On the Sunday following the shootings at Sandy Hook Elementary School, many ministers addressed the killings in pulpits across the United States. Of course, not every sermon or homily that mentioned those killed at Sandy Hook addressed the specific topic of gun control, but many did. And many more Christians debated this topic in blogs and forums on the internet in the days and weeks following the massacre. As one can perhaps guess, the diversity of responses coming from Christians matched the diversity of responses coming from non-Christians. One's identification as a registered Republican or Democrat was probably a more accurate predictor of one's position regarding calls for gun control legislation following Sandy Hook than one's identity as a Christian.

The hard truth is that we do not go to the Bible and derive our values from it. Every one of us has a system of hub symbols formed before we ever consciously engage the Bible as a resource for ethical or theological guidance. Of course, if Bible stories are read to us when we are little and if in other ways we gain knowledge of the Bible's content as we are growing up, our hub symbols can reflect a biblical influence. The Bible itself can be a valued part of the community within which one is raised. But our knowledge of the Bible and the meaning of the Bible for us will be filtered through the lens of the community of which we are a part, and thus any biblical influence upon us will be an *interpreted* influence. Our personal understanding of what the Bible says will be powerfully affected by what *our community says* the Bible says, which may be very different from what other Christian communities say the Bible says.

How, then, can we possibly escape the relativity of our culture? If our hub symbols mold and fashion what we see in scripture, how can the Bible ever be an effective authority source? Part of the answer lies in the fact that although hub symbols shape our understanding of scripture in powerful ways, they do not predetermine either our interpretation or application of the biblical content. We have opportunities to gain new insights. The text itself possesses an integrity that sometimes poses a challenge to one or more of our hub symbols.

Another part of the answer lies in the tension that exists among hub symbols. There is always a degree of dissonance produced by the lack of complete alignment of our hub symbols. When that dissonance grows to the point that we are forced to wrestle with the internal contradictions, creative shifts can occur that produce a new internal landscape. Such shifts are not without emotional pain when they occur, especially when they produce significant realignments, but ultimately, the results can be deeply satisfying as a more harmonic internal configuration of hub symbols is created. In the example above concerning the issue of gun control, we saw that regardless of where one starts on the issue, one does not have to respond in a predictable fashion, following in lockstep with others who share one's hub symbols. We can deviate. Deviation from the crowd can be a sign or evidence of a truth-seeking spirit.

Deviation from our cultural captivity requires critical self-awareness. We need to know, as far as we can determine, who we are and what influences have shaped us into the persons we are. No factor has a more powerful effect on shaping our interpretation of the Bible than the hub symbols (values, beliefs, assumptions, worldview, loyalties) that provide the context within which scripture is read and heard. The task of improving our self-awareness is never complete, nor do we ever have a perfectly clear picture of our hub symbols. We can make great progress, however. And we will only make progress if we are diligent and work hard at it. In order to sustain our motivation to do this hard work, we must be convinced of its importance. Simply put, we will never escape the blinders of our culture unless we have a truth-seeking attitude of curiosity and openness that pushes us to explore the tensions that exist among our hub symbols, as well as to pause and reconsider when our initial emotional reaction to a new idea is to reject it (and often, also, the person or persons who hold it).

We will be more likely to "hit the pause button" on those occasions when a challenge to our hub symbols causes our blood pressure to sky-rocket if we are able to recognize that every hub symbol that is part of the matrix of our worldview is finite. Even our most intense religious beliefs and commitments are part of a perspective that we have constructed.[17] This is the challenge of our finite existence. The Bible did not fall out of the sky. Our most cherished religious beliefs were not handed to us directly from God. As hard as it is for us to accept the idea, we cannot presume that our view of the world can be equated with God's view. We therefore have to take seriously the possibility that in every challenge to our hub symbols we might find the whispering of God's voice, calling us to a better understanding of God's purpose and intention. Every challenge represents an opportunity for growth.

Many Christians seem to want to create a controlled environment—a bubble world—that eliminates the challenges of our pluralistic world. Such approaches are not problematic primarily because they are unrealistic or dishonest or unwelcoming toward others (even though they are all of those things). They are primarily problematic, from a truth-seeking point of view, because they attempt to eliminate the very thing that can be most helpful to us on our truth-journey. Change and challenges are inevitable. They are often hard to face, but they are the raw material for learning and growth.

We need to work as hard as we can to identify the hub symbols that shape our identity. No other factor has as great an impact in determining what we will take away from scripture as the content of the hub symbols that we bring with us to scripture and that provide the filter through which we read or hear the text.

Step Two: As we read the Bible, we become more familiar with it. As we become more familiar with it, themes emerge, we see patterns, and we make connections between different passages. We cannot avoid reading scripture through the lenses of our biases and cultural assumptions (hub symbols), but scripture has a substance and an integrity that resist our tendency to manipulate the text in self-serving directions. There is an objective reality to the text that challenges us to lay aside, as far as we are able, our

17. See Webb, *Preaching and the Challenge of Pluralism*, 58.

presuppositions and to listen to alien voices from long ago. The second step, simply put, is to engage the text: to read it, wrestle with it, and struggle for meanings that challenge us, confront us, confuse us, comfort us, inspire us, and carry us forward into new understandings.

Any serious Bible reader will recognize the biblical message is multifaceted and often internally inconsistent. The authors of the words contained in the Bible were shaped by their own hub symbols. They were historically embedded in the cultural realities of their time and place. Different biblical authors had different hub symbols. And the hub symbols of the communities that produced the biblical literature changed over time.

Our struggle, as we read the Bible, is to find the voice of God among the voices contained in scripture. Any attempt to squash the diversity present in those voices is to be resisted. At the same time, however, we yearn for common threads that unify and integrate. We face an inescapable tension as we seek to honor the integrity of the differing biblical voices while also seeking harmonies among those voices. A guiding principle for truth-seekers is that forced harmonization is never permissible. Our search for harmony will mean that there will be times when we choose to honor some notes over others, but we must be clear that the harmony that results is a constructed harmony—open to revision and correction. The disharmonies of the Bible constantly challenge all of our attempts to construct harmonic frameworks for reading. Our engagement with the Bible takes the form of a constant back-and-forth conversation, as we seek tonic bass notes that reverberate powerfully across cultural divides and limited perspectives.

An example of an impermissible forced harmonization that has been common in the history of Christian interpretation can be found in the way many Christian commentators have tried to make sense of the plural pronouns used in relation to God in Genesis 1:26: "Then God said, 'Let *us* make humankind in *our* image, according to *our* likeness; and let them have dominion'" (emphasis added). Some argue that the *us* and *our* in this verse are references to the trinity. Since the text was composed hundreds of years before the time of Jesus, and since the doctrine of the trinity was not formulated until after the last of the New Testament documents had been completed, we simply cannot claim that the author of Genesis 1:26 was thinking of the trinity and for that reason used the pronouns *us* and *our*. Our interpretation of the text has to begin with an attempt to construct a plausible explanation for these plural pronouns that would have made sense at the time of the text's composition.

Of course, any attempts to reconstruct the meaning intended by the original author are fraught with tremendous difficulties. Our goal cannot be a simplistic attempt to discover authorial intention, as though the interpretive difficulties would be resolved if we could only decipher the meaning intended by the author. Such a goal is impossible to achieve, and even if it were not, tensions would remain among the diverse perspectives present in the Bible. We can, however, rule out some interpretations as invalid, and we can construct a range of plausible ways of understanding a text that are faithful to the historical and cultural realities of its composition.

Bible readers today have a vast amount of resources available to them that can assist them in knowing which interpretations are within the range of plausible possibilities and which are not. These resources are more easily accessible than they have ever been. Truth-seekers must be wary, however, since the quality of these resources varies significantly. Special caution must be reserved for those who claim to have *the correct* interpretation.

More reliable commentators are those who recognize the difficulties involved in understanding and interpreting scripture, who are aware of a range of plausible viewpoints, who are knowledgeable about and take seriously the issues of literary genre and other aspects of modern biblical studies, and who plainly articulate the assumptions that lie behind their approaches. Scholars who devote their lives to academic study of the Bible are not infallible authority sources, but their voices provide essential background knowledge. Checking a variety of perspectives can help correct distortions in any single perspective. For the Old Testament, Jewish perspectives as well as Christian perspectives should be consulted, and for both Old and New Testaments, perspectives from a wide denominational spectrum should be considered.

Reading the Bible and trying to make sense of it for our situation today is not a matter of applying an exact formula. It is more a creative process, with better and worse interpretations rather than unequivocally correct and incorrect understandings. We are adding our own brush strokes to a canvas that has been created out of the lives and stories of communities that claim to have experienced the power and presence of God. There are no precise answers—no definitively settled questions. The traditions passed to us contain a variety of answers that previous communities of faith have found to be attractive. Those answers continue to be tested in the fires of our own experience as we appropriate and reinterpret the traditions for our own time.

The most important aspect of this second step is not the particular interpretive result, but rather the process. We proceed with openness, we strive to learn what we can about the text we are reading, and we allow the text to challenge us. We familiarize ourselves with the stories of the Bible and we allow those stories to shape our own story. Points of difficulty or tension represent opportunities for learning, if we will take them seriously. We can make progress on our journey, but this journey of truth-seeking has no finish line within the confines of our finite existence.

The knowledge we seek has two facets. Some languages have more than one word to describe what, in English, is communicated by the verb "to know." In Portuguese, for example, the word *saber* means "to know" in relation to facts or data. Certainly our truth-seeking journey includes a desire to increase our *saber* kind of knowledge. However, if one wishes to say in Portuguese that one knows *someone*, a different word must be used: *conhecer*. Knowledge of some*one* is a different kind of knowledge than knowledge of some*thing*.

Our truth journey involves learning data, but it is also a relational journey. Relationships change us and shape our identity. A number of English language expressions (other languages have their equivalents) capture this idea. We say, for example, that "you are the company you keep," or "birds of a feather flock together." As we seek to be in relationship with God and strive to hear the whispers of God's voice in scripture (as well as elsewhere), we are invited to learn more than *saber* kind of knowledge. We are encouraged to learn the knowledge that comes in relationship—the *conhecer* kind of knowledge that is discovered through participation in community.

Our approach diverges here from the focus of many "how to read the Bible" books. For a Christian truth-seeker, reading the Bible is not primarily about learning *things*. It is about becoming a certain sort of *person*. It is about living within a certain kind of community. It is about a commitment to be one way and not another—in our personal relationships and in our societal relationships. It affects our priorities, our concerns, our decisions, and our actions. The Bible reveals insight into the character and purposes of a personal being. What we seek, at the end of the day, is participation in a particular sort of community—a community that represents the wholeness of God's intention for us. Bible reading, from a Christian faith perspective, points us toward God's *shalom*.

Shalom is a word found in the Old Testament commonly translated as *peace*. Often, in the English language, we use the word peace to describe the absence of active fighting. Nations sign a peace treaty, for example, or parents tell children to stop fighting so the parents can have some peace and quiet. *Shalom* means much more than *not fighting*. It means wholeness, health, completeness, having one's needs met.[18] The term is closely related to both truth and justice, and is often used in the Bible synonymously with justice. To obtain wholeness and health, we must relate toward one another truthfully and with justice. In the Bible, justice is closely connected with fairness and with the idea of having needs met. *Shalom* is not negative (the absence of certain things) nor is it passive (a byproduct or something that just happens). *Shalom* is active and dynamic. It represents a way of relating to one another—a way of being together in community.

Bible religion is *shalom* religion. And *shalom* religion is religion that emphasizes communities that strive toward the core values of justice, fairness, and truth. It is relational religion, founded on the central premise that God is relational. As we take more seriously the discipline of regularly reading the Bible and engaging it in an ongoing conversation, diligently seeking the truth it contains, our reading will begin to evidence a certain inclination or shape. This shape comes both from the context within which we read the Bible—as part of a community of those committed to following the way of Jesus—and from the content of the Bible itself.

The content of this shape or inclination is not readily available or immediately self-evident. Its discernment requires disciplined study, critical reflection, conversation with others, and the kind of questioning that is part of truth-seeking. Think for a moment about how relationships begin. When we meet someone, we form a first impression. As we spend more time with that person, our first impression may be confirmed, or we may find that we were mistaken. First impressions are hard to overcome, but we can and often do manage to get a more comprehensive, and therefore more truthful, picture of the other person if we are able to maintain an open mind and avoid a rigid labeling that reduces the other person to a category.

First impressions are powerful. They may have nothing to do with the character of the person in front of us, but can be (and often are) affected by the other person's dress, speech pattern, ethnicity, the location and circumstances of the encounter, as well as a myriad of other factors. Once that first impression is formed, however (usually within seconds of meeting

18. See Healey, "Peace," 206–7.

someone, according to research), we tend to look for data that confirms our impression and discount data that contradicts it. Only a truth-seeker's openness to new discoveries combined with an elevated self-awareness can help us overcome our biases.

What do first impressions have to do with the Bible? When we pick up a Bible to read it, whether for the first time or after years of study, we bring an impression of God's character with us. Just as our initial impression of another person may not be a true picture of that person's character, the impression of God that we bring with us to the Bible may have little, if anything, to do with the picture of God presented in scripture. Perhaps our relationship with our parents has played an important role in shaping our view of God. Perhaps cultural symbols such as Santa Claus have shaped our image of God—God rewards good girls and boys and leaves lumps of coal (or worse) for those who misbehave. Whatever its source, we have some preexisting picture of God in our minds that powerfully shapes our Bible reading.

This is where things get really interesting. We cannot avoid a bit of circularity in our approach, but neither must we remain trapped within a circle. We must begin with self-awareness (see step one above). The particular self-awareness question we must ask ourselves in relation to step two is: what is at the heart of our view of God? The question does not call for a list of divine attributes, but rather the identification of the *one* attribute that supersedes all others. If forced to pick one word to describe our view of God, what would it be?

I invite you to stop for a few moments to think about your view of God. You may have difficulty identifying only one attribute in relation to God. Perhaps you can narrow your list to two or three traits, but you find it a struggle to get the list down to only one characteristic. Go with your instincts. Pick one. Do not try to think rationally about your choice. You are trying to identify what your view *is*, not what you would like it to be. Before you read further, I encourage you to formulate a specific word in your mind—or better yet, write it down.

The picture of God we have in our minds before we read the Bible will shape our reading in powerful ways. Our awareness of that picture (and the word that for us best represents it) will help us avoid the circularity trap. Just as truth-seekers try not to allow the biases of a first impression to completely control their second and third, etc. impressions of another person, truth-seekers reading the Bible will strive to allow the text to correct the picture of God they bring with them to scripture. Picking one word to describe God is an exercise in focusing. One word, of course, cannot capture our view of God's essence, but at least it gives us a starting point for understanding what is at the heart of our own conception.

As we read the Bible, we are confronted with images and stories and perspectives representing a diverse array of God-pictures. Not all of them are compatible with each other, much less with the pictures we bring with us to the text. As we read, a process of selection occurs. We emphasize some biblical perspectives over others. We may or may not be aware that as we read, we organize and prioritize. Our interpretations reveal our choices. When we lack self-awareness, we easily fall into the trap of imagining that our interpretations, representing selections we have made from among the diversity of biblical pictures, represent *the* biblical picture of God.

When we recognize that our vision is partial and skewed and when we have at least some awareness of the perspective we bring with us to the Bible, however, we can begin the exciting journey of a conversational engagement with the text. We can recognize when a clash of hub symbols occurs and can begin to ask some interesting questions about which hub symbols seem to characterize the overall perspective of the Bible and how they compare with the hub symbols that we bring with us to the text. As we begin to escape our entrapment within interpretations that represent no more than hall-of-mirror reflections of our own hub symbols and those of our culture, we start to apprehend hub symbols in the biblical material containing a deep and profound resonance. And as our conviction about the truth of those hub symbols strengthens, they stand as challenges to our own hub symbols and the hub symbols of our culture, as well as to alternative hub symbols also present in scripture. At that point, the authority of the Bible comes into full force as it challenges us to correct our faulty hub symbols.

Step Three: Finally, we verify the accuracy and truthfulness of our reading. There are some obvious ways to do this. We rule out interpretations based on faulty assumptions or data by checking commentaries, Bible dictionaries, and other scholarly resources. The more of these we consult, and the broader the representation in terms of denominational perspective, etc., the better. We should learn as much as we can about the historical background of the text, its literary genre, authorship, time and circumstances of writing, intended audience, purpose for writing, editorial shaping, role within the larger canon, etc. that we can. Our own denomination may have interpretive traditions that can guide us and provide helpful insight. The broader traditions within Christian history that call us toward exploration beyond our own denominational boundaries should also be part of our conversation with the text. To the extent that we are able, we should try to become acquainted with alternative interpretive traditions. We should remember that Bible reading is not a solitary task. We should discuss with others the ideas we get from our reading and check our understandings against alternative views.

No one, of course, can do all of these things in relation to every text. But these tests provide us with basic (and adaptable) guidelines for our journey of truth-discovery that are respectful of the data of scripture and cognizant of potential sources of distortion. Even if we do all of these things, we will still likely be faced with a range of plausible interpretations. These interpretations may well be complementary. If contradictory, the test of personal resonance will be the ultimate criterion.

Fortunately, we do not have to apply every test mentioned above in order to gain insight from our reading of scripture. In practice, all Bible-readers use a kind of shorthand most of the time. As we noted in our previous chapter, Glen Stassen argues that our interpretations should be aligned with the *actions and teachings of Jesus, as well as with a view of God that sees God's creative, loving and redemptive activity as being directed toward all persons.*[19] Stassen evidences his hub symbols here, but he is also making a claim about the hub symbols of the Bible itself. In other words, Stassen has developed a criterion for testing interpretations of the Bible based on the kind of engagement with the text that we described in step two above.

I like Stassen's shorthand interpretive criterion. It is more theologically nuanced and comprehensive than the popular WWJD ("What would Jesus do?") that became ubiquitous for a while on wristbands and bumper stickers. WWJD is not a bad shorthand criterion for those who claim to be followers of Jesus. The problem, of course, as Stassen points out, is that our picture of Jesus can be a thin view that is disconnected from the Jesus we encounter in the Bible and ends up being a mirror image of our cultural

19. See Stassen, *A Thicker Jesus*, 20–21. I have restated what I take to be Stassen's point using language that is, from my perspective, less theologically and ethically problematic. See my previous chapter above, note 17.

hub symbols. We cannot avoid operating with a shorthand criterion for most of our Bible reading and interpreting, but we need to be both aware of the criterion we use and open to possible correction as we test our interpretations in the laboratory of life. The exercise in step two above that asked you to identify one word for describing your view of God's essence can be helpful as you think about your own shorthand interpretive criterion.

When we first begin to read the Bible, we cannot avoid bringing with us to the text the hub symbols of our culture and our personal way of viewing the world. As we allow the words of scripture to soak into our souls, however, there is the possibility, if we have a truth-seeker's openness to correction, that hub symbols inherent to the text itself will gradually become more and more powerful in shaping our perspective toward what we read. Just as important as any particular interpretations resulting from our reading is our attention in a more general sense to hub symbols, including the need for their ongoing evaluation and revision. When we read and interpret the Bible, we are making a claim not only about the truthfulness of a particular understanding of a specific text. We are claiming that the criteria that govern our interpretation are not ours alone, but are rather echoes of the voice of God contained in scripture.

This is a bold claim. But there is no getting around it. No one has a "God's eye" view and therefore no one can claim to have an infallible interpretation of the Bible. No one can escape the inherent relativity of human finitude, including the limitations of our hub symbols. Jennifer Wright Knust, in her book *Unprotected Texts: The Bible's Surprising Contradictions About Sex and Desire*, says that when she leads church Bible studies (she is a New Testament scholar and a pastor), she often begins "by asking participants what they wish the Bible said about the topic at hand."[20] She continues:

> Whatever we wish for, I point out, probably can be found somewhere in the Bible, which is why it is so important to admit that we have wishes, whatever they may be. We are not passive recipients of what the Bible says, but active interpreters who make decisions about what we will believe and what we will affirm. Admitting that we have wishes, and that our wishes matter, is therefore the first step to developing an honest and faithful interpretation.[21]

20. Knust, *Unprotected Texts*, 241.

21. Ibid., 241.

Knust is clear in stating her own interpretive principle: "Anyone who would use God and the Bible to deny touch, love, and affection to others has failed to present a valuable interpretation, not only of the Bible but also of what it means to be human, whether or not some biblical passage somewhere can be found to support their claims."[22]

Eric Seibert, in his book *The Violence of Scripture*, also clearly states his interpretative principle: "the Bible should never be used to inspire, promote, or justify acts of violence."[23] Seibert, however, links his interpretative principle to a claim about whether the Bible is authoritative:

> If you want to know whether someone *really* believes in the authority of Scripture, consider how they might answer questions like these: Does your reading of the Bible increase your love of God and neighbor? Does it inspire you to trust God wholeheartedly and to seek God unreservedly? Does it compel you to act justly, love mercy, and walk humbly with God (Mic. 6:8)? Does it move you to behave compassionately toward the most vulnerable members in your community? Does it prompt you to love your enemy and reconcile with your adversary? Does it create in you a desire to do all you can to see God's reign of peace and justice realized in the world? Those who answer "Yes" to such questions embrace the authority of Scripture in a profound way regardless of whether they believe everything in it actually happened or regard all of it as theologically "true." Those who cannot answer questions like these affirmatively, on the other hand, can claim whatever they wish about biblical authority, but their lives ultimately belie their words. The Bible is only truly authoritative in our lives when it functions in ways that transform us into God's image and align our priorities with God's.[24]

Though I am fully sympathetic with the content of Siebert's interpretive criteria, he goes too far in claiming that he has the authority of the Bible behind him while others do not. My point is that all serious biblical interpreters must wrestle with sorting out the difference between authentic and inauthentic biblical hub symbols. The best way to avoid error is to state our assumptions clearly and openly so others can see what guides our interpretation. To his credit, Siebert does this.

22. Ibid., 247.

23. Siebert, *The Violence of Scripture*, 148.

24. Ibid., 161–2.

The likelihood of distortion increases when our assumptions remain hidden or unexamined. Part of the conversation that needs to happen among Christians is at the point of discussing which interpretive criteria are valid. As truth-seekers, we should exercise caution regarding claims to know God's priorities. On the other hand, we must state clearly what we think those priorities are and engage others in conversation as we seek to demonstrate why we think our perspective is truthful. As Knust points out, we are "active interpreters who make decisions about what we will believe and what we will affirm."[25] We choose. Our choices are not blind choices, but neither are they choices made with full knowledge of the ramifications. The real world consequences of our hub symbols are only gradually revealed to us as we discuss them with others, as they become embodied in our lives and the lives of our communities, and as they are tested in the laboratory of our historical existence.

These consequences, either positive or negative, are a form of verification. German Christians following World War II had to ask themselves hard questions about the sources of the theological blind spots that enabled them to be so easily led down the path of Nazi ideology. What was different in the theology of Dietrich Bonhoeffer and Karl Barth that helped them resist the cultural trend? White Christians in the United States, particularly in southern states, have had to ask themselves hard questions about the sources of theological blind spots that enabled first slavery, then ongoing segregation and racism to become so embedded in all aspects of the culture to the point that white churches not only failed to offer resistance, but actively supported structures of oppression. What was different about the theology of people like Clarence Jordan, who spoke and acted so prophetically against those structures?

On the positive side, what was there about the theology of Millard Fuller that led him to start Habitat for Humanity? What in the theology of Dorothy Day led her in the direction of founding the Catholic Worker movement? What hub symbols in the perspective of Arthur Simon led him to take the lead in establishing Bread for the World?

Of course, even the fact that I mention these particular persons and not others reveals assumptions on my part. Another person's list of "heroes of the faith" might include individuals I consider to be seriously problematic as examples to be emulated. This fact reminds us once again that we will not make progress unless our truth-search actively engages the issue

25. Knust, *Unprotected Texts*, 241.

of hub symbols. Hub symbol awareness and analysis is an essential feature of all three aspects of our model: our self-examination, our examination of scripture, and our verification of our interpretations.

6

Applying the Model—Letting the Bible Shape Our Moral Horizon

IN THIS CHAPTER WE will present an argument for why Christians should regard certain specific hub symbols as central to the biblical perspective. We will draw some conclusions in this chapter and the next regarding appropriate Christian responses for issues prominent in our own time. Perhaps you will find yourself in agreement with my claims, perhaps not. The arguments themselves are important, but even more important, if we are to make progress as Christian communities seeking to find ways to make the Bible authoritative in our lives, is our need to have this kind of discussion. This chapter and the next are offered, therefore, both as illustrations and as enticements to join the conversation by engaging scripture yourself and discussing your insights with others in your own community.

The Bible is only authoritative if it is a practical source of guidance in our lives. The nature of the Bible's truth is multifaceted. From a Christian perspective, it provides images for understanding the character of God, contains stories that attest to the activity of God in history, and presents claims concerning God's intentions for us. Often the nature of its message is indirect. A story about an ancient king, for example, might not seem at first glance to offer a relevant message to a twenty-first century audience. Diligent exploration, however, is rewarded with profound insights, as generations of interpreters have attested.

There is no single reason for reading the Bible. Christians often read the Bible, as we have said, to discern more clearly the nature of God and God's intention for us. Sometimes the exploration is more explicitly theological, for the purpose of clarifying one's thinking on a point of doctrine. Sometimes the Bible is read for general edification, with no specific goal. The Bible is read in churches as part of worship services. Sometimes people turn to the Bible for comfort in a time of distress. I argued in the previous chapter that an essential aspect of regular Bible-reading for a truth-seeking Christian is hub symbol analysis and correction.

Accurate identification of the major biblical hub symbols provides us with at least two major advantages. First, it helps us correctly order our priorities. Over time, our priorities should become more closely aligned with biblical priorities, if our claim that the Bible is a genuine authority source has any authenticity. Second, when we face modern issues not addressed explicitly in the Bible, knowledge of biblical hub symbols provides us with clues for a proper Christian response. The Bible has no mention of cloning or global warming, for example, but a biblically-based response to such modern issues can be constructed on the basis of our understanding of the Bible's hub symbols.

In this chapter we want to look at how the Bible can help us sort out correct priorities. If we allow the Bible to shape our perspective and set our agenda regarding matters that ought to take precedence, what issues and concerns will become important for us? Our culture exerts a strong influence in forming our ideas concerning things that have significance. Because critical self-awareness in relation to our culture is difficult to achieve, we often assume that what our culture deems to be important really *is* important, and we are often unaware that those assumptions exist as *assumptions*. As we saw in the previous chapter, our hub symbols can be difficult to identify and are often viewed as simply part of the way the world is. In relation to many of our hub symbols, the issue of whether they are true or good or life-enhancing does not exist for us, since we are not aware that alternative viewpoints are possible. If we have an opportunity to live in another culture for an extended period of time, however, our priorities may shift somewhat as we see the world from a different perspective. Cross-cultural experiences help us to become more self-aware and self-critical.

For example, not too long ago I led a group of students on a five-week study abroad experience. The students encountered a world quite different from the one they had known. Among other things, they confronted a different view of time, a different view about the proper relationship between male and female, a different view about meals and eating, and differing religious perspectives. These differences, combined with the lack of easy access to the internet and various forms of social media to which they had become accustomed, created problems of adjustment for some of the students. At the same time, the appreciation they gained for some aspects of the culture in which they were immersed for five weeks gave them a new perspective. They returned home with an ability to see things that had not been visible to them before. They had a renewed appreciation for some aspects of their home culture, but questioned other aspects in a way that previously had not been possible for them.

You will benefit more from reading this chapter if, before proceeding, you ask yourself two questions:

1. Toward the end of the last chapter you were asked to identify what you consider to be the most important attribute of God. Now write down as many characteristics concerning God as you can come up with. Keep working at it. When you have ten, see if you can think of ten more. Then try to add ten more. Spend some time and try to expand your list as much as you can. Then go back and circle the characteristics you think are most important.

2. Write down what you think are the most important moral or ethical issues presented to us in the Bible.

The biblical world is similar to a foreign culture in that the values and assumptions of that ancient world are drastically different from those characterizing modern society. This fact presents a challenge to modern interpreters, since our tendency is to project our assumptions about reality onto the biblical text. We must work to achieve greater cultural sensitivity to the biblical world, just as we would want to do if immersed in an unfamiliar modern culture. We saw in chapter 3, for example, that adultery had a different meaning in biblical times than it does today. Sexual relations between a married man and a prostitute did not constitute adultery, thus the admonition in Proverbs 6:26 suggesting that prostitution is a preferable alternative to sexual relations with another man's wife. Sensitivity to cultural differences is not the same thing as agreement with differing values. We have to understand before we can evaluate. We cannot engage in an authentic conversation with the biblical text unless we have some knowledge of the perspective of those who produced the writings.

Our search for relevant biblical hub symbols can be compared to a prospector searching for gold in a stream bed. Not every hub symbol in the Bible will be of interest to us. We have noted that the Bible contains hub symbols characteristic of the cultures that produced it, including systems of slavery, patriarchy, and ethnocentrism. Our quest is for hub symbols that are echoes of the voice of God. One method that can help us, therefore, is to look for places where the hub symbols of the Bible seem to diverge in significant ways from those of the surrounding cultures. Slavery, patriarchy, and ethnocentrism were common phenomena in the ancient world. We should not be surprised that many of the biblical voices seem to assume that such things are part of the *way things are*. When we come across a hub symbol that stands out from those that generally characterized ancient cultures, however, we may have a glint of the kind of gold we seek.

We saw an example of an atypical hub symbol in chapter 4 as we examined the first chapter of Genesis. We noted that the depiction of a six-day creation in Genesis was used as the basis for the sabbath command in Exodus 20:10–11. The sabbath command was an innovation in ancient times. The concept of a day of rest was one that benefitted primarily those who were on the bottom of the social scale. Could there be something of the voice of God in a command that benefitted the powerless? Ancient writings, for the most part, preserved the records of the powerful and wealthy. A tradition enunciating a divine command whose practical effect was to establish a right to a day of rest for those who otherwise would have had no relief from relentless harsh labor represents an anomaly.

When we examine the sabbath command in the Deuteronomy version (5:12–15), we see a connection with the Hebrews' experience of slavery in Egypt:

> Observe the sabbath day and keep it holy, as the LORD your God commanded you. Six days you shall labor and do all your work. But the seventh day is a sabbath to the LORD your God; you shall not do any work—you, or your son or your daughter, or your male or female slave, or your ox or your donkey, or any of your livestock, or the resident alien in your towns, so that your male and female slave may rest as well as you. Remember that you were a slave in the land of Egypt, and the LORD your God brought you out from there with a mighty hand and an outstretched arm; therefore the LORD your God commanded you to keep the sabbath day.

Here the appeal to experience is explicit: "Remember that you were a slave in the land of Egypt." Particular concern is expressed that slaves, children, animals, and "aliens" (foreigners) be allowed a day of rest. What do these particular groups have in common? They were the voiceless. Today we might describe them as those with no vote in the ballot box. They had no power and no one to speak on their behalf. In the Bible, God speaks for them and commands that they be given a day of rest.

I have argued that the authority of the Bible is a bottom-up authority derived from the claim that the Bible testifies to God's activity in history. Any truth about God contained in the Bible is truth revealed in the historical experience of those who produced the biblical writings. That truth becomes authoritative as it resonates with and is activated in the lives of contemporary readers. What, then, is revealed in the history of the Hebrews? How is their history, or their interpretation of their history, peculiarly different from the history of other nations of the ancient world? Not many people today are concerned to study the history of the Moabites, Edomites, Ammonites, or other small nations that existed in the same region of the Ancient Near East as Israel and Judah.[1] What was special or noteworthy about the Hebrews?

The Hebrew scriptures themselves preserve a recognition that there was no intrinsic reason for any claim of special status:

> It was not because you were more numerous than any other people that the LORD set his heart on you and chose you—for you were the fewest of all peoples. It was because the LORD loved you and kept the oath that he swore to your ancestors, that the LORD has brought you out with a mighty hand, and redeemed you from the house of slavery, from the hand of Pharaoh king of Egypt. (Deut 7:7–8)

The recorded histories of other nations extol the exploits of their rulers—battle victories, nations conquered, palaces built, and wise governance of the people. They reflect hub symbols of domination and coercive power. They support a status quo with an entrenched power hierarchy blessed

---

1. The term *Israel* is somewhat ambiguous, sometimes referring in the Bible to the northern kingdom that lasted from the death of Solomon to the destruction of Samaria by the Assyrians in 722 BCE, while other times referring more generally to the Hebrews as a people. Unless clearly distinguished as a separate entity in relation to the kingdom of Judah, my use of the term is in its more general sense.

by the gods. Rulers were god-like beings, while slaves were disposable non-persons.

Against this background, the Old Testament presents us with a surprising contrast. The most important events in the history of the Hebrew people as recounted in the Old Testament were their experiences of slavery in Egypt and exile in Babylon. An essential element for understanding the history of the Hebrews was their memory of shared suffering. Much of the perspective of the Old Testament is from the underside of history—the viewpoint of those without power, intimately acquainted with the pain and grief of broken dreams, servitude to others, injustice, and calamities of one sort or another.

The picture of God that developed among the Hebrews, though similar in some respects to that of neighboring cultures, was in many ways remarkably innovative. God was viewed as personal, relational, creative, caring, and forgiving. Several times in the Old Testament we find some version of the formula that God is "ready to forgive, gracious and merciful, slow to anger and abounding in steadfast love" (see, e.g., Nehemiah 9:17). God is pictured as observing "the misery of my people who are in Egypt," God hears "their cry on account of their taskmasters," and God knows "their sufferings" (Exod 3:7–8). God comes "down to deliver them from the Egyptians" (Exod 3:8).

The experience of suffering on the part of the Hebrews became a key element in their depictions of God's intention for the kind of society they should construct amongst themselves. The Hebrews experienced God as a God who heard their cries of pain and who responded to their suffering. Their view of God, therefore, was shaped in the direction of a picture of a caring God who pays special attention to the cries of the suffering and oppressed. God expected the Hebrews to protect the weak and vulnerable. For example, in Exodus 23:9, God gives the following instruction: "You shall not oppress a resident alien; you know the heart of an alien, for you were aliens in the land of Egypt."

The Hebrews experienced God as having a particular concern for hurting people. Their own experience of God's concern, compassion, and mercy was extrapolated into a command to have a similar concern for others, especially those who were more likely to experience pain and oppression. Exodus 22:22 states that "you shall not abuse any widow or orphan." Exodus 22:25–27 commands:

> If you lend money to my people, to the poor among you, you shall not deal with them as a creditor; you shall not exact interest from them. If you take your neighbor's cloak in pawn, you shall restore it before the sun goes down; for it may be your neighbor's only clothing to use as cover; in what else shall that person sleep? And if your neighbor cries out to me, I will listen, for I am compassionate.

Leviticus 19:9–10 instructs: "When you reap the harvest of your land, you shall not reap to the very edges of your field, or gather the gleanings of your harvest. You shall not strip your vineyard bare, or gather the fallen grapes of your vineyard; you shall leave them for the poor and the alien: I am the Lord your God." Among the decrees of the Torah, we find surprising provisions for those who are vulnerable. The reason cited for having a special concern for the weak and defenseless is the experience of slavery in Egypt: "The alien who resides with you shall be to you as the citizen among you; you shall love the alien as yourself, for you were aliens in the land of Egypt: I am the Lord your God" (Lev 19:34).

The historical narrative of the Hebrews emphasized the grace of God, their experience of suffering, the importance of expressing thankfulness for God's provision, and protection of the vulnerable as an expression of devotion to God, who has special concern for such persons. Deuteronomy 26 presents a summary of this narrative:

> A wandering Aramean was my ancestor; he went down into Egypt and lived there as an alien, few in number, and there he became a great nation, mighty and populous. When the Egyptians treated us harshly and afflicted us, by imposing hard labor on us, we cried to the Lord, the God of our ancestors; the Lord heard our voice and saw our affliction, our toil, and our oppression. The Lord brought us out of Egypt with a mighty hand and an outstretched arm, with a terrifying display of power, and with signs and wonders; and he brought us into this place and gave us this land, a land flowing with milk and honey.[2]

Of course, anyone with a superficial knowledge of the Bible knows that these texts are found among other texts that point in a much different direction. There are texts of hatred toward one's enemies, texts of retribution and vengeance, and texts of violence toward others. The mere presence of so much violence in the Bible is not the main issue. More problematic is the fact that God is often pictured in the Bible as condoning or even

---

2. Deut 26:5–9.

commanding acts of violence. The Old Testament is full of examples of what Eric Seibert calls "virtuous violence"—violence that is portrayed positively in the text and seems to be sanctioned by God, is directly commanded by God, or is even committed by God.[3] We are confronted with contradictory pictures of God.

Do we have any warrant for giving preference to texts that speak of God's love, compassion, and concern for the weak and vulnerable when there are numerous texts that present an image of God that seems completely at odds with such a view? Psalm 139 ends with a demand for vengeance against the Babylonians: "O daughter Babylon, you devastator! Happy shall they be who pay you back what you have done to us! Happy shall they be who take your little ones and dash them against the rock!" (139:8–9). Nahum celebrates the destruction of Nineveh in 612 BCE with these words: "I am against you, says the LORD of hosts, and will lift up your skirts over your face; and I will let nations look on your nakedness and kingdoms on your shame. I will throw filth at you and treat you with contempt, and make you a spectacle" (3:5–6). The portrait of God in Nahum is that of a God of vengeance: "A jealous and avenging God is the LORD, the LORD is avenging and wrathful; the LORD takes vengeance on his adversaries and rages against his enemies" (1:2).

Yet the book of Jonah tells a story about how God spares Nineveh from destruction and describes Jonah's subsequent frustration with God's mercy. Jonah petulantly complains to God: "That is why I fled to Tarshish at the beginning; for I knew that you are a gracious God and merciful, slow to anger, and abounding in steadfast love, and ready to relent from punishing. And now, O LORD, please take my life from me, for it is better for me to die than to live" (4:2–3). The book of Jonah concludes with God voicing a question to Jonah (and to the reader of the book): "Should I not be concerned about Nineveh, that great city, in which there are more than a hundred and twenty thousand persons who do not know their right hand from their left, and also many animals?" (4:11).

Sometimes Christians are not fully aware of the stark contrast that exists between the varying images of God found in the Bible. Readings used in worship and Bible study often exclude the most problematic texts, and if one never reads through the Bible on one's own, the challenge presented by these radically differing images of God may not be apparent. Christians who sense the tension sometimes believe the contradictions are potentially

---

3. See Seibert, *The Violence of Scripture*, especially chapter 3.

resolvable, even if they do not see quite how to do it. Sometimes Christians take the attitude that if God did something, or commanded it to be done, it must be okay, even when the actions involved include things such as murder, genocide, and killing innocents.

The view taken here is that the contradictory images of God contained in the Bible are reflections of the contradictory hub symbols existing among those who produced the biblical material. Many of the hub symbols present in the Bible are hub symbols common in societies of the Ancient Near East. Acceptance of slavery, patriarchy, and violence toward one's enemies were common aspects of that ancient world. We should find nothing surprising about the presence of such hub symbols in the biblical material, since the biblical writers were inhabitants of their own time. They shared the general worldview of others living in that time and place. Why should we credit the presence of Ancient Near Eastern hub symbols in the Bible to the revelatory activity of God?

When God's intentions for us are not congruent with the values and structures of our culture, we should expect any revelatory activity of God to represent a challenge to those values and structures. In the Bible, then, when we want to look for hub symbols that express the revelatory activity of God, a good place to focus our search is not in those places where biblical hub symbols were in alignment with the surrounding culture, but precisely in those areas where there was a contrast. There would be nothing distinctive in a claim on the part of the biblical writers that a violent, tribal, vengeful, patriarchal god had revealed himself to them.[4] The pantheon of ancient gods was full of such deities. On the other hand, a picture of a relational God who enters into covenant, makes promises, hears the cries of those who suffer, acts to protect the weak and vulnerable, is merciful, forgiving, and compassionate, and expresses "steadfast love" is an exceptional image worth exploring. If those communities that produced the Bible had anything unique or extraordinary to offer the rest of humanity in relation to our understanding of God, this latter portrait is where it is to be found.

As it turns out, the Bible itself provides us with reasons for emphasizing the loving, compassionate view of God over a violent, vengeful, patriarchal view of God. Most of the biblical quotations until now in this chapter have been taken from the Torah—the first five books of the Bible. When

---

4. I do not use the pronouns "him" or "her" when referring to God since God, as creator of both male and female, cannot be adequately signified by gender-restricted terms. Here, however, the use of "himself" is appropriate.

we look at the prophetic material, we find strong reinforcement of the idea that God has a special concern for the poor and vulnerable. Amos criticizes those who "trample on the needy, and bring to ruin the poor of the land, saying, 'When will the new moon be over so that we may sell grain; and the sabbath, so that we may offer wheat for sale? We will make the ephah small and the shekel great, and practice deceit with false balances, buying the poor for silver and the needy for a pair of sandals, and selling the sweepings of the wheat'" (8:4–6).

Micah preaches against those who "covet fields, and seize them; houses, and take them away; they oppress householder and house, people and their inheritance" (Mic 2:2). God's intention for us is clear, according to Micah 6:8: "He has told you, O mortal, what is good; and what does the Lord require of you but to do justice, and to love kindness, and to walk humbly with your God?"

Isaiah shares the concern of Amos and Micah for the poor and vulnerable: "Wash yourselves; make yourselves clean; remove the evil of your doings from before my eyes; cease to do evil, learn to do good; seek justice, rescue the oppressed, defend the orphan, plead for the widow" (Isa 1:16–17). The prophets are clear in connecting God's displeasure with the failure to care for those who are defenseless: "Ah, you who make iniquitous decrees, who write oppressive statutes, to turn aside the needy from justice and to rob the poor of my people of their right, that widows may be your spoil, and that you may make the orphans your prey! What will you do on the day of punishment, in the calamity that will come from far away? To whom will you flee for help, and where will you leave your wealth, so as not to crouch among the prisoners or fall among the slain?" (Isa 10:1–4).

Jeremiah linked knowledge of God with the practice of justice: "Are you a king because you compete in cedar? Did not your father eat and drink and do justice and righteousness? Then it was well with him. He judged the cause of the poor and needy; then it was well. Is not this to know me? says the Lord. But your eyes and heart are only on your dishonest gain, for shedding innocent blood, and for practicing oppression and violence" (Jer 22:15–17). Jeremiah is here addressing King Jehoiakim. He praises Jehoiakim's father, King Josiah, as an example of a king who practices justice. In contrast to Josiah, Jehoiakim's policies led to disaster. Jerusalem was captured by the Babylonians in 597 BCE and some inhabitants were carried into exile. The last king of Judah, King Zedekiah, was no better than Jehoiakim. Jeremiah lived to see the destruction of Jerusalem in 586 BCE.

For Jeremiah, the cause of that catastrophe was obvious: the exile was God's punishment for the failure to practice justice.

The Babylonian exile, usually dated to the destruction of Jerusalem in 586 BCE even though there were additional occasions (597 BCE and 582 BCE) when Hebrews were taken into captivity by the Babylonians, was a time of intense crisis for the Hebrew people. Two narratives had been vying for supremacy in their religious self-understanding. In one narrative, often referred to as the "royal ideology" or "Davidic covenant" view since it legitimized and was supported by the power of the monarchy, the Hebrew people were specially chosen by God for eternity. God's choice in favor of Israel had nothing to do with the moral character or any other special quality of the Hebrews. It was simply God's decision to grant special protection and preferential treatment to the Hebrews. God's choice was unconditional and eternal. Psalm 89 is a clear presentation of this viewpoint. The psalmist declares, "You said, 'I have made a covenant with my chosen one, I have sworn to my servant David: "I will establish your descendants forever, and build your throne for all generations"'" (Ps 89:3–4). Referring to the Davidic dynasty (house of David), the psalmist continues:

> Forever I will keep my steadfast love for him, and my covenant with him will stand firm. I will establish his line forever, and his throne as long as the heavens endure . . . . I will not violate my covenant, or alter the word that went forth from my lips. Once and for all I have sworn by my holiness; I will not lie to David. His line shall continue forever, and his throne endure before me like the sun. It shall be established forever like the moon, an enduring witness in the skies. (89:28–29, 34–37)

This narrative stands in contrast to another, often referred to as the "Sinai covenant" perspective, which emphasized the conditional character of God's promises to Israel. The Sinai covenant harkened back to the covenant God made with the people during the time of Moses, when Moses said to the people:

> See, I have set before you today life and prosperity, death and adversity. If you obey the commandments of the LORD your God that I am commanding you today, by loving the LORD your God, walking in his ways, and observing his commandments, decrees, and ordinances, then you shall live and become numerous, and the LORD your God will bless you in the land that you are entering to possess. But if your heart turns away and you do not hear, but are led astray to bow down to other gods and serve them, I declare to

> you today that you shall perish; you shall not live long in the land
> that you are crossing the Jordan to enter and possess. I call heaven
> and earth to witness against you today that I have set before you
> life and death, blessings and curses. Choose life so that you and
> your descendants may live, loving the LORD your God, obeying
> him, and holding fast to him, for that means life to you and length
> of days, so that you may live in the land that the LORD swore to
> give to your ancestors, to Abraham, to Isaac, and to Jacob. (Deut
> 30:15–20)

In the Sinai covenant the people have a choice. God is not indifferent about that choice. God's desire is that the people choose the way of life and blessings. The people must decide for themselves, however, and they will experience the consequences of the choice they make. In the royal ideology narrative, God unconditionally and permanently supports the hierarchical structures of the monarchy and the status quo. In the Sinai covenant narrative, all human institutions are relativized; even the king must stand in judgment before a God who demands justice.

These competing narratives struggled against one another for dominance during the period of history when the Hebrew people were moving in the direction of establishing a monarchy as their form of government. Political structures possess ideological underpinnings, and the politics of monarchy led to reflection on the nature of the Hebrews' relationship with God. Those associated with the monarchy, which controlled the institutions connected to the temple in Jerusalem, favored the royal ideology which legitimized their claim to power and authority. The prophetic tradition arose as a challenge to the royal claim to possess unconditional divine favor and approval. In his famous Temple Sermon, for example, Jeremiah challenged the idea that Jerusalem possessed immunity from destruction simply because the temple, viewed as God's place of residence, was located there:

> Thus says the LORD of hosts, the God of Israel: Amend your ways
> and your doings, and let me dwell with you in this place. Do not
> trust in these deceptive words: "This is the temple of the LORD,
> the temple of the LORD, the temple of the LORD." For if you truly
> amend your ways and your doings, if you truly act justly one with
> another, if you do not oppress the alien, the orphan, and the
> widow, or shed innocent blood in this place, and if you do not go
> after other gods to your own hurt, then I will dwell with you in this
> place, in the land that I gave of old to your ancestors forever and
> ever. (Jer 7:3–7)

The prophets harkened back to the Sinai covenant, claiming that the fulfillment of God's promises was conditional upon whether God's care for all persons was made concrete in the way society was structured. Or, to put it another way, from the perspective of the prophetic tradition the answer to the question of whether God's blessings were upon the people was to be found in whether or not justice was practiced in Israel.

The challenge presented by the biblical prophets to the royal claim that the king possessed unlimited authority blessed by God was not simply a matter of a political power struggle, although it was that. It was grounded in a struggle over which conception of God would ultimately win out among the Hebrews. In order to fully understand the nature of what was at stake we need some knowledge of the changes in Hebrew society that accompanied the rise of the monarchy. The picture presented in the Old Testament of the twelve tribes of Israel emerging from their wilderness wanderings is one that portrays a relative equality among the people. The land was distributed among the various tribes on a roughly equal basis and people began to shift from a nomadic existence to a mainly agrarian life, occasionally needing to band together during the period of the judges to repel an invader.

Gradually there arose among some of the people a desire to have a king. Judges 8:22 tells us that "the Israelites said to Gideon, 'Rule over us, you and your son and your grandson also; for you have delivered us out of the hand of Midian.'" Gideon refused, saying that "the LORD will rule over you" (8:23). Gideon's son Abimelech did not possess his father's scruples, however, and killed seventy of his brothers in an attempt to become king (Judges 9:1–6). Eventually Saul was anointed the first king over Israel, but not before Samuel warned the people what would happen should they decide to have a king:

> "These will be the ways of the king who will reign over you: he will take your sons and appoint them to his chariots and to be his horsemen, and to run before his chariots; and he will appoint for himself commanders of thousands and commanders of fifties, and some to plow his ground and to reap his harvest, and to make his implements of war and the equipment of his chariots. He will take your daughters to be perfumers and cooks and bakers. He will take the best of your fields and vineyards and olive orchards and give them to his courtiers. He will take one-tenth of your grain and of your vineyards and give it to his officers and his courtiers. He will take your male and female slaves, and the best of your cattle and donkeys, and put them to his work. He will take one-tenth of your

> flocks, and you shall be his slaves. And in that day you will cry out because of your king, whom you have chosen for yourselves; but the LORD will not answer you in that day." But the people refused to listen to the voice of Samuel; they said, "No! but we are determined to have a king over us, so that we also may be like other nations, and that our king may govern us and go out before us and fight our battles." (1 Sam 8:11–20)

Although there are positive depictions in 1 Samuel of the idea of having a king, the Bible also preserves a tradition that interpreted the choice to have a king as a rejection of God's rule:

> Samuel summoned the people to the LORD at Mizpah and said to them, "Thus says the LORD, the God of Israel, 'I brought up Israel out of Egypt, and I rescued you from the hand of the Egyptians and from the hand of all the kingdoms that were oppressing you.' But today you have rejected your God, who saves you from all your calamities and your distresses; and you have said, 'No! but set a king over us.' Now therefore present yourselves before the LORD by your tribes and by your clans." (1 Sam 10:17–19)

Samuel, seeking to justify his own leadership of the people, insists that he has not been a king, nor has he acted like a king: "Whose ox have I taken? Or whose donkey have I taken? Or whom have I defrauded? Whom have I oppressed? Or from whose hand have I taken a bribe to blind my eyes with it? Testify against me, and I will restore it to you" (1 Sam 12:3).

Stories of kingly abuse of power appear in the Bible almost from the beginning of the establishment of the monarchy. David's relationship with Uriah's wife Bathsheba and subsequent plot to have Uriah killed is well known (see 2 Sam 11), though many interpretations focus narrowly on the sexual aspect of the relationship in a way that ignores the issue of power. Solomon's reign was so harsh that when Solomon died, the northern tribes submitted a request to Solomon's son Rehoboam to "lighten the hard service of your father and his heavy yoke that he placed on us" (1 Kings 12:4). Rehoboam's response to the request ("My father made your yoke heavy, but I will add to your yoke; my father disciplined you with whips, but I will discipline you with scorpions") led directly to rebellion on the part of the northern tribes and to a division between the northern kingdom of Israel and the southern kingdom of Judah.[5]

---

5. 1 Kings 12:14.

When Naboth refused to sell his vineyard to King Ahab, Ahab's wife Jezebel made arrangements to have Naboth executed following a sham trial on trumped-up charges so that there would be no impediment to Ahab's taking the vineyard for himself. In the ancient world, kingly power was absolute. In Israel and Judah, the prophets, serving as God's representatives, challenged those with political and religious power (the religious authorities were subject to and closely aligned with the monarchy) to respect a higher power. When Elijah confronted Ahab for what he had done, Ahab's response was, "Have you found me, O my enemy?" (1 Kings 21:20). Elijah was direct: "I have found you. Because you have sold yourself to do what is evil in the sight of the LORD, I will bring disaster on you; I will consume you" (1 Kings 21:20–21).

The rise of the monarchy in Israel and Judah coincided with rising levels of extreme inequality. The prophetic critique can only be properly understood when set against this background. The prophetic critique was not addressed to *all* Hebrews; it was addressed to the wealthy and powerful. When Amos says, for example, "I will tear down the winter house as well as the summer house; and the houses of ivory shall perish, and the great houses shall come to an end" (Amos 3:15), he is not speaking to the poor. When he says, "Hear this word, you cows of Bashan who are on Mount Samaria, who oppress the poor, who crush the needy, who say to their husbands, 'Bring something to drink!'" (Amos 4:1), he is not addressing the hungry. Isaiah makes clear his audience: "The LORD enters into judgment with the elders and princes of his people: It is you who have devoured the vineyard; the spoil of the poor is in your houses. What do you mean by crushing my people, by grinding the face of the poor? says the Lord GOD of hosts" (Isaiah 3:14–15).

The irony of the desire of the Hebrews to be "like other nations" was that they succeeded all too well—in the ways predicted by Samuel. A people who had been delivered from crushing oppression at the hands of the Egyptians had now become themselves practitioners of oppression. The enormous inequity and resulting injustice were an affront to God. Injustice was a *religious* issue in Israel and Judah in a way that it was not among other nations. Among other nations, religion supported and legitimized the royal power and the wealthy elite. We do not find in the history of the Hebrews a significant difference from the surrounding nations in the areas of the quality or character of its kings and leaders or the beauty of its temple or the superiority or significant dissimilarity of its social institutions or in unusual claims for the power of its deity. In all of these areas the Hebrews were unremarkable. The history of the Hebrews stands out because a prophetic tradition arose that challenged the power of the elite and called it to accountability to a higher power.

The prophets reminded the wealthy and powerful of Israel and Judah of the covenant God had made with the people during the time of Moses in the desert—a covenant that demanded a special concern for the vulnerable and weak. When the exile occurred, the Old Testament prophets provided an explanation. The exile was God's punishment for the failure to practice justice:

> The word of the LORD came to Zechariah, saying: Thus says the LORD of hosts: Render true judgments, show kindness and mercy to one another; do not oppress the widow, the orphan, the alien, or the poor; and do not devise evil in your hearts against one another. But they refused to listen, and turned a stubborn shoulder, and stopped their ears in order not to hear. They made their hearts adamant in order not to hear the law and the words that the LORD of hosts had sent by his spirit through the former prophets. Therefore great wrath came from the LORD of hosts. Just as, when I called, they would not hear, so, when they called, I would not hear, says the LORD of hosts, and I scattered them with a whirlwind among all the nations that they had not known. Thus the land they left was desolate, so that no one went to and fro, and a pleasant land was made desolate. (Zech 7:8–14)

The narrative of the royal ideology was challenged in the Old Testament by the narrative of the Sinai covenant, which placed all human power relationships in the context of God's care and concern for all people, including especially the most vulnerable. Ancient Near Eastern societies were highly stratified. Israel and Judah were no different in that respect. But unlike the religions of the surrounding peoples, which provided religious support for social inequality, the Hebrew religion leveled a critique against abuse of power and mistreatment of the poor and defenseless.

The prophets prominent in the books of the Bible were not the only prophets practicing in Israel or Judah. Kings had their court prophets who were paid to tell them what they wanted to hear. One famous example is found in the confrontation between Elijah and the prophets of Baal and Asherah on Mount Carmel (1 Kgs 18:17–40). Another example can be seen in Jeremiah 28, where the prophet Hananiah challenged Jeremiah, predicting that God would "break the yoke of King Nebuchadnezzar of Babylon from the neck of all the nations within two years" (Jer 28:11). Two narratives vied for preeminence among the Hebrews. At stake was the understanding of God that would characterize the Hebrew people.

Was God a tribal god who for some arbitrary reason favored the Hebrews? Did God unconditionally endorse the monarchy? Could one assume that power and wealth were signs of God's favor? Or did God's authority relativize all earthly authorities, including the authority of the king? Were power and wealth accountable to the demands of God's justice? Did God's love extend beyond the Hebrews to the other nations, including those nations the Hebrews regarded as their enemies?

These were open questions until the horrific events of 586 BCE. History has a way (eventually) of validating one side or another of our political and moral debates. Today we honor Dietrich Bonhoeffer and André Trocmé and their opposition to Hitler rather than theologians such as Paul Althaus, Emanuel Hirsch, and Gerhard Kittel who supported Hitler.[6] We honor Martin Luther King Jr. for his struggle in favor of civil rights rather than Bull Conner who tried to preserve segregation.[7] We have in the Bible a book named Jeremiah rather than a book named Hananiah. In their own time, these voices that we honor today were a small minority facing entrenched, powerful opposition. They spoke courageously, placing their lives at risk in the process. Yet they did so because their view of God required it.

Before 586 BCE, the arguments of Hananiah against Jeremiah seemed plausible to many. After all, when the northern kingdom of Israel was destroyed in 722 BCE by the Assyrians, had not God preserved the southern kingdom of Judah? Did not Judah possess the temple? Was not Judah blessed with an unbroken line of rulers in the lineage of David? One could almost say that the northern kingdom had deserved what it got. Had it not shown evidence of disobedience to God? Judah had faced grave threats before. Surely God would act once again in order to preserve the promises made to Abraham and Moses!

The destruction of Jerusalem and the temple in 586 BCE was a shock to the soul of the Hebrew people. How could God have allowed such a thing to happen? The post-exilic writings contain powerful literature pondering

---

6. See Ericksen, *Theologians Under Hitler*. See also the documentary film "Theologians Under Hitler" based on the book, produced by Steven D. Martin.

7. For insightful discussion of history's validation of Bonhoeffer, Trocmé, and King Jr. (among others), see Stassen, *A Thicker Jesus*. A brief synopsis of Stassen's discussion regarding history's corroboration of a certain ethical perspective was presented in chapter 4.

the meaning of life in the face of great loss and tragedy. The Sinai covenant and the prophetic tradition represented by persons such as Amos, Hosea, Micah, Isaiah, Jeremiah, and Ezekiel, among others, provided a way forward. Between the alternative perspectives of the Sinai covenant on the one hand, and the royal ideology of the Davidic covenant on the other, one was now revealed by the events of 586 BCE to be gravely inadequate for helping people understand their new situation, while the other held promise for a creative vision moving forward.

The Old Testament reflects the struggle between these two alternative ways of thinking about God. Both are preserved in the literature. We have seen an example of the royal ideology's tendency toward tribalism in Psalm 89. There are plenty of passages in the Old Testament that call upon God to take vengeance upon the enemies of the Hebrews. Yet there are texts such as Jonah that depict God as loving those whom the Hebrews considered enemies. The book of Ruth asserts God's care and protection for a Moabite woman who, according to the text, became the great-grandmother of David. As creator of all that exists (see Genesis 1), God's concern extended beyond tribal barriers. Isaiah describes the mission of the servant in chapter 49 as extending to all people: "It is too little a thing that you should be my servant to raise up the tribes of Jacob and to restore the survivors of Israel; I will give you as a light to the nations, that my salvation may reach to the end of the earth" (49:6–7).

What is the salvation being described here? The Old Testament picture of salvation is a vision of a particular kind of community where *shalom* is present.[8] Zechariah describes the *shalom* community as one where "old men and old women shall again sit in the streets of Jerusalem, each with staff in hand because of their great age. And the streets of the city shall be full of boys and girls playing in its streets" (8:4–5). In the *shalom* community, people prosper: "For there shall be a sowing of peace [*shalom*]; the vine shall yield its fruit, the ground shall give its produce, and the skies shall give their dew; and I will cause the remnant of this people to possess all these things. Just as you have been a cursing among the nations, O house of Judah and house of Israel, so I will save you and you shall be a blessing" (8:12–13). How are members of the *shalom* community supposed to live? "These are the things that you shall do: Speak the truth to one another, render in your gates judgments that are true and make for peace [*shalom*],

---

8. See my discussion of *shalom* in chapter 5.

do not devise evil in your hearts against one another, and love no false oath; for all these are things that I hate, says the LORD" (8:16–17).

The practice of justice was a prerequisite for *shalom*. Practicing justice meant having no extreme inequities. When the prophets criticized extreme inequality, they stood in the tradition of Leviticus 25, which established structures for ensuring, if faithfully practiced, that a relative equality would continue among the Hebrews. Leviticus 25 (see also Deuteronomy 15) set the requirements for the sabbath year and the year of jubilee, which required the restoration of land to its original owners and the release of indentured servants. Land ownership was the primary source of wealth and security. Loss of land meant vulnerability. After the land had been relatively equally distributed among the people by Joshua, the practice of sabbath year and jubilee year would provide regular occasions for leveling wealth and status among the Hebrews. Leviticus 25 called for nothing less than a *redistribution* of wealth among the Hebrews so that a relative equality would be reestablished. The prophetic concern for justice was firmly rooted in provisions set forth in the Torah. The harshness of the prophetic critique can only be rightly understood when connected to their view that injustice was an offense against God.

A strong case can be made, therefore, that the unique contribution of the Hebrew scriptures to any conversation about the nature of God and the intentions of God for this world lies in their portrayal of God as loving creator who desires *shalom* as the pattern for human relationships. God's love for God's creation grants worth and value to it, including those parts of God's creation that seem not to have any particular usefulness to human beings (Psalm 104 celebrates various aspects of God's creation, including the Leviathan, or sea monster, that God formed "to sport," or play, in the sea[9]). As bearers of God's image (Gen 1:27), human beings occupy a special place of value and worth. That worth transcends national and tribal boundaries. The salvation (*shalom*) God intends for humanity in the Old Testament is a salvation that extends to all persons. The narrative inherited from the surrounding cultures—the narrative of the royal ideology and a permanent covenant that viewed God as being on the side of the Hebrews and against their enemies—had proven insufficient in the wake of the tragic events of 586 BCE. An alternative narrative found in the prophets hearkened back to Sinai and pointed forward toward the universal reach of God's love and the role of the Hebrews as agents in the extension of that love.

9. See Psalm 104:26.

What about the New Testament? How does its view of God compare to that of the Old Testament? Since Christians affirm the authority of both the Old and New Testaments, holding that both possess truth about God and God's intentions for humanity, one might think that all Christians see a fundamental congruence between the portraits of God presented in the two parts of the Christian Bible. Since many Christians are aware of passages in the Old Testament depicting a tribalistic, vengeful, and often apparently arbitrary God, however, in practice many Christians view the Old Testament portrait as flawed. They give preference to what they perceive to be the loving God of the New Testament. They speak of the covenant in the Old Testament as having been "set aside," "invalidated," "substituted," or "superseded" by a new covenant given to the church. This new covenant, from their perspective, is obviously superior. The Old Testament is like a winding detour one has to follow while a new superhighway is being built. Once the highway is finished (i.e., once we have the New Testament), the detour is no longer necessary.

Jesus himself, however, affirmed the validity of the revelation of God in the writings of the Old Testament, stating in Matthew 5:17–18: "Do not think that I have come to abolish the law or the prophets; I have come not to abolish but to fulfill. For truly I tell you, until heaven and earth pass away, not one letter, not one stroke of a letter, will pass away from the law until all is accomplished." We misread both the Old Testament and the New Testament if we fail to see the close relationship between the view of God predominant in the teachings of Jesus and the view of God characteristic of the Torah, prophets and writings of the Old Testament.

In Matthew 22, when Jesus is asked to identify the greatest commandment, he responds, "'You shall love the Lord your God with all your heart, and with all your soul, and with all your mind.' This is the greatest and first commandment. And a second is like it: 'You shall love your neighbor as yourself.' On these two commandments hang all the law and the prophets" (Matt 22:37–40). The lawyer questioning Jesus in Matthew's story, who was apparently hoping to trap Jesus with his question (see verses 34–35), had no response. We can presume, therefore, that Jesus's view regarding the basic message of the law and prophets was shared by the Pharisees of his day, at least according to Matthew's understanding. Jesus and his opponents all agreed that "Love God, and love your neighbor as yourself" was a summation of the Old Testament perspective. But if we can say that Jesus and his opponents were agreed on their understanding of the basic meaning of the law and the prophets, where was the point of conflict? Why was Jesus seen as such a threat by the religious authorities of his day?

Luke provides a clue in his account of the story, since he adds that the lawyer follows up on Jesus's response with an additional question: "But wanting to justify himself, he asked Jesus, 'And who is my neighbor?'" (Luke 10:29).[10] Jesus's response to this additional question is to tell the well-known parable of the Good Samaritan. A man is robbed, beaten, and left "half dead" along the side of the road going from Jerusalem to Jericho. Jesus describes three travelers who come upon the man. The first is a priest, the second a Levite. Both represent religious authority among the Jews of Jesus's day, and as such, would be expected to act correctly in an ethical case study such as Jesus presents here. Both pass by the injured man on the other side of the road.

The third person in Jesus's parable is "moved with pity" for the injured man and takes action: "He went to him and bandaged his wounds, having poured oil and wine on them. Then he put him on his own animal, brought him to an inn, and took care of him. The next day he took out two denarii, gave them to the innkeeper, and said, 'Take care of him; and when I come back, I will repay you whatever more you spend'" (Luke 10:34–35). Jesus then inquires of the lawyer: "Which of these three, do you think, was a neighbor to the man who fell into the hands of the robbers?" (36). The lawyer responds, "The one who showed him mercy." Jesus tells the lawyer to "Go and do likewise" (37).

Nicholas Wolterstorff has pointed out that the way in which Jesus phrases the question is important. Jesus's question

> was not the lawyer's question rephrased in the light of the story. Jesus did not ask, "To which of the three passersby was the wounded man a neighbor?" Instead he asked, "Which of the three passersby was a neighbor to the wounded man?" Rather than employing the traditional category that the lawyer had employed, that of *being a neighbor of* someone, Jesus employed the related but different category, *being a neighbor to* someone.[11]

What is the difference Wolterstorff is highlighting here? To phrase the question as "Who is my neighbor?" (or as "Who was a neighbor *of* the wounded

---

10. In Luke's version of the story, the initial question put to Jesus by the lawyer is different from that found in Matthew: "'Teacher,' he said, 'what must I do to inherit eternal life?'" (Luke 10:25).

11. Wolterstorff, *Justice in Love*, 131–2.

man?") is to conduct a passive inquiry into relationship status. It opens the door to the possibility of an abstract discussion of social affiliations that ignores the pain and hurt of the man lying at the side of the road. To ask rather, "Who was a neighbor *to* the wounded man?" puts the pain and hurt of the wounded man front and center and explicitly addresses the issue of whether or not assistance and aid were rendered. The moral claim consists in the condition of the man as an injured person requiring assistance, not in the man's membership or non-membership in any of the artificial categories we create in the way we socially construct our relationships. Wolterstorff concludes:

> I take Jesus to be enjoining us to be alert to the obligations placed upon us by the needs of whomever we happen on, and to pay no attention to the fact, if it be a fact, that the needy person belongs to a group that is a disdained or disdaining out-group with respect to oneself. Every society has derogatory terms for members of one and another out-group: wop, dago, Hun, Jap, nigger, "Dutchman belly full o' straw." Whether we ourselves employ such terms or they are applied to us, they prevent us from recognizing our obligations to aid those in need. Discard them all, says Jesus. Do not let them deafen your ear to the cry for help or harden your heart.[12]

We see, then, that responding to the needs of those who are hurting and in pain was an important part of Jesus's view of what it meant to be obedient to the God revealed in the Torah and the prophets. The foundational experience in the life of the Hebrew people had been their conviction that God had heard their cry when they were slaves in Egypt and had responded to deliver them. Their conviction had grown that God demanded of them a similar concern for responding to the pain of hurting people as a condition for achieving God's desired *shalom*. Likewise in the New Testament we see an emphasis on God's care and concern for the weak and vulnerable. In Luke's "Sermon on the Plain," Jesus says,

> Blessed are you who are poor, for yours is the kingdom of God. Blessed are you who are hungry now, for you will be filled. Blessed are you who weep now, for you will laugh. . . . But woe to you who are rich, for you have received your consolation. Woe to you who are full now, for you will be hungry. Woe to you who are laughing now, for you will mourn and weep. (Luke 6:20–21, 24–25)

---

12. Ibid., 132.

The sort of social reversal we find here is similar to many texts found in the prophets. Jesus did not stand outside of, but rather fully within, that tradition. Jesus begins his ministry in Luke with a quotation from Isaiah (see Luke 4:18–19), and when John the Baptist sends two disciples to inquire of Jesus whether he is "the one who is to come, or are we to wait for another?" (7:19), Jesus responds with references drawn from Isaiah: "Go and tell John what you have seen and heard: the blind receive their sight, the lame walk, the lepers are cleansed, the deaf hear, the dead are raised, the poor have good news brought to them" (Luke 7:22).

Jesus's critique of the religious leaders and institutions of his day echoes the critique of the Old Testament prophets: "As [Jesus] taught, he said, 'Beware of the scribes, who like to walk around in long robes, and to be greeted with respect in the marketplaces, and to have the best seats in the synagogues and places of honor at banquets! They devour widows' houses and for the sake of appearance say long prayers. They will receive the greater condemnation'" (Mark 12:38–40). Matthew's famous passage concerning the judgment says that those who enter the kingdom are persons who give food to the hungry, welcome strangers, clothe the naked, care for the sick and visit those in prison (see Matt 25:31–40). Those who do not do these things are condemned to "eternal punishment" (see Matt 25:41–46).

John's gospel depicts Jesus as healing the sick and giving sight to the blind. His religious opponents, concerned as they were with theological classifications, are portrayed as being at a loss as to how to categorize Jesus, and thus are not sure how to respond to him. We read in John 10:

> So the Jews gathered around him and said to him, "How long will you keep us in suspense? If you are the Messiah, tell us plainly." Jesus answered, "I have told you, and you do not believe. The works that I do in my Father's name testify to me . . . . If I am not doing the works of my Father, then do not believe me. But if I do them, even though you do not believe me, believe the works, so that you may know and understand that the Father is in me and I am in the Father." (John 10:24–25, 37–38)

Jesus says in John 14 "If you love me, you will keep my commandments" (14:15), and in chapter 15 says that those who keep his commandments "abide in my love, just as I have kept my Father's commandments and abide in his love" (15:10). What does "abiding" in Jesus's love mean concretely? 1 John 3:17–18 provides this clarification: "How does God's love abide in anyone who has the world's goods and sees a brother or sister in need and yet refuses help? Little children, let us love, not in word or speech, but in truth and action."

The New Testament contains numerous passages indicating that authentic Christian discipleship involves acting in particular ways. James is famous for his declaration that Christians ought to be "doers of the word, and not merely hearers who deceive themselves" (James 1:22). What particular sorts of actions are enjoined? James 1:27 states: "Religion that is pure and undefiled before God, the Father, is this: to care for orphans and widows in their distress, and to keep oneself unstained by the world." James 2:15–16 adds: "If a brother or sister is naked and lacks daily food, and one of you says to them, 'Go in peace; keep warm and eat your fill,' and yet you do not supply their bodily needs, what is the good of that?" James 5 contains one of the most vehement denouncements of wealth to be found anywhere in the Bible:

> Come now, you rich people, weep and wail for the miseries that are coming to you. Your riches have rotted, and your clothes are moth-eaten. Your gold and silver have rusted, and their rust will be evidence against you, and it will eat your flesh like fire. You have laid up treasure for the last days. Listen! The wages of the laborers who mowed your fields, which you kept back by fraud, cry out, and the cries of the harvesters have reached the ears of the Lord of hosts. You have lived on the earth in luxury and in pleasure; you have fattened your hearts in a day of slaughter. You have condemned and murdered the righteous one, who does not resist you. (Jas 5:1–6)

The prophetic concern for justice, including special attention to the cries of those who suffer, finds clear resonance in the New Testament generally and is unquestionably present in the portraits of Jesus contained in the Gospels. Biblical interpreters differ in their estimation of whether and to what extent a tension exists within the New Testament between those texts that highlight this concern for justice and action directed toward helping those who are vulnerable and other texts that seem less concerned or even unconcerned about Christian involvement in alleviating injustice or in striving to achieve the kind of *shalom* community that seems to be an important desire of God in the Old Testament. For example, whereas James rhetorically asks, "What good is it, my brothers and sisters, if you say you have faith but do not have works? Can faith save you?" (2:14), Paul seems to take the opposite view: "We have come to believe in Christ Jesus, so that we might be justified by faith in Christ, and not by doing the works of the law, because no one will be justified by the works of the law" (Gal 2:16).

What can be said about this apparent difference between the perspectives of James and Paul? The question of whether such a tension actually exists is, first of all, not bothersome since we have seen that the Bible is filled with tensions of various sorts. The issue must be explored using the tools available to the modern interpreter, examining the evidence and drawing conclusions that can be reasonably supported. Second, we can be sure that Paul clearly was not saying that actions do not matter, since he has a lot to say on the subject of ethical action and was concerned to follow the example of Jesus: "Be imitators of me, as I am of Christ" (1 Cor 11:1). Third, the writings of the New Testament represent differing genres and have differing purposes, so there should be no surprise in finding varying emphases among the various writings. Fourth, there may be real tensions of viewpoint within the New Testament related to the question of whether the church is to attempt in any way to strive toward the Old Testament vision of a *shalom* community, but I have made a plausible case, I believe, for seeing a continuity of emphasis in the Old Testament and New Testament writings on the importance of attention to the concerns of justice and meeting the needs of the vulnerable in the community as essential aspects for achieving God's desire regarding how we are to live in this world.

There is nothing novel in the claim I am making here, though it will be resisted by some Christians. I said earlier that some Christians see a radical difference between the Old and New Testaments. In practice they set aside the Old Testament as an authoritative guide, since it has been superseded by a new covenant given to the church. Interpreting Paul to mean works are irrelevant and possessing a view of faith that reduces it to a matter of mental assent ("Yes, I agree that Jesus is Lord" or "Yes, I accept Jesus into my life"), Christians who hold this view find no obligation within the pages of the Bible for concern about justice issues. Feeding the hungry, fighting for those whose rights are being abused, and standing up for the weak and vulnerable are *optional* for Christians who want to live exemplary lives, but one's salvation is in no way dependent upon whether one engages in such activity. In fact some Christians, desiring to avoid any hint of "works righteousness," explicitly and adamantly deny any connection whatsoever between moral concerns and actions, on the one hand, and our salvation as Christians on the other. Salvation, in this view, has been shifted entirely out of this life into a future existence and thus possesses little or no relevance for how we are to live our lives here and now beyond a vague admonition to "try to be a good person."

How can we know which perspective is correct—or closer to the truth? In chapter 5 I suggested three steps for interpreting the Bible if we want to have some concern for the integrity of the text and appreciation for the difficulties presented by our limited perspective. I said that the steps are not necessarily to be followed in sequential order, and as a matter of fact, we have been occupied primarily with the second step so far in this chapter (engagement with the text). We need to give some consideration to step one—"know thyself." What can we say about the cultural values that shape our perspective? If there is any "skewing" of our interpretation of the Bible as a result of the influence of those values, what is its likely direction?

I recall sitting in a Sunday School class on one occasion when the text for our study was the story in Luke 18 of Jesus's encounter with a wealthy ruler. The ruler questions Jesus about what he must do "to inherit eternal life," and Jesus tells him to obey the commandments (Luke 18:18–20). The ruler says he has "kept all these since my youth." Jesus responds: "There is still one thing lacking. Sell all that you own and distribute the money to the poor, and you will have treasure in heaven; then come, follow me." The ruler cannot bring himself to do it. He goes away sad, "for he was very rich." Seeing him leave, Jesus comments: "How hard it is for those who have wealth to enter the kingdom of God! Indeed, it is easier for a camel to go through the eye of a needle than for someone who is rich to enter the kingdom of God" (Luke 18:24–25).

In the discussion of the text, most in the group agreed that Jesus really did not mean what Luke quotes him here as saying. Surely Jesus did not mean that his disciples should sell all of their possessions and give the money to the poor! Jesus must have meant something else. He must have meant that we should not be *attached* to our possessions. Possessions are okay as long as we are not *attached* to them. They should not *rule our hearts*. Jesus knew that this ruler was attached to his possessions, so he gave him this command. It is not a command, however, that applies to all Christians. In fact, those present in the discussion that morning seemed to think that it is not a command that applies to many Christians at all. For the majority of people in that class, the possibility that the command should be understood literally by Christians today was not even a conceivable consideration. If my personal experience in other churches is any indication, I do not think their view of Luke 18 is particularly unusual among North American Christians generally.

Whether or not most people sitting in that Sunday School class were correct in their interpretation of Luke 18 is beside the point. I mention this example simply for the purpose of illustrating how difficult it often is for us to give any consideration to alternative readings that challenge our social status. Certain questions never confront us because we rule them out of order before they can be put on the table for discussion. Yet people in a different social location have no trouble at all raising those questions or coming up with alternative readings of scripture. Our social location makes a great difference in how we read the Bible.

When we compare the social location of many North American Christians to the social realities standing behind the texts of the Bible, we find that many North American Christians, generally speaking, are in a difficult place for properly understanding the message of the Bible. We have many reasons for trying to avoid hearing what the text says, because what the text says often contains a harsh critique of persons who, in biblical times, had access to great power and wealth. Today, that social location among the wealthy and powerful is precisely where many of us—most North American Christians—find ourselves.[13] We often deny the reality of our social location to ourselves. We often do not commonly think of ourselves as privileged. We certainly do not generally categorize ourselves as oppressors. Yet from the perspective of many in the world, that is what we are.

We are often blind to our participation in structures of oppression. We generally have no idea how vast is the gulf between our standard of living and that of most persons in the world. We lack knowledge of the mechanisms that ensure that our wealth is preserved through oppression of others. We are forgetful of our history, and most forgetful of those parts of our history that remind us that our access to wealth and power was gained through brutality and violence. For the most part, we have no idea that our view of Jesus is slanted, and therefore we find ourselves shocked and offended when someone says to us that our view of Jesus is false.

Miguel De La Torre, for example, writing from a Hispanic perspective, says "the Jesus of the dominant Euroamerican culture" must be rejected. He writes,

---

13. I myself am white, male, a US citizen, and wealthy in comparison to the vast majority of people in the world.

> Hispanics (as well as Euroamericans) must avoid the Jesus of history that launched crusades to exterminate so-called Muslim infidels; the sexist Jesus that burned women seeking autonomy as witches; the genocidal Jesus who decimated indigenous people who refused to bow their knees to the European God; the capitalist Jesus who justified kidnapping, raping, and enslaving Africans; and today's neoliberal Jesus who is blinded to the pauperization of two-thirds of the world's population so that a small minority of the planet can consider themselves blessed by God.[14]

As difficult as it may be for us to hear it, De La Torre claims that "all too often, the Jesus articulated within traditional Christian institutions tends to justify oppression."[15] Hispanics should reject the Euroamerican Jesus and follow instead the Hispanic Jesús:

> Salvation for Hispanics will never be found in the divine symbols of the Euroamerican culture. To commune with a Hispanic Jesús is to incarnate the gospel message within the marginalized spaces of the *barrios* so that the actions and words of Jesús can infuse *la comunidad* (the community) with the hope of survival and liberation. For this reason, the Euroamerican Jesus which has served as the Hispanic anti-Christ, needs to be rejected for a Jesús constructed from within the Latino/a ethos.[16]

These are strong words. The Euroamerican Jesus is the Hispanic anti-Christ? If such words provoke within us a strong emotional reaction, we must remind ourselves that a hub symbol is probably being threatened. We must work to identify the hub symbol and then assess whether or not the hub symbol is one we wish to consciously defend. At the very least, De La Torre's perspective puts questions on the table for our discussion we might not otherwise consider. He challenges us to spend more time on step one of our model. We must understand ourselves better, including the hub symbols that so powerfully shape our perspective, if we are to avoid a kind of blindness—an inability to see certain perspectives or questions or facts—resulting from an unexamined loyalty to our culture's values.

Engagement with perspectives such as those represented by De La Torre also move us into step three of our model, since verification of our assumptions about the biblical message requires openness to and dialogue

14. De La Torre, "A Thick Hispanic Jesús," 133.

15. Ibid.

16. Ibid, 136.

with a wide variety of viewpoints. We must persistently search for the truth in viewpoints that differ from ours, always willing to have needed corrections in our own perspective pointed out to us.

My own response to De La Torre's critique of Euroamerican Christianity, as should be obvious from what I have presented above regarding what I see to be the voice of God in the Bible's overarching perspective, is that he is correct in what he says about the ways in which we have been blind to our participation in injustice and oppression. I have argued that a concern for justice and for meeting the needs of the vulnerable are central biblical hub symbols. Were we to take those hub symbols seriously as helpful guides for setting our course, what might be some appropriate directions for Christian moral concern? Another way to phrase the question is: What issues and concerns ought to be important to us if we allow prominent biblical hub symbols to shape our perspective?

In view of what I said previously about the rise of the monarchy in ancient Israel/Judah and the prophetic critique leveled against the resulting social inequity and injustice, as well as the clear presence of a concern for social inequity in the Torah and the teachings of Jesus, one contemporary issue in the United States today fairly jumps out at us, though admittedly few Christians seem to be much concerned about it. A search of the internet using the query "inequality in the US" reveals information that my students often find both astounding and troubling. Both income inequality and wealth inequality have been rising for decades in the United States. The US now stands among the world's worst countries in its Gini index—a measure of inequality in the distribution of family income. Ranking countries by wealth distribution is difficult due to problems of gathering and interpreting comparable data, but no one questions the fact that wealth inequality in the US is at high levels and is increasing rather than decreasing.[17]

The economic crisis beginning in 2008 stimulated interest in discussions concerning the "1 percent" and the "99 percent," but those discussions among Christians seemed to be more related to trending news cycles than to an analysis of what ought to be prominent moral concerns for

---

17. Wealth inequality is related to the distribution of assets among a given population (what people "own"), whereas income inequality is related to income distribution (what people "earn"). Although there are usually correlations between the two measures, there can be important differences as well. Relative equality in relation to one measure is no guarantee of relative equality in the other. In the United States as of 2010, the top 20 percent of households owned roughly 90 percent of privately held wealth, and about 95 percent of privately held financial wealth (wealth minus the value of one's home).

Christians. Part of the reason may be that Christians in the United States are not inclined, generally speaking, to think that following Jesus has much to do with attention to matters of justice. In the minds of many, love and justice are separate matters, and Jesus was concerned about the former, not the latter.

There are many possible reasons why Christians in the United States tend to define love and justice in ways that remove an ethical obligation for working for justice. The matter is complicated, since one's views about love and justice are necessarily interconnected with one's theological assumptions in relation to God, salvation, atonement, the nature of the church, and the nature and purpose of evangelism. Our analysis of hub symbols has alerted us, however, to the possibility that our theological views are affected by biases that may blind us to the truth. Our views may have more to do with where we stand in relation to the way power is distributed in our society than with a dispassionate analysis of the intellectual issues involved. As truth-seekers, we should be particularly suspicious of beliefs that justify our own privilege at the expense of others who are suffering and hurting.

Martin Luther King Jr. had harsh words in his "Letter from Birmingham Jail" (written from his jail cell in April, 1963) for Christians who stood by during the civil rights campaigns of that time and did nothing to help reduce injustice and oppression. King expresses particular disappointment with white Christians and white religious leaders:

> I have heard numerous southern religious leaders admonish their worshipers to comply with a desegregation decision because it is the law, but I have longed to hear white ministers declare: "Follow this decree because integration is morally right and because the Negro is your brother." In the midst of blatant injustices inflicted upon the Negro, I have watched white churchmen stand on the sideline and mouth pious irrelevancies and sanctimonious trivialities. In the midst of a mighty struggle to rid our nation of racial and economic injustice, I have heard many ministers say: "Those are social issues, with which the gospel has no real concern." And I have watched many churches commit themselves to a completely other-worldly religion which makes a strange, un-Biblical distinction between body and soul, between the sacred and the secular.[18]

18. King Jr., "Letter from Birmingham Jail," 90. If you have not read this entire letter, I strongly urge you to do so. Although versions are available online, they are not always reliable. A trip to the library to find the volume *Why We Can't Wait* will be well worth your time.

King rightly discerns that the issue at stake is more than how one defines justice. The real question is: *Who is our God?* Is the God we worship the same God who is revealed in the pages of the Bible? If justice is a central concern in the Bible, and if the Bible links justice to the character of God, how can Christians claim to worship the God revealed in scripture when they either ignore or are blind to injustice around them? Does not the evidence of our actions speak more loudly than the testimony of our lips when it comes to the identification of our true allegiances?[19] Worship of the God of the Bible cannot be separated from the practice of justice. Although King wrote these words fifty years ago, one wonders to what extent the implicit charge of idolatry (worship of a god other than the God revealed in the Bible) might still valid:

> I have traveled the length and breadth of Alabama, Mississippi and all the other southern states. On sweltering summer days and crisp autumn mornings I have looked at the South's beautiful churches with their lofty spires pointing heavenward. I have beheld the impressive outlines of her massive religious-education buildings. Over and over I have found myself asking: "What kind of people worship here? Who is their God? Where were their voices when the lips of Governor Barnett dripped with words of interposition and nullification? Where were they when Governor Wallace gave a clarion call for defiance and hatred? Where were their voices of support when bruised and weary Negro men and women decided to rise from the dark dungeons of complacency to the bright hills of creative protest?"[20]

If we claim to worship a God who hears and responds to the cries of the oppressed and suffering, we should be particularly careful to identify places in our thinking that have the potential to serve as ear plugs preventing us from hearing those cries. An insensitivity to the pain of those who suffer is a sure sign of an anemic faith.

An extensive analysis of the concepts of love and justice is not possible here, nor is it necessary. Suffice it to say that a compelling case can be made for seeing love and justice as integrally connected with one another and for viewing the biblical perspective, both in the Old and New Testaments, as promoting such an understanding.[21] The existence of high levels

19. See Amos 5:21–24.

20. King Jr., "Letter from Birmingham Jail," 90–91.

21. See, for example, Wolterstorff, *Justice: Rights and Wrongs* and Wolterstoff, *Justice in Love.*

of inequality in the United States today is an issue of justice. This inequality is causing massive amounts of pain. The recent economic crisis has exacerbated that pain. Economic inequality is not something that happened spontaneously or unexpectedly, such as a bad storm that could not have been predicted. Inequality happens and is sustained because certain structures are in place that cause it and in fact ensure that it will exist. Carole Shammas has written, for example (more than twenty years ago, when both wealth and income inequality were much less severe than they are today):

> The most salient characteristics of the wealth distribution, namely the consistently large chunk of wealth held by the top 1 percent and the improvement noticeable by the mid-twentieth century in the share of wealth held by the lower 80 percent, can be associated with specific governmental policies. The share claimed by the top 1 percent is highly correlated with progressive tax rates. A whole group of such levies—the estate tax, tax on capital gains, gift tax, and income tax—were introduced on the eve of World War I and then sharply increased in progressivity and impact during the Great Depression and World War II. The effectiveness of these taxes can be measured by the post-1945 growth in those occupations—estate planners, tax accountants, and tax lawyers—created to counteract them. As exemptions increased in the 1950s and rates of taxation fell in the 1960s, the share claimed by the top 1 percent climbed back up. As the government granted further tax benefits to wealthy groups in the 1980s, the share claimed by the top 1 percent climbed to historic highs.[22]

A bit of research into historical patterns of inequality in the United States reveals that progress was made in the mid-twentieth century in reducing inequality. Most of my students are surprised to learn that top marginal income tax rates in the US were higher than ninety percent from 1944–1964 and stood at seventy percent or higher until 1982. The Gini index measure of inequality shows that inequality in the United States improved markedly in the period from the early 1940s to the early 1980s, when inequality began to get worse. Our tax structure is not the only factor in the generation of inequality, of course, but it must certainly be considered an important factor. What can be said with relative certainty is that the causes of the inequality we observe in our society are *political* in nature.

22. Shammas, "A New Look at Long-Term Trends in Wealth Inequality in the United States." 428. See also Marsh, *Class Dismissed;* Rieger, *No Rising Tide;* and Schwalbe, *Rigging the Game.*

They are the result of policies and structures that resulted from particular decisions. In other words, *they can be changed.* As Shammas states:

> It is not that technological progress, the demographic profile, and capital availability are inconsequential in determining the wealth distribution. Rather, it is that their effects cannot be assessed outside the political system that apportions the resulting assets and liabilities among the population. Wealth inequality is not the product of some inexorable economic development process but the outcome of specific laws regarding property rights, the tax structure, and public expenditures.[23]

If Christians possess a set of theological beliefs or an ideological framework that encourages them to think of inequality as something outside their control or influence—it is part of "human nature" or part of "the way the world is," for example—they will not be inclined to engage in action that challenges the structures that sustain and increase inequality. Similarly, if Christians possess a set of theological beliefs or an ideological framework that encourages them to think of inequality as a matter of optional interest but not a matter of obligatory moral concern, little will likely happen in the way of organized efforts on their part to bring about change.

For a change of attitude among Christians to occur, we need to be enabled to hear the cries of those who are suffering. Since the injustice of inequality in the United States is at a point now where it is causing pain not only for those on the bottom, but also for large numbers in the middle, an awareness of the pain is growing. As awareness of the pain grows, the potential for sharper analysis of the causes of the pain rises. Sharper analysis helps us to see both that the problem is multifaceted—with linkage to a large number of issues—and also solvable. Many other nations, for example, are democratic and prosperous yet have much less inequality.[24] We can actually see what less inequality looks like in a society. We know that gross inequality is not a necessary evil. The fact that the problem is linked to a large number of issues has the positive implication that engagement with the problem can begin from a variety of different angles.

At the beginning of this chapter we said that regular, attentive Bible reading that includes the steps of know thyself, engagement with the text,

23. Shammas, "A New Look at Long-Term Trends in Wealth Inequality in the United States" 429.

24. See, for example: Inequality.org Staff, "ILO: U.S. Inequality Now Literally Off the Chart," http://inequality.org/ilo-report-inequality-literally-chart/.

and ongoing verification can help us sort out correct hub symbols and thus help us sort out what ought to be matters of priority for us. Through this process, the Bible becomes authoritative as it changes the focus of our attention. It becomes a guide—a north star helping us to chart our course and set our direction. We have uncovered an example of an issue that is unquestionably prominent in both the Old and New Testaments, but which has been largely ignored by most North American Christians. Here is a place, therefore, where our model can help us increase the authority of the Bible in our lives. If the Bible is our guide, as Christians claim it to be, our concerns ought to be grounded in biblically revealed hub symbols rather than the headlines of our culture. Sustained attention to the situation of those who are vulnerable and in danger of having their needs disregarded—those who in biblical times were identified as the orphans, widows, foreigners, and poor—ought to lead North American Christians, I have argued, to place the issue of inequality and problems related to that issue (as well as, more generally, issues that have to do with situations of injustice) high on their list of important moral concerns. For many North American Christians, one has to say, doing so would involve a radical change of course.

7

Applying the Model—How Can the Bible Speak to Contemporary Issues?

CONTEMPORARY CHRISTIANS FACE MANY issues for which there is no explicit biblical guidance. Our world of today is a very different place from the world of two thousand years ago. How can the Bible provide us with guidance regarding questions that are peculiarly modern? What is a proper Christian response to cloning? What should Christians think of *in vitro* fertilization? What about global warming? Is the increasing use of genetically modified foods a topic that should concern Christians? We face end-of-life decisions today that our forebears could never imagine. The challenges of modern living confront us with questions unimaginable to persons living in biblical times. In this age of increasing global population and dwindling global resources, is my choice concerning which car to purchase morally neutral? Is the choice to buy a car versus consideration of other modes of transportation a morally neutral matter for followers of Jesus?

How can the ancient collection of documents we call the Bible assist us with such questions? The previous chapter addressed the question of how the Bible can shape our moral horizon by helping us reorient our hub symbols and rearrange our priorities. The direction of our investigation was from biblical hub symbols to the kind of concerns that ought to be important to us today. This chapter reverses the direction of inquiry. It begins with a contemporary concern and goes to the Bible seeking assistance for how best to construct an appropriate Christian response.

There is no particular reason why we should pick one issue over another. Any issue can serve as an example of how to apply our model to contemporary concerns. Rapid change is characteristic of our modern world, and we know that fifty or one hundred years hence many of the issues that will generate contention and controversy within society in general and among Christians in particular will be matters we cannot imagine today, just as many of the most prominent contemporary issues in our society were not matters of major concern to people fifty or one hundred years ago. As we shall see in this chapter, the advantage of our model is that its focus on hub symbols allows the Bible to speak a relevant word to any issue, since every issue is ultimately a test of the identity of our hub symbols.

We will take a look at the issue of homosexuality because it is causing divisions within numerous denominations today (and thus, from our modern perspective, is an important topic), because the Bible is not much concerned about the matter, and because Christians often assume that the Bible treats the subject rather straightforwardly.[1] For many Christians the primary question is not, "What does the Bible say about homosexuality?" Since they are certain the Bible condemns homosexuality, they ask only, "Is the Bible going to be our authority on this topic, or not?" They assume that Christians who approve of same-sex marriages, for example, have abandoned the Bible as an authority source—at least as far as this issue is concerned.

Interestingly, Christians on opposite sides of this issue often agree that the Bible condemns same-sex sexual activity. Christians who support same-sex marriages will often say they think the Bible is wrong on the topic of homosexuality. To think that the Bible could be interpreted as supporting the view that same-sex marriage is morally on an equal footing with opposite-sex marriage is inconceivable for many Christians, no matter what position they take in their own views on the matter. This topic thus offers interesting possibilities for exploring the use of our model as a way of

---

1. The matter of what ought to be a proper Christian response to questions arising in relation to the topic of homosexuality is part of the larger issue of a proper Christian response to questions currently being debated concerning LGBTQ (Lesbian Gay Bisexual Transgender Questioning) persons. Considerable change and diversity of usage has characterized terminology for non-heterosexual persons, due both to the diversity that exists among non-heterosexuals and to the tendency for the terminology that has existed to carry derogatory implications. LGBTQ is currently widely accepted, though not without debate. Whatever terminology is used, one should keep in mind that every person is a unique individual and temptations toward stereotyping should be avoided.

bringing the authority of scripture to bear on divisive contemporary concerns.

You might want to pause for a few minutes and give some thought to your own views on the topic of homosexuality. Can you state your position with some clarity? Try writing down a short summary of your position.

Do you know the basis for your position? Does that basis include biblical support? If so, look up and read what you believe to be pertinent verses.

What do you think might be other factors that have shaped your views on this topic? To what extent has the Bible been an important source influencing your position? To what extent have non-biblical sources been important in influencing your position?

Have your views changed over the course of time? If so, what factors have caused your views to change? Do you think it likely that your views will be different ten years from now? Why or why not?

The first step of our model is *know thyself*. The importance of this step is immediately apparent when one examines polling on the issue of homosexuality. Most people are aware that attitudes are changing, and since there is a significant gap between the views of older adults in the United States and those of young people, attitudes will continue to shift over the next several decades. A colleague suggested to me once that one of the best predictors of the stance one takes on the issue of homosexuality is whether there is within the circle of friends with whom one regularly shares meals someone who openly identifies as LGBTQ. Young people tend to have more friends who are openly LGBTQ than do older adults. Fear has been a major component of past attitudes toward LGBTQ people (they have been falsely tagged as more likely than heterosexuals to molest children, abuse drugs, and suffer from mental illness, among other things). Familiarity with openly LGBTQ persons has reduced fear and thus also reduced prejudice in our attitudes, even if it has not eliminated it.

Since prejudice against LGBTQ people has been part of the cultural background of this issue, we have to begin by asking honest questions of ourselves. What comes to mind when we think of LGBTQ persons? Are the images primarily negative or positive? What are the influences most responsible for shaping what we think about LGBTQ people? What kinds of personal experiences have we had with LGBTQ persons? How many openly LGBTQ persons do we know? How many of our friends or work colleagues do we know are LGBTQ? Whether our impressions are positive or negative, the point is that we already have formed impressions of LGBTQ people as a group or category of persons, and those impressions shape how we respond to LGBTQ people as individuals, as well as to such issues as same-sex marriage and LGBTQ persons in church leadership positions. As honestly as we can, we should attempt to assess the sorts of attitudes we bring with us to a discussion of this topic.

Another important aspect of self-understanding related to this matter is connected with what William Countryman in his book *Dirt Greed & Sex* has called "purity codes."[2] Countryman writes that "what marks particular sexual acts as violations of purity rather than of some other ethic is that the acts are deemed repellent in and of themselves, like snails or slugs on a dinner plate. One rejects them because they seem self-evidently unacceptable, not because of any identifiable, concrete harm which they threaten to a society or to a person participating in them."[3] Purity codes have to do with what is considered *dirty*, or out of place, within a particular society.

An informal gauge for identifying our purity codes is to use the *ick* factor—what are those things that cause us to respond with "that's icky" or "yucky." What are the things that cause a reaction of disgust? Many Europeans are not bothered by women who do not shave their legs and underarms, but North Americans tend to be horrified by such behavior. Many of our reactions to smells are connected with purity codes. Travelers from the United States to other countries will often find themselves disgusted by smells in a marketplace that are not regarded negatively at all by native residents. The common factor about purity codes is that they are learned reactions. We are not born with them. Countryman notes, however, that we learn them "at such an early age that we tend to regard them, ever after, as self-evident."[4]

Because purity codes are learned at such a young age, because we almost never attempt to identify or reflect on the content of our purity codes,

2. See Countryman, *Dirt Greed & Sex*, chapter 1.

3. Ibid, 18.

4. Ibid, 11.

and because they operate at such a deep emotional level, purity codes are resistant to change. We tend to think that they are not even subject to change since they are part of *the way things are* rather than culturally learned responses. Purity codes are so engrained within us that they seem to have the characteristics of universal truths. We only begin to recognize their relation to our cultural context when we are able to get some distance from them—either through cross-cultural experience or through the perspective provided by changes that occur over time.

For example, not too long ago interracial relationships were considered "icky" by many (white persons) in the United States. Forty-one states at one time or another passed anti-miscegenation laws outlawing interracial marriages, including in some cases bans on interracial cohabitation or interracial sexual relations. In its 1883 *Pace v. Alabama* decision, the US Supreme Court upheld those laws, saying they did not represent a violation of the Fourteenth Amendment's equal protection clause. Gradually attitudes changed. States began to repeal their anti-miscegenation laws. In 1967 the Supreme Court struck down anti-miscegenation laws in the sixteen states that still had them at that time in its *Loving v. Virginia* decision, arguing that such laws were indeed a violation of the Fourteenth Amendment's equal protection clause as well as its due process clause.

A purity code against interracial relationships still exists within certain segments of US culture.[5] Most people today, however, find it difficult or impossible to imagine the level of revulsion felt by many people just a few decades ago toward the idea of interracial relationships. Today, many think of such attitudes as odd or even bizarre. If we can acknowledge the high probability that we would have shared such attitudes ourselves had we been born in a different place and time, we can begin to understand the power of purity codes and the magnitude of their impact on our views toward moral questions that evoke an emotional response connected with such codes.

Any attempt to analyze our own purity codes is extremely difficult, in part because identifying our purity codes is challenging and in part because deep-seated emotional reactions are not subject to easy scrutiny or modification. Awareness is the first step, however, and we can make progress if we are able to recognize reactions that are the result of culturally learned responses. Attitudes toward homosexuality have certainly been affected by

---

5. South Carolina and Alabama did not amend their state constitutions to remove bans on interracial marriage until 1998 and 2000, respectively, even though the legal force of those bans was nullified by the 1967 US Supreme Court decision.

purity codes. Feelings of revulsion are evidence of the presence of purity codes. Truth-seekers will want to be attentive to the presence of such feelings and to the power they have to interject a particular cultural bias into our perspective.

Our emotional reaction to purity code violations has an intellectual counterpart in the argument that certain ways of relating are part of the way things are, or at least part of the way things are intended to be. Such arguments are known in the disciplines of theology and ethics as *order of creation* arguments. They claim that there is something in the very structure of creation itself that suggests that one way of arranging our relationships is superior to others. Many arguments presented in favor of anti-miscegenation laws were based on the premise that mixing races was destructive to civilization and against the natural order. Arguments against women in positions of church leadership, or more generally in favor of particular roles for men and women are often natural order arguments. Likewise, many have argued that certain types of sexual activity ought to be labeled immoral or sinful or at least unnatural since they are violations of God's intention in creation.[6]

Natural order arguments are fear-based arguments. They make a claim that terrible things will happen unless we preserve certain artificial social constructions. One problem with all such arguments is that they fail the test of experience. In every instance, the imagined collapse of civilization fails to occur. Interracial relationships do not destroy society. As women have moved into professions and roles traditionally occupied by men—including preaching from pulpits on Sunday mornings—the sky has not fallen. As people realize their fears are baseless, opposition gradually changes to acceptance. In relation to the issue of same-sex marriage, we now have a variety of examples of nations and US states where same-sex marriage is legally permitted. The horrors predicted by opponents of such laws have not materialized. The fact that they have not materialized is not an argument in favor of permitting same-sex marriages. It simply proves the insufficiency of fear-based threats predicting chaos resulting from the dissolution of some supposed natural order.

Natural order arguments fail to recognize the cultural relativity of whatever is claimed to be revealed in nature. Such arguments are, in

---

6. A well-articulated example of this line of reasoning can be found in Grenz, *Sexual Ethics*. See especially 211–5. Note that this argument rules out many types of sexual behavior no doubt commonly practiced by couples in heterosexual marriage relationships.

essence, attempts to forestall debate through a claim of divine sanction for one's own viewpoint. Because they do not admit or recognize that all of our thinking about ideal human relationships is symbolic, metaphorical, and constructed from our experience, they do not recognize that the actual choice confronting us is not one between *revealed in nature* versus *human social construction*, but rather *which* of various humanly constructed ideals will we choose, and why? A Christian approach, of course, will attempt to discern symbols and metaphors that express the revelatory activity of God. One must make a case, however, for why some symbols and metaphors should be accepted over others. A claim that the divine intention is clearly revealed in nature is insufficient. Many patterns of interaction can be found in nature, none of which can claim to be self-evident examples of divine intention for human social interactions.

Nothing in what we have said thus far provides us with much help in knowing what position Christians should take on the topic of homosexuality. Our exploration of the first step of our model, know thyself, has primarily served a negative purpose of identifying pitfalls to avoid as we proceed. We have identified examples of reactions and responses that contain high probabilities for truth distortion. Of course, an important aspect of step one is the identification of one's personal hub symbols (see chapter 5). Only you can identify those for yourself. You will be much better prepared to explore this issue (or any other) if you have at least a general awareness of the content of your most important hub symbols.

The second step of our model is engagement with scripture. In relation to the subject of homosexuality, the first thing we notice when we get to this step is that the Bible has almost nothing explicit to say on the topic. There is no word for *homosexual* or *homosexuality* in the biblical languages of Hebrew and Greek.[7] The Old Testament contains two texts in Leviticus (18:22 and 20:13) that speak of lying "with a male as with a woman." The first text forbids the act; the second commands the death penalty for anyone who commits such an act. The Old Testament says nothing about female homosexuality. The New Testament contains two texts (1 Cor 6:9 and 1 Tim 1:10) that use grammatical constructions which seem to derive from the Septuagint (Greek translation of the Old Testament) language of

---

7. See Soards, *Scripture & Homosexuality*, 15, and Hays, *The Moral Vision of the New Testament*, 382. The English term "homosexuality" itself is of modern origin.

Leviticus.[8] These two texts contain lists of "wrongdoers" (1 Cor) and of the "lawless and disobedient" (1 Tim).

These texts (and a few others that are sometimes thrown into the mix) have been closely scrutinized by numerous scholars. For the most part scholars agree, regardless of their final conclusions about the content of a proper biblical perspective toward contemporary questions about homosexuality, that none of these texts can be directly applied to modern discussions on the topic.[9] The single text that seems, for some scholars, to have some applicability to current debates is found in Romans 1:26–27. The Romans text is also the only place in the entire Bible that appears to mention female same-sex activity.

Romans 1:26–27 reads as follows:

> For this reason God gave them up to degrading passions. Their women exchanged natural intercourse for unnatural, and in the same way also the men, giving up natural intercourse with women, were consumed with passion for one another. Men committed shameless acts with men and received in their own persons the due penalty for their error.

What can we say about this text? First, there is no consensus among scholars about how to apply this passage to contemporary discussions related to homosexuality. Scholars have interpreted it in different ways.[10] Second, a single text is hardly a firm basis for claiming a biblical position. The model we have developed suggests that no matter how one interprets these particular verses, one must set them against the background of what one deems to be the major biblical hub symbols. Indeed, one's understanding of particular verses is inevitably shaped by one's perception of the larger context within which the verses are set (chapter, section, book, group of books, Old Testament/New Testament, Bible as a whole), including one's view of the hub symbols characterizing that larger context. Third, all scholars interpret this text, as well as the others mentioned above, from the perspective provided by the framework of their own hub symbols. Scholars vary in the extent to which they acknowledge and identify the content of their hub

8. Soards, 19.

9. This is true for scholars such as Soards (*Scripture & Homosexuality*, 16–17, 20) and Hays (*The Moral Vision of the New Testament*, 382–3) who conclude that sexual activity between persons of the same gender is always wrong.

10. For one view, see Hays, *The Moral Vision of the New Testament*, 383–9. For a different perspective, see Rogers, *Jesus, the Bible, and Homosexuality*, 76–79.

symbols. Identification of the hub symbols of the interpreter is a key factor for evaluating any interpretation offered, however, since interpretations are always shaped by one's general frame of reference. There is no such thing as pure, unbiased, value-free, neutral interpretation.

Scholarly investigations of the biblical texts we have mentioned tend to fall into two distinct categories. On the one hand are scholars such as Jeffrey Siker, who argues that the issues addressed in the few biblical texts that can be claimed to have anything at all to do with same-gender sexual behavior do not in fact have any relevance to our modern questions. In his discussion of Romans 1:26–27 he notes:

> What stands out most are the contrasts between the presupposi-
> tions Paul and his contemporaries had about [same-sex] relations
> with the presuppositions we have today. Paul saw homoerotic rela-
> tions as a free choice against natural law. We see homosexual rela-
> tions primarily in terms of sexual orientation, which one does not
> choose but of which one naturally becomes aware in the process
> of maturation. Paul knew only of exploitive forms of homoerotic
> expression—particularly pederasty and prostitution—and then
> probably indirectly. We know of forms of homosexuality where
> the relationship is one of mutuality, commitment, and care. Paul
> saw all forms of homoeroticism as expressions of insatiable lust.
> We know of homosexual relationships where the sexual aspect
> is no more or less obsessive than in comparable heterosexual
> relationships. Paul presumed that all homoerotic relations were
> a consequence of Gentile idolatry. We know of gay and lesbian
> Christians who truly worship and serve the one true God and yet
> still affirm in positive ways their identity as gay and lesbian people.
> Paul apparently knew of no homosexual Christians. We do. What
> we can affirm with Paul is his condemnation of exploitive forms
> of homoeroticism, which are the consequence of human sinful-
> ness in refusing to acknowledge God as God. What we cannot
> and must not do is anachronistically to condemn gay and lesbian
> Christians in our age and with our understandings on the basis of
> what Paul says about non-Christian homoerotic activity in *his* age
> with *his* understandings.[11]

On the other hand are scholars who argue that the questions posed in contemporary discussions about homosexuality are sufficiently analo-gous to issues presented in texts such as Romans 1:26–27, 1 Corinthians 6:9, 1 Timothy 1:10, Leviticus 18:22 and Leviticus 20:13 that one is able to

11. Jeffrey S. Siker, "Gentile Wheat and Homosexual Christians," 143.

draw specific guidance from them. Marion Soards, for example, argues that Paul's opposition to same-gender sexual activity remains relevant to our situation today:

> Paul was not concerned with the origins, motivations, or gratifications of homosexual activity, nor were other ancient thinkers interested in these issues. Arguments about the genetic or sociological origins of homosexuality, about the phenomenon of mutual consent between adult homosexual partners, about genuinely loving homosexual relationships—none of these would impress Paul. He would simply understand the use of such information in arguments for the acceptance of homosexual behavior as further evidence of the blindness of humanity in bondage to sin.
>
> As Paul discerned and declared God's relationship to humans, homosexual acts were outside the boundaries of God's intentions for humanity . . . . On the matter of homosexuality, we should see clearly that the biblical understanding of homosexual behavior is univocal (although this issue is at most a minor concern). Homosexual activity is not consistent with the will of God; it is not merely a sin but evidence of sin, and there is no way to read the Bible as condoning homosexual acts.[12]

The few biblical texts that appear to mention same-gender sexual activity view it negatively. As we can see in the arguments of Siker and Soards, however, a key question is whether these texts can be viewed as applicable to our contemporary debates. Does the sort of same-gender sexual activity these biblical texts had in view have any relation at all to "a mutually consensual, monogamous, loving, and committed relationship between an adult gay couple or an adult lesbian couple"?[13] Because Siker concludes it does not, he says we must look to "the larger context of what the Bible has to say about human sexuality overall."[14] Soards, on the other hand, interprets these verses as applicable to the contemporary debate. His claim is that we need proceed no further to find the "biblical view" on the matter.

As with many ethical conundrums, on this topic Christians—and Christian scholars—disagree. The Bible, rather than providing clear and straightforward answers convincing to all parties, is interpreted in ways that lead to differing conclusions. Christians on various sides of the debate claim that the authority of the Bible is on *their* side of the issue. When an

12. Soards, *Scripture & Homosexuality*, 23–24.

13. Siker, 141.

14. Ibid.

issue touches deeply-held hub symbols, tempers rise. The debate can become highly polarized. On the issue of homosexuality, the polarization has led to division within congregations and denominations. What approach should truth-seeking Christians take in relation to such disputes?

The model we presented in chapter 5 provides a way forward. It helps us understand the importance of the influence of our personal and societal hub symbols and calls us to ongoing analysis and correction of faulty hub symbols. It helps us place the interpretation of any particular biblical texts within the larger picture of the prominent hub symbols characteristic of the entire biblical narrative. It calls us to verify our readings of scripture and the views we develop from our reading against the knowledge we have from other sources—both within and without the larger Christian tradition. The ultimate verification of truth comes in the resonance we detect between a particular stance and our view of God as one who loves every person unconditionally and who calls us all to live in a love/justice community as neighbors, friends, and family—a community where the possibilities for the prospering of each is maximized.

This community is represented in the Bible as the *shalom* community. A key ingredient for achieving a *shalom* community is the need for love to become embodied in an ongoing concern for justice.[15] A community concerned for justice will be a community sensitive to the pain of those who suffer. It will be particularly keen to listen for the voices of the oppressed. We have noted that where those voices were not heard by majoritarian Christian communities in the past (e.g., Germany before and during World War II and white churches in the United States during the civil rights era), massive moral failures occurred.[16]

A key diagnostic tool for testing the adequacy of our position, therefore, is to ask ourselves whether the stance we take evidences sufficient awareness of and responsiveness to the pain of those who are negatively affected by positions adopted by Christians and Christian institutions. The importance of this step cannot be overstated. I believe one of the primary deficiencies of most Christian treatments of the topic of homosexuality is

15. See Wolterstorff, *Justice in Love.*

16. I have pointed out previously that Glen Stassen presents an excellent analysis of these and other historical examples where majoritarian Christian morality failed miserably. Those who followed a model of devotion to a "thick Jesus" that evidenced what Stassen calls "incarnational discipleship," however, withstood the pressures of those times of historical testing in a way that can serve as a model for us today. See Stassen, *A Thicker Jesus.*

the failure to consider sufficiently the ways in which our beliefs, attitudes, and positions cause actual harm.

For example, even though the consensus within the scientific community for more than forty years has been that homosexuality is not a mental disorder, many Christians continue to think of it in that way. The American Psychiatric Association, the American Medical Association, the American Psychological Association, the American Counseling Association, the National Association of Social Workers, and the American Academy of Pediatrics have all criticized the "assumption that people who are homosexual should and can change their sexual orientation."[17] Yet many Christians believe otherwise, thanks at least in part to misinformation disseminated by organizations such as Focus on the Family.[18] In his book, *Stranger at the Gate*, Mel White describes his own suffering at the hands of misinformed and misguided Christians in a letter written to a pastor who produced a TV special condemning homosexuality:

> Like hundreds of thousands of your fellow Christian Americans, I spent twenty-five years trying to be an "ex-gay." Even after my conversion experience, I spent tens of thousands of dollars on Christian therapy. Repeatedly, I was counseled, exorcised, electric-shocked, medicated, and prayed for by the saints. Like the young people in your TV special, I began each new day really believing that God had "healed me," when in fact, I was simply refusing to face the facts.
>
> Finally, I realized that my sexual orientation was permanently and purposefully formed in my mother's womb or in my earliest infancy. Because of simplistic, well-meaning, but uninformed teachings on homosexuality like your own, I wasted thirty-five years in guilt, fear, and personal agony. And though there were times I could not feel God's presence, God never left my side. God's Spirit was there always to comfort and to guide me. Now I have accepted my sexual orientation as a gift from my loving Creator. Finally, as our Savior promised, the truth has set me free to be a productive, responsible, Christian gay man.[19]

I have no idea what Mel White's pain was like. What I do know, however, is that virtually every one of my Christian LGBTQ friends, colleagues

17. Rogers, *Jesus, the Bible, and Homosexuality*, 100.

18. See documentation of Focus on the Family's misrepresentation of data and use of violent rhetoric in Rogers, *Jesus, the Bible, and Homosexuality*, 98–101.

19. White, *Stranger at the Gate*, 314.

and acquaintances has a story to tell that involves pain and hurt at the hands of other Christians or Christian institutions. Our view of God as one who hears the cries of the oppressed and knows the suffering of the downtrodden should encourage us to train our ears to be especially alert to stories of pain.

We must take into account the history of violence and oppression against LGBTQ persons. Heterosexuals for the most part tend to be unaware of this history or do not consider its intimate connection with majoritarian cultural attitudes. An internet search on "history of violence against LGBTQ people in the United States" yields a heartbreaking list representing only the most visible and heinous aspects of a pattern of violence that cannot be separated from our culture's definition of LGBTQ persons as a class against whom discrimination and violence are permissible. Christians have been almost uniformly silent about this violence. The complicity of many Christians in attitudes that have encouraged or at least tolerated violence toward those whose sexual identity does not fit the majority's definition of normal is part of the background of our discussion of this topic.

The kind of pain we are discussing here, it is important to note, is of a particular sort. The pain of those who have suffered because of their LGBTQ identity is in a different category from the pain of a community that has been devastated by a tornado, for example. The pain of a storm can be exacerbated by the effects of injustice, as was evident with Hurricane Katrina in 2005, but the destruction of a storm is not intrinsically unjust, precisely because there is a random character to the destruction. When we discuss the topic of homosexuality and the pain experienced by LGBTQ people, however, we cannot avoid a discussion of injustice. The pain that is part of the story of LGBTQ people is not pain distributed at random among the general population that only coincidentally happened to affect LGBTQ persons. It has a target and has specific causes that ensure its continuance among a specific minority group as long as those causes remain in place. We cannot understand this issue unless we understand why justice has to be part of the discussion.

Nicholas Wolterstorff has argued that justice "prevails in human relationships insofar as persons render to each other what they have a right to."[20] And what are those things to which persons have a right? "Someone's rights are what respect for his or her worth requires. Or to put it from the shadow side: to wrong someone is to treat her with less respect than befits

20. Wolterstorff, *Justice in Love*, 90.

her worth—to treat her with under-respect, to treat her as would only befit someone of less worth."[21] Justice, in other words, depends on attributing to persons the value due them and treating them accordingly.

Marvin Ellison has written that the goal of justice is "to empower disenfranchised persons and groups so that they may live as respected, participatory members of the community, empowered to pursue their own life projects . . . . Doing justice means working not just for the *inclusion* of some, but for the *transformation* of community itself so that all may participate meaningfully and share enough resources to thrive."[22] In order for that to happen, we need

> to have a feel for actual experiences of injustice, of the pain and suffering incurred not only because of individual acts of meanness and cruelty, but also as a consequence of status quo power arrangements that grant privileges to some at the expense of others. Gaining a cognitive and affective appreciation of injustice as lived reality requires, first and foremost, listening to the pain-filled stories of those who have experienced an injustice. Second, we must rely on the social sciences to demonstrate how structural dynamics of power and oppression have perpetuated that pain. For this reason, what churns at the heart of every justice struggle is conflict over how to interpret the world and whose authority counts in that naming.[23]

Ellison makes the same connection between justice and the worth of persons that Wolterstorff makes: "Justice is . . . about recognition of persons *as* persons. Based on indebtedness or owingness, justice is grounded in the perception that others, too, are persons of worth. As part of the community, they have a right to make claims on others."[24] Following Karen Lebacqz's argument in *Justice in an Unjust World*, Ellison says that a helpful way to clarify the meaning of justice is to begin with the "lived experience of injustice in its multiple dimensions: as political disenfranchisement, economic disadvantage, and cultural marginality."[25]

---

21. Ibid., 89–90.

22. Ellison, *Same-Sex Marriage?*, 49. Note the similarity between Ellison's view of the ideal toward which justice strives and what I have described as the characteristics of the *shalom* community.

23. Ibid, 48.

24. Ibid., 49.

25. Ibid., 48.

Ellison defines heterosexism as "the institutionalizing of heterosexuality as the exclusively normative way to be human" and says it is

> constructed on the basis of devaluing sexual difference. It involves the universalizing of heterosexual experience and cultural norms from a supposedly neutral, but in fact privileged position of power, and "normalcy," the measuring of those who are different as deviant ("failed" heterosexuals) and inferior (sinful, criminal, mentally ill). Resistance to heterosexual oppression requires, on the part of the culturally defined Other, a subversive move to become self-defining.[26]

Heterosexism is more than an attitude. Like racism and ageism, it involves unequal distributions of power in society. It is an issue of justice.

There ought to be no debate among Christians that discrimination against any class of people is not only impermissible but intolerable. Christians ought to join in the defense of legal rights for others who face unequal treatment, no matter who they are. Sadly, we must admit that as far as the issue of homosexuality is concerned, even such a modest and seemingly obvious step would entail an enormous change in attitudes and actions for many Christians.

The enormity of the change required, as well as the fact that we are dealing with power relationships and not simply individual attitudes, can be seen in a relatively common response-pattern on the part of those who benefit from structural advantages when the assumptions underlying their position of institutionalized privilege begin to be challenged. Interestingly, those who are in positions of privilege will often claim to be persecuted or will in other ways blame those who have been the true sufferers of oppression.[27] When those with unfair advantages make such a claim they are not necessarily lying in the sense that they are saying something they know to be untrue. They may well feel and believe themselves to be persecuted. The facts do not support their case, however. Their response is (sometimes unconsciously) an attempt to justify the perpetuation of arrangements that have provided them with access to advantages denied to others and which

26. Ibid., 51.

27. Martin Luther King Jr. pointed out in his "Letter from Birmingham Jail" that he was blamed for stirring up trouble in Birmingham, Alabama. His response was that "we who engage in nonviolent direct action are not the creators of tension. We merely bring to the surface the hidden tension that is already alive." See King, "Letter from Birmingham Jail," 85.

have sometimes (even though sometimes unknown to them) been made possible through harsh oppression.

Often we are only dimly aware of the extent of the injustice embedded within the structures that provide us with privileges that are part of our daily living. For example, when buying a chocolate bar, how many of us consider whether the cocoa beans used to make the chocolate may have been harvested by children or persons in situations of virtual slavery?[28] Those with privilege seldom give sustained thought to the mechanisms that perpetuate their privilege. Frequently structures of injustice remain invisible to us. Invisibility is not the same as nonexistence, however. When those who are harmed by oppressive structures engage in the struggle to change those structures, they encounter stiff resistance. Those who stand passively on the sidelines do not play a neutral role. Passivity reinforces current power arrangements and makes the struggle against injustice more difficult.

In relation to the issue of homosexuality, I have heard Christians who are opposed to same-gender sexual activity say that they feel "oppressed" by the "gay agenda." What is the nature of this feeling of oppression? They say that "gay rights" is the "new normal" and they feel like their own perspective is a minority view. Words matter, and we need to be careful to define what we mean by *oppression*, as well as to distinguish between the right to one's opinion and the right to be treated equally. Regardless of whether there is truth in the claim that opposition to same-gender sexual activity is a minority opinion, having a minority opinion is not the same thing as experiencing oppression.

As I stated above, there ought to be no debate among Christians that discrimination of any sort is impermissible. Christians ought to be able to agree that equal treatment of all persons is a value we support. We ought to advocate for laws that reflect this value. The question of homosexuality as a moral concern is a topic we can discuss with full recognition that differences of opinion exist and that those differing opinions are held by equally devout Christians seeking to follow Christ. When laws treat one category of persons differently from everyone else, however, the biblical call toward sensitivity to the experience of those who are wronged and harmed ought to cause us to respond not defensively, but rather with concern to check the

---

28. Fortunately, greater awareness and public pressure are having an impact on the policies of food companies, but much work remains to be done. See website of Slave Free Chocolate: http://www.slavefreechocolate.org/.

validity of our assumptions and with open ears to hear the complaints of those who accuse us of supporting injustice.

We turn now from the topic of equal treatment under the law—an issue which ought not to be a subject of debate for Christians—to an exploration of our theological understanding of homosexuality. A question much debated among Christians is the matter of whether homosexuality ought to be considered sinful. On this point, many scholars distinguish between homosexual orientation and sexual activity between persons of the same gender. I am aware of no contemporary Christian scholar who labels homosexual orientation as sinful. Scholars on all sides of the debate recognize, in agreement with science, that (1) human sexuality is not bipolar but characterized by enormous variety, encompassing not only heterosexuality and homosexuality but also bisexuality and asexuality, with people ranging along a spectrum rather than always clearly at one end or another of the scale, that (2) sexual orientation is set at a very early age (no matter which side one takes in the *genes* versus *environment* debate) and is not a matter of choice, and that (3) sexual orientation is part of a person's identity in the sense that it fundamentally affects how one relates to others. Sexual orientation shapes our self-understanding in powerful ways.[29]

A number of Christian scholars argue, however, that sexual *activity* involving persons of the same gender is intrinsically sinful—they claim that there is no context in which it could *not* be viewed as sinful—and thus ought to be always condemned. The only sinless option for homosexually oriented persons is abstinence (or also, according to Stanley Grenz, fidelity within heterosexual marriage!).[30] There are two reasons generally given for why homosexual expression should be seen as always sinful. One is that scripture and tradition view it as sinful. The other is that it is unnatural or against the created order.

We have already seen that the Bible is variously interpreted on the subject of homosexuality, so the question of whether or not we can assert

29. Although scholars on all sides of the debate are agreed on these points, conversation among non-scholars reveals that many people are misinformed. Many people believe, for example, that sexual orientation is a matter of choice. As I pointed out in chapter 1, however, truth-seekers are respectful of data, seek to understand the scholarly consensus, and know that should they wish to stake out a position contrary to that consensus, the burden of truth rests on them to show on the basis of evidence why the consensus view is mistaken. Progress in conversations on this topic cannot be made when the basis for discussion is ill-informed opinion rather than research-based knowledge.

30. See Grenz, *Welcoming but Not Affirming*, 125, and Hays, *The Moral Vision of the New Testament*, 400.

unequivocally that the Bible (or tradition, for that matter) condemns all same-gender sexual expression in our contemporary context is at least an open one. We have also observed that there are problems with created order arguments. Many sermons have been preached against same-gender sexual expression. I have never heard (or heard of) a single sermon targeting oral sex practiced by heterosexual married couples. Both types of sexual activity would be excluded by the created order arguments. Why the one-sided attention to one form of "sin" over another? I daresay the reason is not for lack of oral sexual activity among heterosexual Christians!

The real issue here has to do with our view of sin. And our view of sin is related to our understanding of human nature and our concept of salvation. We have argued that the biblical view of salvation is linked with a vision that favors and strives to achieve a certain sort of community—a community of *shalom*. Sin, in this view, would be anything that blocks or lessens or distorts our achievement of such a community. Christians recognize that the power of sin is such that we will never be free of its influence in this world. The challenge of our calling as citizens of God's *shalom* community, however, is to live our lives according to the rules and principles of God's kingdom—in the here and now, not the by and by. Christian salvation is not good news only for the time after we die.

Jeffery Siker's definition of sin is similar to mine. He says it is "that which goes against our understanding of God's intentions for faithful human existence."[31] Siker reminds us that Christian "notions of sin have changed significantly over time."[32] What can we say, then, as Christians living in the twenty-first century concerning the question of whether same-gender activity should be labeled as always sinful, given our understanding of God's intention for us as including a desire for our prospering in a community where people love one another as neighbors?

We have found the witness of scripture and tradition to be at least ambiguous. That is especially the case when we look at the biblical witness as a whole, focusing on the primary hub symbols. Arguments from nature or the created order are not convincing. Those who condemn same-gender sexual expression expend much effort attempting to show that it is harmful. The harm is supposedly intrinsic to the action. Those who adopt this position do not think that sexual activity between persons of the same gender can ever be an expression of physical love-making in the same way as

---

31. Siker, in Brawley, ed., *Biblical Ethics & Homosexuality*, 137.
32. Ibid. See also Fredriksen, *Sin: The Early History of An Idea*.

heterosexual love-making. Stanley Grenz calls same-sex intercourse a "deficient act"; Richard Hays calls it "a distortion of God's order for creation."[33] There is no evidence, however, that same-gender sexual activity is intrinsically harmful, either to the individuals engaging in such activity or to the larger community. In fact, the evidence points in the opposite direction.

All "love the sinner but hate the sin" arguments depend on the assumption that there is something sinful about same-gender sexual activity. Such arguments view the sin as connected specifically with the activity; there is no context—even a context involving two persons who love each other—wherein the activity itself can ever be viewed as positive or life-giving or an embodied expression of mutual love. The *intention* of those engaged in the activity matters not. There is an objective quality to the act itself that makes it sinful.

The view of sin I have advocated, however, makes understanding context essential for judging the sinfulness of an action. If the sinfulness of an action has some connection to its effects on others and oneself and if the effects that matter are those related to that which blocks or lessens or distorts our achievement of a *shalom* community, where is the basis for the claim that same-gender sexual activity is always sinful? Truth-seekers must consider the possibility that the majority of Christians, up until now, have been wrong about the intrinsic sinfulness of same-gender sexual activity, just as the majority viewpoint has turned out to be wrong in relation to a number of issues in the past. We know that the track record of Christians is not good when it comes to challenging false cultural hub symbols. In fact, often Christianity has served as a barrier to progressive change. Christian attitudes tend to follow rather than lead the culture, with some built-in lag time.[34]

There is another serious problem with "love the sinner but hate the sin" arguments. They have a faulty view of human nature in that they fail to recognize the power of the connection between our sexuality and our identity as persons. Since few today (and no scholar of which I am aware) wish to condemn homosexual orientation since orientation is recognized to be in the category of things-not-chosen (such as, e.g., eye color), a distinction is made between same-gender sexual activity and same-gender attraction.

33. Grenz, *Welcoming but Not Affirming*, 110, and Hays, *The Moral Vision of the New Testament*, 396.

34. The reader can no doubt think of examples. I discovered the truth of this statement as a graduate student in my study of Baptist attitudes toward the Vietnam War. See Blevins, "Southern Baptist Attitudes Toward the Vietnam War in the Years 1965–1970."

The former is placed in the category of *sinful* while the latter is placed in the category of *not sinful*. The distinction is untenable, however.

Christian scholars agree (for the most part) that not all sexual attraction is lustful. Sexual attraction *can* be lustful when we objectify the other, and sexual activity certainly has the potential to be distorted by sin. But our creation as sexual beings who have sexual impulses and who find pleasure in responding to those impulses is not an evil thing in itself. The love to which God calls us can find legitimate, life-affirming, celebratory, and joyful affirmation in the passionate embrace of another.

The nature of our sexual attraction is given to us. It is part of our identity. We do not choose it. Truth-seekers who pay attention to the findings of science recognize these facts and accept them. Any assertion that we can affirm the full human value of a homosexually-oriented person while at the same time denying that there is any possibility that such a person can express his or her sexual impulses in a legitimate, life-affirming, celebratory, and joyful same-sex sexual encounter is disingenuous, illogical, and unjust. Scholars who label same-gender sexual activity as sinful claim that such activity is always infected by lust. The claim is unconvincing. It devalues the full personhood of LGBTQ persons, since it fails to account for their creation by God as whole persons. Our sexual identity is part of the goodness of our creation in God's image, including impulses that draw us toward one another and toward covenants of intimacy that can be enhanced through sexual expression.

There is no hierarchy of better and worse forms of sexual expression. We do not invade heterosexual bedrooms to ensure that proper forms of sexual expression are being utilized. Sexual intimacy can be expressed in enormously diverse ways, no matter one's sexual orientation. The attempt to label certain forms as legitimate and others as illegitimate is arbitrary. As far as I can tell after examining all of the arguments and the history of the majority tradition, the true reason for the claim that same-gender sexual activity is immoral seems to lie in the power of the majority to define the limits of legitimate behavior. The majority tends to label the minority—the Other—as *deviant*. Behavior associated with the Other is labeled sinful, thus helping ensure that the boundary between normal/legitimate and Other/illegitimate remains clear.

The cultural attitude toward homosexuality is changing. Fewer people, especially young people, believe that same-gender sexual activity is intrinsically harmful or sinful. My view is that eventually the change taking place in societal attitudes will be reflected in the majority view of Christians. In the meantime, Christian truth-seekers have good *theological and biblical* reasons for leading rather than resisting the movement toward recognition and protection of the rights of LGBTQ people to enjoy and express their sexuality without restrictions except for those we commend for sexual expression in general.

I see no reason why sexual activity between persons of the same gender cannot be viewed as serving potentially similar purposes in a same-sex relationship as heterosexual activity does in a heterosexual relationship. Arguments related to the supposed procreative purpose of sexual activity fail, since plenty of heterosexual sex happens in the absence of procreative possibilities. Arguments that same-sex marriage violates some supposedly intrinsic aspect of the nature of marriage fail, since a study of the history of marriage reveals a tremendous variety of understandings and practices. Arguments related to any attempt to elevate one view of family over others fail, since family life in the United States today is diverse, is changing rapidly, and nothing indicates that families composed of same-gender partners are any more or less healthy than families composed of heterosexual partners. And, as we have seen, arguments from nature, from the claim that same-gender sexual behavior is necessarily harmful, and from the need for obedience to a supposed biblical command all fail. In sum, there is no good reason to view same-gender sexual activity as *intrinsically* sinful.

If we are correct in saying that the language of sin should not automatically be applied to same-sex activity, there are implications for how we think about the topic. Language matters, as do the analogies we use to frame our discussion of issues. The analogy of alcoholism has been used in relation to homosexuality by those who wish to suggest that while we should not condemn LGBTQ persons (just as we do not condemn alcoholics for their alcoholism), we should properly condemn same-gender sexual practice, just as we condemn drinking by alcoholics, since drinking, for alcoholics, leads to destructive consequences for themselves and others in a way similar to same-gender sexual activity on the part of LGBTQ persons. Jeffrey Siker argues the analogy is flawed for a number of reasons. First, same-gender sexual activity is not intrinsically harmful or destructive. Second,

> while most recovering alcoholics recognize that their alcoholic orientation is potentially debilitating and destructive, unless they abstain from drinking, most persons who are homosexual do not

see their sexual orientation as anything from which they need to recover. Rather, contrary to the alcoholism analogy, they would argue that abstaining from homosexual activity itself is what is potentially most debilitating because to do so is to deny a significant expression of their identity as human beings who seek out intimate and committed relationships with other persons, just as heterosexual people do . . . .

Finally, alcoholism is a disease from which some people suffer that is triggered by the act of drinking alcoholic beverages. The focus in alcoholism is on the act: either drinking or abstaining from drinking. But gays and lesbians repeatedly remind us that while heterosexuals tend to focus on homoerotic acts whenever discussing homosexuality, gays and lesbians are much more concerned with the whole range of factors that comprise relationships. Homosexual acts (just like heterosexual acts) are but one feature of a much larger complex of factors that contribute to the makeup of relationships. To focus on the sexual act is to miss the point of the larger context of the relationship. It is to dehumanize and depersonalize gays and lesbians, caricaturing them only in terms of their sexual activities rather than seeing them as whole persons with lives that include more than sex.[35]

Siker's reasoning convincingly reveals the faults of analogies such as alcoholism in relation to this topic. Siker offers as an alternative analogy the situation of Gentile Christians in the early church.[36] Initially viewed by early (Jewish) Christians as sinners and outside the bounds of God's love, eventually Gentile Christians were fully received as brothers and sisters in Christ—without having to conform to Jewish practices. Though this analogy has been critiqued by some, the critiques depend on arguments we have already judged wanting.[37] Siker's argument reminds us of the need for openness to the movement of God's Spirit in helping us to see from new perspectives.

We have seen that we have good reasons to be suspicious that traditional Christian perspectives toward the topic of homosexuality have been distorted by cultural hub symbols. We know that our sexuality is a vitally important part of our identity as persons created in the image of God. The Bible offers no support for an argument that our existence as sexual persons

---

35. Siker, "Homosexual Christians, the Bible, and Gentile Inclusion," 183.

36. Ibid, 187–90.

37. See, e.g., Hays, 395–6 and Soards, 61–63.

is evil. The sexuality we have is the sexuality given to us. We do not choose it. What we choose is how to express our sexuality.

If the *shalom* community to which God calls us is a community designed to foster the prospering of all, and if there is nothing intrinsically harmful in same-gender expressions of love, why should either LGBTQ persons or *LGBTQ persons in same-sex relationships* be considered anything other than an example of the amazing diversity of God's family? A key element in the verification of the truthfulness of our position is the need to look at real-life consequences. Consequences cannot be the only measure of the correctness of our view, but neither should we ignore the implications regarding the kinds of communities that tend to result from the positions we hold.

A heterosexual visitor attending a church service where the majority population is composed of LGBTQ persons is likely to be impressed with the joy, vitality, welcoming spirit, and committed spirituality of those present—the same sorts of things one would hope to find in any worship service. Imagine, if you are heterosexually oriented, standing next to an LGBTQ person as you sing God's praises in a worship service. Which viewpoint do you think is more likely to enhance the possibilities for a stronger, more intimate and life-affirming community? A presumption that God's curses rather than God's blessings are upon the sexual activity of the one standing next to you? Or a presumption that you are both whole persons striving to follow Jesus in every area of life, including openness to possibilities for sharing sexual intimacy in a variety of life-affirming, joyous and celebratory ways? Can the former viewpoint be attributed to anything other than self-righteousness and arrogance? Which person, of the two of you, is more in need of repentance for harmful and destructive attitudes and beliefs?

We know that one of the most surprising and impressive things about Jesus's ministry was his inclusiveness, especially his inclusion of those regarded at the time as outside the boundaries of God's love. We also know that among the most grievous sins for which the church must repent is its history of exclusion, persecution, and oppression. In our discussion of justice, we noted that justice is essentially treating persons according to the value due them. I have seen no scholar argue that LGBTQ persons have less value than heterosexual persons. Treating LGBTQ persons with the value due them means heterosexuals must be extremely cautious about setting a standard of behavior for all that matches the majority's narrow definition of normal/legitimate. Treating LGBTQ persons with the value due them means heterosexuals must be willing to consider the possibility of forms of life-affirming sexual expression that fall outside of their own experience. Treating LGBTQ persons with the value due them means heterosexuals must be ready to answer the charge of injustice when they advocate "abstinence only" for LGBTQ folk, since such advocacy targets a minority class for deprivation of a good they (the majority) reserve for themselves.

As truth-seekers, we know that whatever stance we take leaves us open to the possibility of error. The question we face is not whether we risk error. Nor can we choose neutrality. There is no "live and let live" position, because if the arguments about heterosexism and injustice are correct, we contribute to injustice when we fail to stand with those being oppressed. "Do nothing" is only a moral option for the one who has examined all of the evidence and concluded that there is no injustice in setting heterosexuality as the standard by which to judge personal behavior as well as legal codes relating to marriage, inheritance, next-of-kin, adoption, etc.

The question we face is: on which side do we want to risk error? On which side do we run the gravest risk of violating our central calling to be followers of Jesus? As truth-seekers, we do our best to account for all of the evidence before us. As *Christian* truth-seekers, we seek to emulate the love, grace, compassion, and justice that we have experienced personally and to which scripture and Christian tradition testify. Our model pushes us to seek verification of claims and counter-claims. It also pushes us to give particular attention to the claims of those who say they have been *wronged* by us.[38] LGBTQ persons claim they have been treated *unjustly* by the heterosexual majority. For Christian truth-seekers, this is among the most serious accusations that can be made against us, since it challenges our assertion that we are Christ-followers and that the Bible is authoritative for us. Heterosexual Christians cannot assert that they have done the work necessary for a full exploration of the topic of homosexuality until they have looked LGBTQ persons in the eyes, listened to their stories, and attempted to offer some response to the claims LGBTQ people have against heterosexuals for the injustices they have suffered.

The purpose of our examination of the topic of homosexuality has been to provide an example of how the model presented in chapter 5 can help us bring the authority of scripture to bear in relation to contemporary

---

38. See Wolterstorff, *Justice: Rights and Wrongs*, 292–300 and Wolterstorff, *Justice in Love*, 85–90.

issues that are modern in the sense that they either did not exist in former times or they did not exist in the way they challenge us today. We have discovered that our model is useful in applying the authority of the Bible to *any* issue since it is grounded in a vision of what God desires for the kinds of communities we ought to be constructing. The measure of faithful discipleship is not an abstract norm seemingly dropped from the heavens. The norms that seem so obvious to those in the majority are often nothing more than the reflection of our cultural hub symbols. Rather, we are called to follow the Christ who set an example for us in both attitude and action as one whose love was abundantly and radically inclusive. A key test of our success is the presence or absence among Christians of a love that so values every member of the community that it is sensitive to the places of pain, able to hear the cries of those who have been wronged, and aroused to action by a righteous anger wherever there is injustice or wherever the prospering of any person or group of persons is blocked or inhibited or distorted. Perhaps one way to sum up the verification question would be to ask: If we wish to stand with Jesus, where should we place ourselves?

8

Following Jesus with Heart and Mind

THIS BOOK HAS BEEN an exploration of the thesis that logic and intellectual inquiry are not antithetical to biblical faith. We have argued that truth is accessible to us, yet we have also argued that all of our truth claims are subject to scrutiny and open to challenge. The truth search must begin with the recognition that we are finite and thus our knowledge is fallible. The search for truth calls for hard work and an open mind. We make progress as we gain confidence in the ability of our truth claims to withstand ongoing analysis and challenge.

Some will argue that the outcome of the search is more important than the process. They are afraid that following some paths might lead us astray. They are happy to affirm truth-searching *as long as* it leads to their idea of what constitutes truth. They want to set parameters on which claims for truth are acceptable. They are more concerned with gate-keeping than with opening doors. Their motivation is grounded in fear, their in-group conversations tend to emphasize admonitions not to wander too far from the safety of the fold, and their attitudes toward those outside the group tend to fall on a spectrum between suspicion and outright condemnation.

We have already identified problems with an outcome-oriented approach. It petrifies a given conception of truth and is unable to adjust to new knowledge and fresh movements of the Spirit. Truths that are vigorously defended as universal and eternal are often, over long periods of time, revealed to be perspectives of particular times and cultures. The gate-keeping required by this approach leads to abuses of power as those with authority strive to suppress dissent. The attractiveness of one's truth claims diminishes as one's views become more rigid, less open to challenge, and increasingly reactionary.

Those who are more concerned with repelling dangerous ideas than exploring new pathways have a tendency to focus on boundary markers. They look for "friend or foe" signals that will enable them to categorize others as in-group or out-group. Their fear generates insecurity, resulting in a constant need to reassure themselves that they are right and others are wrong. A consequence can be self-righteousness, along with judgmental attitudes toward others.

The word that comes to my mind when I think of this approach is *shriveling*. A shriveling of one's soul takes place as one breathes the stale air trapped behind closed windows and shut doors. The fear that drives one to seek safety and security results in self-imposed confinement within a prison of one's own construction. The "house of outcomes" in which one seeks safety can be built of doctrines, rules, prejudices, inherited patterns and beliefs, or anything else one might cling to as a defense against change. The irony is that fear can never be eliminated. The deadbolt locks and alarm systems we install only provide an illusion of safety. The storms of life and the change that inevitably comes with the passage of time conspire to dilapidate all such houses—eventually.

In the meantime, those living in such houses miss the joy of exploring the vast spaces that lie just beyond their locked doors. Houses intended to protect from danger become grave threats to our spiritual well-being. Those raised within such houses have their views distorted by a perfect sunshiny-day-with-a-rainbow-and-happy-smiling-faces vision that attempts to substitute wishful thinking for the messiness of real life. Invariably, some with sufficiently inquisitive minds will recognize that the house that is supposed to provide all of the answers is incapable of doing so and will leave, setting forth on their own journeys of discovery. Such departures tend to reinforce the feeling on the part of those remaining in the house of the need for further vigilance against the entrapments of the world outside.

I have emphasized process rather than outcome. I am less concerned with whether we agree on a particular topic than I am with the sorts of questions we are asking and the spirit with which we ask them. Truth-seeking is collaborative. Others—including others with whom we disagree—are not opponents. They are fellow sojourners. Other viewpoints are not threats. They are opportunities for learning and growing. The image

I used in chapter one is that of a journey. As we explore, we are open to new knowledge, new perspectives, and new relationships. Truth-seeking is open-ended. We do not know, nor can we know, the directions in which our explorations may take us.

The end of our inquiry brings us back to something we noted at the start. Truth-seeking requires a certain attitude. It manifests itself in a kind of spirit more than in the quantity of one's knowledge. It sets forth on a journey of inquiry with no preconceptions about the final destination. When it encounters differing perspectives, it sees opportunity rather than threat. When it senses fear, it pauses to examine the source of the fear, for it knows that fear inhibits the search for truth. When it senses anger, it seeks to identify the hub symbols that are behind the angry response. The truth-seeker knows that emotions can be helpful tools in the search for truth. But emotions can also lead us into error when we fail to recognize the source of our emotional reactions.

The most important aspect of a truth-seeking spirit is the humility that grows out of a deep recognition of the limitations of one's knowledge. Certainty begets judgmentalism. A judgmental attitude leads to a defensive stance against other viewpoints. It seeks to refute rather than to understand. If we see other viewpoints as offering potential corrections to our own distorted and finite vision, we will be more likely to receive them with gratitude as opportunities for interesting exploration.

Some might criticize the view I have presented as anti-evangelistic. After all, how can one evangelize if one cannot claim absolute certainty regarding one's beliefs? The question reveals a misunderstanding of the true nature of evangelism (and, indeed, the true nature of Christianity). True Christian evangelism is witnessing to the truth of God revealed in one's encounter with the person of Jesus. To witness it to testify—to tell the story of one's own truth search. Genuine truth-seeking and true evangelism are, in fact, perfectly compatible.

I believe we are hard-wired for truth-seeking. There is an urge within us that pushes us toward greater consistency of belief and more complete knowledge. The source of this drive is what we might call, in theological language, the image of God within us. Truth-seeking is immensely satisfying, since it is linked with our discovery of our true self. To a much greater extent than most of us realize, we are part of the world in which we live. Our bodies constantly exchange matter with the world around us. Every atom in our bodies will continue to exist within this universe long after we are dead. We are part of an ongoing story. Our personal experience is set within that larger story and adds new content. Our truth-seeking is rooted in our drive toward discovering who we are within the context of the world within which we find ourselves.

Truth, therefore, is not abstract. It is embedded in the history of a universe created by God and is inseparable from our experience as embodied, finite persons. The most important truths we can discover are relational. We tell our stories and we listen to the stories of others. Christians read the Bible expecting to learn something of the story of God's interaction with people who have lived before us. Those stories help shape our interpretation of events happening in our lives today. Our narrative is set within a larger narrative. The placement of our personal stories within a larger story is what makes us who we are.

Our identity cannot be separated from the larger story that provides the basis for our self-understanding. Events and experiences provide raw data. Our interpretation of those experiences becomes the narrative that gives our experiences significance. Our personal narrative—the narrative we adopt as meaningful for explaining our own journey—provides a framework that shapes our interpretation and integration of new experiences. Our identity unfolds as we interact with the world around us.

Telling our stories makes us vulnerable. When we honestly share our experiences we risk rejection, since inevitably our stories include cowardice as well as courage, meanness as well as kindness, and wasted opportunities as well as significant achievements. When we are honest with one another, however, learning takes place. Ultimately our only hope for gaining true knowledge is in paying close attention to our own experiences and the experiences of others (past and present). Those with the most potential to teach us are those whose perspectives most differ from our own. When we respond to those who are different with closed-mindedness rather than openness, we block potential learning. As we tell our stories and listen to the stories of others, fear is reduced and new learning is made possible.

A significant aspect of the truth contained in the Bible is that it is communicated primarily through narrative. The Bible is not a theological textbook with nicely defined terminology and a well-constructed presentation of creedal statements. Even the most fundamental and dearly-held Christian affirmations, such as the idea of the trinity and the affirmation of the full humanity and full divinity of Jesus are the result of post-biblical theological reflection. Those doctrines are not explicitly found in the Bible itself. The Bible gives us stories, and those stories provide a resource for Christians today as we seek to identify the direction of God's ongoing activity.

Of course, discerning the truth contained in the Bible is complicated by the fact that it contains a multiplicity of perspectives that are often in tension with each other, as we have seen. We have also seen, however, that we can make progress in resolving those tensions as we work to identify major biblical hub symbols and as we pay careful attention to our own primary hub symbols. There is an unavoidable messiness to this process. Truth-claims must be validated in the laboratory of life. Ongoing correction is essential. Defensiveness impedes our progress. Openness and receptiveness to hearing and exploring viewpoints that differ from or are in opposition to our own is vital for the search for truth.

Unfortunately, such openness is not in plentiful supply these days. Our society is becoming increasingly polarized. Perhaps one reason for this polarization is actually to be found in our desire for community. We long for a connection with others, as evidenced in the popularity of various sorts of social media. Ironically, however, research shows that we feel increasingly lonely.[1] Rather than sitting down together and enjoying long conversations, we send clipped messages electronically. Rather than engaging one another eye-to-eye, our eyes are distracted by messages received and sent on our technological devices. In the absence of real community—which includes real vulnerability—we look for a pseudo-community composed of those who agree with us. Like-mindedness substitutes for genuine relationships. Consensus substitutes for love. Forwarding or posting a link to a blog or article that supports our own viewpoint substitutes for frank and open dialogue or the sort of digging into data that the truth-search requires.

Group membership is fragile when it depends on agreement with a narrow agenda or restrictive group identity markers. We intuitively sense the threat of its dissolution. Our desire for acceptance drives us toward conformity. Fear of group rejection causes repression of ideas we sense might damage our relationships within the group. Obviously, such an atmosphere lacks the oxygen needed for truth-seeking to flourish.

Truth-seeking requires a community of loving acceptance. Not too long ago I was leading a group discussion at a church's Wednesday night

---

1. See, e.g., Maria Konnikova, "How Facebook Makes Us Unhappy," http://www.newyorker.com/online/blogs/elements/2013/09/the-real-reason-facebook-makes-us-unhappy.html.

Bible study and admitted to those gathered that I was surprised at the range of viewpoints expressed and impressed with the way the group accepted a broad divergence of opinion. One person in the group responded, "We disagree, but we love each other." Would that more churches evidenced such a spirit! Truth-seeking is not a solitary venture. In order to risk the sort of exploration truth-seeking requires we need to feel the safety of knowing we will continue to be loved and accepted even when—especially when— we disagree with one another. Genuine community creates bonds of trust. Those bonds act as a safety net that provides the confidence we need to try new thought experiments. We can be honest and vulnerable, knowing we will continue to be loved and accepted.

Truth-seeking is enhanced by exposure to a broad diversity of perspectives. If the primary trust-communities to which we belong are relatively homogeneous, we will need to work especially hard to overcome the limitation of restricted horizons. In such situations, our only hope for escaping our myopic vision is to open ourselves to encounters with those who are Different or Not-like-us. We will need to seek out opportunities for genuine dialogue and conversation. We will need to take advantage of opportunities for friendship with persons with whom we might not normally associate.

We need exposure to alternative perspectives because we know that our viewpoint is distorted and in need of continual correction. Our vision is selective. Whenever people disagree, the facts they cite in support of their position reveal a particular interpretation of reality. Our conclusions may seem reasonable given the data we have included in our examination of a particular matter, but we may have excluded from our deliberations data that would fundamentally challenge our conclusions.

Data must be handled with care. Truth-seekers must be careful to avoid manipulation of data. Rather than striving to suppress data which challenges our understanding, truth-seekers must be especially attentive to give due consideration to facts and information that do not seem to fit with our view and which call our conclusions into question.[2] The views of experts may not be infallible, but when we encounter a consensus view held by knowledgeable people we must consider it with great seriousness. Any challenge to such a consensus must convincingly show that important data has been ignored or insufficiently taken into account or else must be able to make a compelling case that the existing consensus regarding the proper interpretation of the data has been faulty. A big difference between

2. See Stassen, "Critical Variables in Christian Social Ethics," 70–71.

strong arguments and weak arguments lies in the comprehensiveness of their explanatory power in relation to the relevant data. Explanations that account for a broader range of data will be judged to be superior to those that obviously exclude inconvenient facts.

Liberationist perspectives have much to teach us at this point concerning the clearer vision of truth often possessed by those who are vulnerable. Those who are poor, who suffer unjust treatment, who are without power, who are discriminated against, and who are denied opportunities available to others possess a truer understanding of the harmful effects of unjust power structures than do those who benefit from those structures. Jack Rogers rightly reminds us that an important test of our theology and our ethics is to ask the question: "Who bleeds?"[3] If God is one who hears the groans of those who suffer and are oppressed (see Exod 3:7–9), any inability on our part to hear such groans is a clear sign of deficiency in our theological perspective.

Rogers notes that the Bible has often been used by those with power to justify their oppression of those who are vulnerable. His analysis is limited to the Presbyterian Church in the United States, but it is relevant to most US denominations during the time period he examines. On the issues of slavery/segregation and the role of women, Rogers says that "at one point the church had near unanimity of opinion and then, over time and painfully, changed its mind to almost the exact opposite view."[4] He says that in each case, "we accepted a pervasive societal prejudice and read it back into Scripture. We took certain Scriptures out of their context and claimed to read them literally with tragic consequences for those to whom these verses were applied."[5]

Christians living today can see in hindsight that those who used the Bible to defend slavery were wrong. Abolitionists were right. But two hundred years ago the kind of clarity we now have about this issue did not exist for many people. What was different about the way Christian abolitionists read the Bible? Rogers says that "their method of biblical interpretation looked at the Bible as a whole and gave priority to its central themes, especially that Jesus was the central figure in Scripture and the one we should seek to emulate."[6]

3. Rogers, *Jesus, the Bible, and Homosexuality*, x.
4. Ibid., 17.
5. Ibid., 18.
6. Ibid., 33.

We have seen that Glen Stassen's analysis of those who were faithful in times of testing, including people such as Dietrich Bonhoeffer, André Trocmé, Martin Luther King Jr., Clarence Jordan, Dorothy Day, etc., has produced a similar assessment. Stassen identifies loyalty to Jesus with particular attention to Jesus's actions and teachings as a critical factor that enabled these people, who we now recognize as "heroes of the faith," to break free of the distorting effects of their particular cultural contexts.[7] Stassen argues that in order to overcome the distorting effects of our own cultural context, we need a "thicker Jesus" and an ethic of "incarnational discipleship."[8]

This book has been addressed to Christians who claim the Bible as an authority source. Christians who wish to take the authority of the Bible seriously face tremendous challenges. When Christians defend contrasting and even contradictory theological and ethical viewpoints, all claiming biblical support for their positions, how can a truth-seeker sort things out? I have argued for a view that takes seriously the limitations of our existence within history. No one can claim that her or his finite, culturally-limited perspective is the same as God's view. No one can claim to have complete knowledge of the truth. On the other hand, I have argued that there are things that are truthful, and they can be apprehended. We can make progress on our journey.

The way forward is to work toward clarity in relation to both our own hub symbols and central biblical hub symbols, as we saw in chapter 5. We argued in chapter 6 that a major concern throughout the Bible is that human communities should not be characterized by extreme inequalities and that the Bible proclaims God's special concern for those who are vulnerable and thus more likely to suffer from unjust power distributions. If pressed for a theological rationale lying behind these biblical concerns, one could argue that they are based on a more fundamental claim: God is a loving God. Love demands fair treatment. Thus love is closely related to justice.[9] A love that requires fair distribution and meeting the needs of the vulnerable is an essential aspect of God's character. If we accept this affirmation as truthful, we have a starting point for evaluating specific issues. Much more can be said, and more criteria can and must be developed. The implications of this simple affirmation are enormous. We have much work to do

---

7. See discussion of Stassen in chapter 4 above.

8. See Stassen, *A Thicker Jesus*.

9. See Wolterstorff, *Justice in Love*.

as we explore the meaning of this affirmation in specific situations. The affirmation itself, however, provides us with a useful criterion for judging alternative perspectives.

This book provides you with a methodology for applying the Bible effectively, authoritatively, and with integrity to issues that arise in your life and in the larger society. Knowledge, however, is not the same as action. To verbally assert the Bible's importance as an authority source is not the same thing as having the Bible function effectively in guiding our thinking and our action. Knowing how to read the Bible is not the same thing as reading the Bible. A tool is effective only when put to use.

Bible reading, for most Christians, is not an end in itself. Its purpose is to help us in our spiritual journey to know God better and to follow God's will for our lives. George Barna, founder of the Barna Research Group (now The Barna Group) has said his research shows that "most Christians mirror cultural goals, desiring happiness, comfort, security, belonging, and popularity. Surprisingly few are focused on completely cooperating with God to experience the kind of whole-life transformation described in the Bible and made possible only through a partnership with God."[10] A 2009 report from The Barna Group, summarizing research conducted throughout the previous year, concludes that

> Bible reading has become the religious equivalent of sound-bite journalism. When people read from the Bible they typically open it, read a brief passage without much regard for the context, and consider the primary thought or feeling that the passage provided. If they are comfortable with it, they accept it; otherwise, they deem it interesting but irrelevant to their life, and move on. There is shockingly little growth evident in people's understanding of the fundamental themes of the scriptures and amazingly little interest in deepening their knowledge and application of biblical principles . . . . The problem facing the Christian Church is not that people lack a complete set of beliefs; the problem is that they have a full slate of beliefs in mind, which they think are consistent with biblical teachings, and they are neither open to being proven wrong nor to learning new insights.[11]

10. "Research on How God Transforms Lives Reveals a 10-Stop Journey," https://www.barna.org/transformation-articles/480-research-on-how-god-transforms-lives-reveals-a-10-stop-journey.

11. "Barna Studies the Research, Offers a Year-in-Review Perspective," https://www.barna.org/barna-update/faith-spirituality/325-barna-studies-the-research-offers-a-year-in-review-perspective#.UokfkxAueLw.

The fact that you are reading this book is evidence that you are looking for more than "sound-bite journalism" in your Bible reading. I believe the majority of Christians *want* to read the Bible in a meaningful way, but they are confused by much that is contained in the Bible and not sure what to do when their internal sense of what is truthful seems contradicted by a particular biblical passage.

The importance of having a rationally coherent and spiritually satisfying approach to reading the Bible cannot be overstated. For example, although we noted in chapter 7 that our cultural attitudes regarding the issue of same-sex marriage are moving in the direction of greater acceptance, we argued that a biblically-grounded ethic should have been ahead of our societal values in affirming that loving relationships ought to be supported and encouraged, regardless of the sexual orientation of the persons involved. In those cases where Christians invoke the Bible to support their position, the focus generally tends to be on a few verses from which universal rules are derived rather than on an analysis of hub symbols, including those of the Bible, our culture, and our own.

For the most part young heterosexual Christians, like young heterosexuals generally in the US today, tend to be more accepting of same-sex marriage and LGBTQ persons than older heterosexual Christians. In other words, they tend to reflect the general cultural attitudes of their peers, just as their elders did before them.[12] Many of my students believe (because they have been told by those in leadership positions in their churches) that the Bible condemns all homosexual practice. Yet the heterosexually-oriented among those same students have LGBTQ friends whom they are less and less willing to condemn when they see them in relationships that look every bit as loving as heterosexual relationships. The result, for students who are Christians, is an undermining of the authority of the Bible, since the supposed teaching of the Bible is pitted against their intuitive sense of what is truthful.[13]

12. Cody Sanders rightly reminds us that young people are just as likely to evidence tendencies toward hatred, prejudice, violence, and injustice as are their elders and that the struggle for justice is an ongoing task. See Sanders, *Queer Lessons for Churches on the Straight and Narrow*, Epilogue.

13. See Kinnaman, "America's Change of Mind on Same-Sex Marriage and LGBTQ Rights." Kinnaman states, "Our research on younger Christians shows many leave the church over questions on these complex [LGBTQ-related] issues. And unless they are given a robust and compelling vision for why they need to hold to those views—and how to embrace them in a humble-yet-livable way—we expect even more disaffection between young adults and the Church in the years come."

Faulty thinking about the biblical message is leading many younger Christians to disregard the Bible in the formulation of their core theological and ethical affirmations. When the Bible is disregarded, other authority sources fill the vacuum. Sometimes those authority sources are personal—a pastor or authority figure within the church. Sometimes they are creedal—a list of doctrines or statement of ethical guidelines. Often, however, Christians end up with authority sources that are essentially secular.

I have argued that "Christian" ought to be defined as "Christ-follower."[14] Christians affirm that Jesus represents the fullest revelation of God in history. Christians are those people who seek to pattern their lives after the example of Jesus and who strive to follow the teachings of Jesus. They turn to the Bible as the best source of information about the life of Jesus and the story of God's revelatory activity surrounding Jesus. The story of Jesus is part of a larger story told in the pages of the Bible. Grasping the key elements of that story is a vital task for Christian truth-seekers.

False narratives can lead us astray. A primary narrative for many Christians is that the world will be ending soon. Such a narrative leads to a bunker mentality. The world is literally going to hell, so the task of Christians is to remain faithful while we wait for the fireballs to start falling. Another primary narrative for many Christians is that salvation is entirely personal. The focus of salvation is to get your own heart right with God. The biblical sense of a *shalom* community is entirely absent in this view. Neither of these narratives will lead Christians to wonder, as the biblical narrative would seem to lead us to do, whether excessive wealth might be wrong or might be something that Christians ought to challenge. Narratives matter. Getting our narratives properly aligned with the biblical narrative is an essential task for Christians.

Our lives can either be lived in autopilot mode or we can take control of our thinking and our actions. Most people's values and beliefs tend to echo those of the surrounding culture. Most people tend to accept the values and beliefs of their culture without serious questioning. God gave us brains, however, and we can put them to use. The Bible can provide an invaluable resource to Christians who take it seriously as part of the unfolding story of God's self-revelation.

This book provides you with a model that focuses on hub symbols, enabling the Bible to speak a relevant word to the issues of our day. Alignment of our hub symbols with biblical hub symbols is the real test of the Bible's

14. See my discussion in chapter 4 above.

authoritative power. The stories of God's activity recorded in the pages of the Bible, and in particular the story of God's activity revealed in the life of Jesus, provide us with a powerful counter-cultural—and potentially culture-transforming—resource.

My parting prayer for you, my fellow traveler on this journey of truth-seeking, is that you find your voice. And that you speak it. And that in the conversations that ensue, you are enabled to hear the whisperings of God's voice as it comes to us from unexpected directions, enigmatically, some-times comforting and reassuring, but often challenging and confronting. The ultimate test of our truth-seeking will be found in the kinds of lives that we live, the kinds of relationships we develop, and the kinds of communi-ties we build along the way. May God's *shalom* be with you on your way.

Study Guide
Prepared by Gail Peace

REFLECTING ON YOUR EXPERIENCES can be invaluable in mining the gold found in your story. Our stories inform how we experience and read the Bible. The following questions can help prompt your exploration regarding matters discussed in the book. Use them as a guide and alter them to fit your situation, whether for personal reflection or group study.

Chapter 1: To Be a Truth-Seeker

1. Describe your childhood experiences related to church. Did you go to church as a child? Did your family attend church, or was your knowledge of church obtained through friends who attended church?

2. How were you exposed to the Bible as a child? Was the Bible read in your home? What were the attitudes communicated to you about the Bible by your family? How are those attitudes reflected in your thinking as an adult?

3. What questions related to God, the Bible, or church do you remember asking yourself or others when you were a child? Did you verbalize your questions to anyone? Who? Do you recall anything about the responses you received?

4. How would you describe your attitude about the Bible? For example, do you think it is a guidebook for living? Do you think it is God's

infallible word? Have your attitudes and thinking about the Bible changed as you have grown older? If so, how?

5. How do you approach reading the Bible? Do you "open and point"? Do you use a devotional book to help you? Do you have a specific system for reading the Bible? Do you avoid reading the Bible? If so, why do you think that is the case? Why do you think you use the method that you do?

Chapter 2: Map for a Journey or Fortress to be Defended?

1. What do you know about the origin of the Bible? Where did you learn this information?

2. What questions did you have about where the Bible came from when you were a child or teenager?

3. Is the argument in Chapter 2 that says the Bible was not directly delivered from God in agreement with your own thinking or do you feel uncomfortable with that idea? If you feel uncomfortable, what do you think causes the discomfort?

4. Define the word *inspiration*. In what way is that word connected with your thinking about scripture?

5. Define the word *authority*. In what way is that word connected with your thinking about scripture?

6. Do you sometimes feel as though the Bible needs defending? When? Why?

7. Discuss how the knowledge of the history of the Bible informs your reading of the Bible.

8. Respond to the following quote from Chapter 2: "The Bible is authoritative to the extent that contemporary Christian communities allow it to change them and guide them."

Chapter 3: Storybook or Textbook?

1. Is the evidence presented in this chapter regarding contradictions in the Bible problematic for you? If so, explain how. If not, why not?

2. What are your early memories of the attitudes of Christians in your community regarding faith questions? Did you feel free to ask such questions of adults around you?

3. What are your attitudes today regarding faith questions? Do you feel like some questions are off limits or out of bounds? Which?

4. Which is a greater motivator for you: fear or discovery? Explain with some personal examples.

5. Which scripture passages are most meaningful to you? Why? Which scripture passages are most troublesome to you? Why?

6. Is it frightening or invigorating to entertain the idea that the Bible is contradictory? Explain.

7. How would you describe the Bible to someone totally unfamiliar with it?

8. Do you relate to the Bible as *your story*? Do you view it more as a list of rules? Describe your view about how the Bible can be meaningful for us today.

Chapter 4: Biblical Authority is *Bottom-Up*

1. How often do you read the Bible? Would you say that you study the Bible? How do you decide what to read or study in the Bible?

2. Do you use outside sources, such as commentaries and dictionaries, to aid you in your Bible reading or studying? If you do, do you find them to be helpful, and if so, how do they help you?

3. What sort of authority, if any, would you say the Bible has in your life?

4. At this point in your life, would you describe your attitude toward the authority of the Bible as more *top down* or *bottom up*? Explain.

5. Do you trust yourself to read and interpret scripture on your own, or do you seek guidance from another authority source? What assistance do you think Christians ought to have when reading the Bible?

6. Do you engage in group Bible study and discussion? If this is helpful to you in finding meaning in scripture, explain how. Where and with whom does this happen? How would you describe the relationship you have with this group of learners?

7. Discuss authority sources other than the Bible that have power in your life.

8. Identify three people you feel live as though the Bible is a primary authority source for them. Discuss common characteristics you find among these people.

Chapter 5: A Model for Reading, Reflecting On, and Living in Tune with the Bible

1. What do you think is the most important personal quality one should bring to the reading of the Bible?

2. Do you tend to avoid texts in the Bible you find problematic? Can you think of some? Do these texts have common characteristics or a common theme?

3. What are your favorite biblical passages? Do these have a theme? Why do you think these are your favorites? Do you tend to read your favorite passages more than others?

4. Identify at least two of your own hub symbols. How do you think these hub symbols hinder or enhance your reading of the Bible?

5. Do the themes you identified in your favorite and problematic texts in questions two and three above seem to have a connection with your hub symbols?

6. Describe your vision of a *shalom* community.

Chapter 6: Applying the Model—Letting the Bible Shape our Moral Horizon

1. How did you think of God when you were a child? How has your thinking changed? What do you think brought about that change in thinking?

2. What image of God do you focus on most often? What images of God do you tend to avoid or find less attractive? Why do you think you focus on or avoid these particular images? Can you connect these images to any of your hub symbols?

3. Think of a time when you would say the Bible directly guided your behavior. Describe what that was like.

4. Do you tend to read the Old Testament or New Testament more frequently? Why? Do you think one is more important than the other? Why?

5. Has working for justice played an important role in your personal faith journey? What part do you think seeking justice *should* play in the life of a faith community? Explain your answer.

Chapter 7: Applying the Model—How Can the Bible Speak to Contemporary Issues?

1. Do you have friends or family members who are LGBTQ? What is your relationship to these persons?

2. What do you recall about the first time you became aware of the distinction between heterosexual and homosexual?

3. How do you think having persons who are LGBTQ as friends or family members might change one's feelings about homosexuality?

4. If you are involved with a faith community, what is the attitude of that community toward LGBTQ persons? Would a person who identifies as LGBTQ be welcomed and affirmed in your faith community? Why or why not? Do you know persons who identify as LGBTQ who are part of your faith community?

5. How have your own attitudes about homosexuality changed through the years? If your views have changed, what would you say has brought about that change? To what extent do you think your view is biblical? Explain.

6. How do you think Jesus would treat LGBTQ persons living in our world today? Explain your answer.

7. Are you comfortable and confident with your attitudes and actions regarding the treatment of persons who are LGBTQ? Why or why not? How do you think this issue will affect churches in the future?

Chapter 8: Following Jesus with Heart and Mind

1. What are your attitudes about truth-seeking? Do you think a truth-seeking approach is necessary in order to read the Bible effectively? Explain.

2. Does the thought of exploring uncharted waters in the search for truth excite you or do you feel like you would rather stay safely on shore? What might either of these attitudes cost you?

3. How do you think Jesus lived his life in relation to the truth? Did he tend more in the direction of venturing out or more in the direction of staying safe? Do you think Jesus resided in a "house of outcomes"? Explain your answer.

4. How do you handle disagreements? What do feel when disagreements surface? Do you avoid them or confront them? Can you think of specific examples? What about your church community? Do you think it handles disagreements constructively? Why or why not? What implications do you see for the task of truth-seeking?

5. Do you spend much time with people who have a significantly different perspective from yours, or with people who are in other ways significantly different from you? How do you handle those differences? Are you comfortable with the differences, or do they cause you discomfort? Be specific. Is there anything you would like to change about the way you relate to people who are significantly different from you?

6. Who are your heroes of the faith? What is it about these people that you admire? What biblical themes do you think are reflected in their lives? Explain.

7. Now that you have finished the book, what questions do you have? How can you find answers to them?

8. Has reading this book changed the way you think about what it means to be a follower of Jesus? How, specifically? The title of the last chapter is "Following Jesus with Heart and Mind." What does that mean to you? In what way do you see these as related?

9. In what way do you see *thinking* as related to *actions*? Do you agree with the statement at the end of the book that "the ultimate test of our truth-seeking will be found in the kinds of lives that we live, the kinds of relationships we develop, and the kinds of communities we build

along the way"? Can you think of anything in relation to your actions
or the actions of your church that you would like to change? What do
you think is the best way to get change to happen?

Bibliography

Achtemeier, Paul J. *Inspiration and Authority: Nature and Authority of Christian Scripture.* Peabody, Massachusetts: Hendrickson Publishers, 1999.

Ackroyd, P. R. and C.F. Evans, eds. *The Cambridge History of the Bible: From the Beginnings to Jerome.* Vol. 1. Cambridge: Cambridge University Press, 1970.

"Barna Studies the Research, Offers a Year-in-Review Perspective." Report published online by the Barna Group on December 18, 2009, https://www.barna.org/barna-update/faith-spirituality/325-barna-studies-the-research-offers-a-year-in-review-perspective#.UokfkxAueLw.

Blevins, Kent. "Southern Baptist Attitudes Toward the Vietnam War in the Years 1965–1970." *Foundations* 23, no. 3 (July–September 1980): 231–44.

Brady, Sarah. "The Time for Debating is Over—We Need Action." Blog post in *The Huffington Post*, December 16, 2012, http://www.huffingtonpost.com/sarah-brady/gun-control_b_2313088.html?utm_hp_ref=tw.

Cobb, John B., Jr. *The Process Perspective: Frequently Asked Questions About Process Theology.* St. Louis: Chalice Press, 2003.

Coogan, Michael. *The Old Testament: A Historical and Literary Introduction to the Hebrew Scriptures.* Third Edition. New York: Oxford University Press, 2014.

Countryman, L. William. *Dirt Greed & Sex: Sexual Ethics in the New Testament and Their Implications for Today.* Philadelphia: Fortress Press, 1988.

Coyne, Jerry A. *Why Evolution is True.* New York: Penguin Books, 2009.

De La Torre, Miguel A. "A Thick Hispanic Jesús." *Perspectives in Religious Studies* 40, no. 2 (Summer 2013): 131–42.

De Santillana, Giorgio. *The Crime of Galileo.* Chicago: The University of Chicago Press, 1955.

Dungan, David L. *Constantine's Bible: Politics and the Making of the New Testament.* Minneapolis: Fortress Press, 2007.

Ehrman, Bart D. *Lost Christianities: The Battles for Scripture and the Faiths We Never Knew.* New York: Oxford University Press, 2003.

———. *Lost Scriptures: Books that Did Not Make It into the New Testament.* New York: Oxford University Press, 2003.

Eighmy, John Lee. *Churches in Cultural Captivity: A History of the Social Attitudes of Southern Baptists.* Revised edition. Knoxville: The University of Tennessee Press, 1987.

Ellison, Marvin M. *Same-Sex Marriage? A Christian Ethical Analysis.* Cleveland: The Pilgrim Press, 2004.

Ericksen, Robert P. *Theologians Under Hitler*. New Haven, CT: Yale University Press, 1985.

Erickson, Millard J. *Christian Theology*. Second edition. Grand Rapids, MI: Baker Academic, 1998.

"Evolution and Creationism in Schools." On website of the National Academy of Sciences, http://www.nationalacademies.org/evolution/InSchools.html.

"Evolution, Creationism, Intelligent Design." Undated report published online by Gallop, http://www.gallup.com/poll/21814/evolution-creationism-intelligent-design.aspx.

Fredriksen, Paula. *Sin: The Early History of An Idea*. Princeton, NJ: Princeton University Press, 2012.

Freeman, Curtis W., James William McClendon Jr., and C. Rosalee Velloso da Silva, editors. *Baptist Roots: A Reader in the Theology of a Christian People*. Valley Forge: Judson Press, 1999.

Fretheim, Terence E. "The Book of Genesis." In *The New Interpreter's Bible*, edited by Leander E. Keck, 1:319–674. Nashville: Abingdon Press, 1994.

Friedman, Richard Elliott. *The Bible with Sources Revealed: A New View Into the Five Books of Moses*. New York: HarperSanFrancisco, 2003.

————. *Who Wrote the Bible?* New York: HarperSanFrancisco, 1987.

Gallop. "Evolution, Creationism, Intelligent Design." No pages. Online: http://www.gallup.com/poll/21814/evolution-creationism-intelligent-design.aspx.

Goodfriend, Elaine Adler. "Adultery." In *The Anchor Bible Dictionary*, edited by David Noel Freedman, 1:82–86. New York: Doubleday, 1992.

Grant, Robert M. with David Tracy. *A Short History of the Interpretation of the Bible*. Second edition revised and enlarged. Minneapolis: Fortress Press, 1984.

Grenz, Stanley. *Sexual Ethics: A Biblical Perspective*. Dallas: Word Publishing, 1990.

————. *Welcoming but Not Affirming: An Evangelical Response to Homosexuality*. Louisville, KY: Westminster John Knox Press, 1998.

Harris, Stephen L. *The New Testament: A Student's Introduction*. Sixth edition. New York: McGraw Hill Higher Education, 2009.

Haught, John F. *Science and Religion: From Conflict to Conversation*. New York: Paulist Press, 1995.

Hays, Richard B. *The Moral Vision of the New Testament: Community, Cross, New Creation; A Contemporary Introduction to New Testament Ethics*. New York: HarperSanFrancisco, 1996.

Healey, Joseph P. "Peace." In *The Anchor Bible Dictionary*, edited by David Noel Freedman, 5:206–7. New York: Doubleday, 1992.

Helwys, Thomas. *The Mistery of Iniquity*. In Leon H. McBeth, *A Sourcebook for Baptist Heritage*, 70–72. Nashville: Broadman Press, 1990.

————. *The Mystery of Iniquity*. In Curtis W. Freeman, James William McClendon, Jr., and C. Rosalee Velloso da Silva, editors. *Baptist Roots: A Reader in the Theology of a Christian People*, 84–87. Valley Forge: Judson Press, 1999.

Inequality.org Staff. "ILO: U.S. Inequality Now Literally Off the Chart." Report published online by Inequality.org on June 6, 2013, http://inequality.org/ilo-report-inequality-literally-chart/.

Kimball, Charles. *When Religion Becomes Evil*. New York: HarperSanFrancisco, 2002.

King, Martin Luther, Jr. "Letter from Birmingham Jail." In *Why We Can't Wait*, 76–95. New York: The New American Library, Inc., 1964.

Kinnaman, David. Quoted in "America's Change of Mind on Same-Sex Marriage and LGBTQ Rights." Report published online by the Barna Group on July 3, 2013, https://www.barna.org/barna-update/culture/618-america-s-change-of-mind-on-same-sex-marriage-and-lgbtq-rights#.UokckRAueLw.

Knight, Douglas A. and Amy Jill-Levine. *The Meaning of the Bible: What the Jewish Scriptures and Christian Old Testament Can Teach Us.* New York: HarperOne, 2011.

Knust, Jennifer Wright. *Unprotected Texts: The Bible's Surprising Contradictions About Sex and Desire.* New York: HarperOne, 2011.

Konnikova, Maria. "How Facebook Makes Us Unhappy." *The New Yorker,* September 10, 2013, http://www.newyorker.com/online/blogs/elements/2013/09/the-real-reason-facebook-makes-us-unhappy.html.

Kugel, James L. *How to Read the Bible: A Guide to Scripture, Then and Now.* New York: Free Press, 2007.

———. *The Bible as it Was.* Cambridge, MA: The Belknap Press of Harvard University Press, 1997.

Lampe, G.W.H., ed. *The Cambridge History of the Bible: The West From the Fathers to the Reformation.* Vol 1. Cambridge: Cambridge University Press, 1969.

Leland, John. "The Rights of Conscience Inalienable." In L.F. Greene, editor, *The Writings of the late Elder John Leland,* 177–192. New York: G.W. Wood, 1845.

Leonard, Bill. *Baptist Ways: A History.* Valley Forge: Judson Press, 2003.

Luther, Martin. *Luther's Works.* Edited by Jaroslav Pelikan (vols. 1–30) and Helmut T. Lehmann (vols. 31–55). Vol. 35, *Word and Sacrament I,* edited by E. Theodore Bachmann. Philadelphia: Muhlenberg Press, 1960.

Marsh, John. *Class Dismissed: Why We Cannot Teach or Learn Our Way Out of Inequality.* New York: Monthly Review Press, 2011.

Newport, Frank. "In U.S., 46% Hold Creationist View of Human Origins." Report on Gallop website, June 1, 2012, http://www.gallup.com/poll/155003/hold-creationist-view-human-origins.aspx.

Niebuhr, Reinhold. *Moral Man and Immoral Society: A Study in Ethics and Politics.* New York: Charles Scribner's Sons, 1932.

Pelikan, Jaroslav. *Whose Bible is It?* NewYork: Viking, 2005.

Polkinghorne, John. *Science and Religion in Quest of Truth.* New Haven: Yale University Press, 2011.

———. *Theology in the Context of Science.* New Haven: Yale University Press, 2009.

"Research on How God Transforms Lives Reveals a 10-Stop Journey." Report published online by the Barna Group on March 17, 2011, https://www.barna.org/transformation-articles/480-research-on-how-god-transforms-lives-reveals-a-10-stop-journey.

Rieger, Joerg. *No Rising Tide: Theology, Economics, and the Future.* Minneapolis: Fortress Press, 2009.

Rogers, Jack. *Jesus, the Bible, and Homosexuality: Explode the Myths, Heal the Church.* Louisville, KY: Westminster John Knox Press, 2006.

Ruggiero, Vincent Ryan. *Beyond Feelings: A Guide to Critical Thinking.* New York: McGraw Hill, 2008.

Sagan, Carl. *The Demon Haunted World: Science as a Candle in the Dark.* New York: Ballantine Books, 1996.

Sanders, Cody J. *Queer Lessons for Churches on the Straight and Narrow: What All Christians Can Learn from LGBTQ Lives.* Macon, GA: Faithlab, 2013.

Sanders, James A. "Canon." In *The Anchor Bible Dictionary,* edited by David Noel Freedman, 1:837–52. New York: Doubleday, 1992.

Bibliography

Schwalbe, Michael. *Rigging the Game: How Inequality Is Reproduced in Everyday Life*. New York: Oxford University Press, 2008.

Shammas, Carole. "A New Look at Long-Term Trends in Wealth Inequality in the United States." *The American Historical Review* 98, no. 2 (April 1993): 428–29.

Siebert, Eric A. *The Violence of Scripture: Overcoming the Old Testament's Troubling Legacy*. Minneapolis: Fortress Press, 2012.

Siker, Jeffrey S. "Gentile Wheat and Homosexual Christians: New Testament Directions for the Heterosexual Church." In *Biblical Ethics and Homosexuality: Listening to Scripture*, edited by Robert L. Brawley, 137–151. Louisville, KY: Westminster John Knox Press, 1996.

———. "Homosexual Christians, the Bible, and Gentile Inclusion: Confessions of a Repenting Heterosexist." In *Homosexuality in the Church: Both Sides of the Debate*, edited by Jeffrey S. Siker, 178–194. Louisville: Westminster John Knox Press, 1994.

Soards, Marion. *Scripture & Homosexuality: Biblical Authority and the Church Today*. Louisville, KY: Westminster John Knox Press, 1995.

Spoto, Donald. *Reluctant Saint: The Life of Francis of Assisi*. New York: Viking Compass, 2002.

Slave Free Chocolate. Online: http://www.slavefreechocolate.org/.

Stassen, Glen Harold. *A Thicker Jesus: Incarnational Discipleship in a Secular Age*. Louisville, KY: Westminster John Knox Press, 2012.

———. "Critical Variables in Christian Social Ethics." In *Issues in Christian Ethics*, edited by Paul D. Simmons, 57–76. Nashville: Broadman Press, 1980.

Sullivan, Clayton. *Toward a Mature Faith: Does Biblical Inerrancy Make Sense?* Decatur, GA: SBC Today, 1990.

Swartley, Willard M. *Slavery, Sabbath, War and Women: Case Issues in Biblical Interpretation*. Scottdale, PA: Herald Press, 1983.

Vauchez, André. *Francis of Assisi: The Life and Afterlife of a Medieval Saint*. Translated by Michael F. Cusato. New Haven: Yale University Press, 2012.

Webb, Joseph M. *Old Texts, New Sermons: The Quiet Revolution in Biblical Preaching*. St. Louis, MO: Chalice Press, 2000.

———. *Preaching and the Challenge of Pluralism*. Saint Louis, MO: Chalice Press, 1998.

White, Mel. *Stranger at the Gate*. New York: Penguin, 1994.

Wolterstorff, Nicholas. *Justice in Love*. Grand Rapids, MI: William B. Eerdmans Publishing Company, 2011.

———. *Justice: Rights and Wrongs*. Princeton: Princeton University Press, 2009.